THE
NEW
HOSPITAL

Future Strategies
for a Changing Industry

Russell C. Coile, Jr., MBA
Health Forecasting Group
Alameda, California

AN ASPEN PUBLICATION®
Aspen Publishers, Inc.
1986

Rockville, Maryland
Royal Tunbridge Wells

Library of Congress Cataloging-in-Publication Data

Coile, Russell C.
The new hospital.

"An Aspen publication."
Includes bibliographies and index.
1. Hospitals—Administration. 2. Strategic planning. I. Title. [DNLM: 1. Delivery of
Health Care—trends—United States. 2. Economics, Hospital—trends—United States.
3. Hospital Administration—trends—United States. WX 157 C6793n]
RA971.C685   1986   362.1'1'068   86-7907
ISBN: 0-87189-363-0

Editorial Services: Marsha Davies

Library of Congress Catalog Card Number: 86-7907
ISBN: 0-87189-363-0

Printed in the United States of America

1   2   3   4   5

To Lori, Courtney, and Zac, who will create the future

Table of Contents

Foreword

These are changing times. There has been more change since 1982 than in the previous 25 years. The health industry today is in transition. The past is gone, but the future is not yet clear.

Health care is not the only industry experiencing turbulent times: "Have you ever paddled a canoe along a smooth, placid river and then suddenly entered a long stretch of boiling, rushing, churning white water filled with rocks—some seen, and some unseen? Competition in the banking industry today is like a white-water river. Once in it, the only choice is to get through without swamping. There's no turning back" (Bleeke 1983, 15). Like the airlines, banking, and communications industries, hospitals are entering the white water of competition. It will leave no hospital untouched.

In this time of uncertainty and transition, which way should hospitals turn? There are many possible directions, and hospitals are trying them all. Diversification abounds, leaving some observers to wonder who's minding the store: the base business of hospitals, inpatient care (Witt 1985, 45).

Since 1920, the Lutheran Hospital Society of Southern California has been in the forefront of new ideas, probing the future. In the process the organization has grown and diversified through formation of a for-profit management and consulting subsidiary, a health maintenance organization, and a preferred provider organization.

In 1984 LHS joined with other regional health providers to form American Healthcare Systems, a national network of premier nonprofit hospital systems. Already AHS has grown to the largest health system in the nation, with 35 participating systems including nearly 1,500 owned or aligned facilities. In 1985 the Lutheran Hospital Society moved again, taking its health maintenance organization public and completing a corporate restructuring. LHS Corp. is the new multihealth corporation. You can see my bias for the future: the conglomerates scenario.

Prediction, then, is not an unlikely role for LHS. The society engaged Russ Coile, long-time architect of future trends, as the first corporate futurist in the health industry and initiated a foresight process to pull back the curtain that obscures tomorrow. With the insights of our futures research, we are building the next generation of health organizations. A number of driving forces will shape the health care marketplace in the near and midrange future. We cannot predict exactly how they will affect the future of health care, only that they will.

We are within sight of the next century. The period before 2000 promises to be the most challenging hospitals has ever faced. Hospitals have two choices: to be pushed around by competitors and market forces or to steer their own course inspired by the scenario of the future they prefer. The signals of change are contradictory. Every market is different, and there are no simple formulas for success. Hospitals must chart their own strategic path, defining their vision of tomorrow's health care organization that will best fit the evolving needs of its customers.

I like the prospects of those hospitals willing to design their own future. They will be the New Hospitals, to whom this book is dedicated.

Samuel J. Tibbitts
President
Lutheran Hospital Society of Southern California

REFERENCES

Bleeke, Joel. "Deregulation: Riding the Rapids," *Business Horizons,* May–June 1983, p. 15.

Witt, John. "Free Enterprise vs. Fake Enterprise," *Healthcare Forum,* November/December 1985, p. 45.

Preface

We should all be concerned about the future because that's where we'll have to spend the rest of our lives.
—William F. Kettering, president, General Motors

A hospital is a human invention, and as such can be reinvented at any time.
—Leland R. Kaiser

On the product life-cycle curve the hospital industry is mature and declining. Under pressure from major employers, insurers, and government, America's hospitals in the 1980s are experiencing a deep decline in admissions and revenues. There is a good chance this recession in the hospital industry is permanent, reflecting a major shift in consumption patterns.

For the nation's nearly 7,000 hospitals, the doomsday forecasts of massive hospital closures are frightening. For health care managers and trustees, the future of hospitals appears grim and foreboding. That vision is too limited. The good news is that the health industry is growing, with the potential of continuously increasing revenues at rates of 10 to 15 percent through the year 2000. While hospitals continue to be buffeted by government regulation and consumer resistance, many other health and related services can anticipate a major boom.

The New Hospital: Future Strategies for a Changing Industry is the first comprehensive forecast of the health industry for the near and midrange future to the year 2000. The data base is three years of futures research sponsored by the Lutheran Hospital Society of Southern California.

There are trends and countertrends in today's health care marketplace. Selection of those macrotrends that will have the greatest impact on the future reflects extensive dialogue with hospital managers, trustees, consultants, academics, and government officials. Most importantly the book sets forth the implications of these driving forces for tomorrow's hospitals and the health industry and advances a portfolio of strategic management options for health care executives.

The New Hospital is organized in four parts. Part I focuses on the challenge of managing tomorrow's health care organizations, and introduces the concept of futures management—reconceptualizing the future as a resource to be managed, just as hospitals now strategically manage their capital and human resources.

Part II profiles emerging macrotrends in tomorrow's health care marketplace, illuminating the influence of key factors such as shifting patterns of health care expenditures, new intellectual and diagnostic technologies, telecommunications, patient noncompliance, and ethical issues raised by the new medicine.

Part III focuses on management strategies for the new age CEO and health care manager. In a complex environment there is no simple prescription. Many strategies are promising: nichemanship, innovation and intrapreneurship, and building multihealth corporations. All can be paths to the future.

Of course there are many possible futures. Part IV illustrates four plausible scenarios. Each hospital and health care organization must design its own unique future and aim its business and management strategies toward its preferred scenario, prudently avoiding others less favorable.

The New Hospital is a symbol of all hospitals that seek to design their own future. Through futures management, tomorrow's health care organizations will realign management styles, investment and market strategies, and organizational structure toward a desired future form—the future by design.

The New Hospital: Future Strategies for a Changing Industry is written for health care managers, purchasers, physicians, and trustees to illuminate key macrotrends emerging from the confusion of the present and to suggest advanced management strategies for the competitive future. This book owes a substantial debt to the Lutheran Hospital Society of Southern California and to Samuel J. Tibbitts, its visionary president since 1966. LHS is a health care company with a sense of the future. In 1982 LHS created the first corporate futures program in the health industry, inspired by the innovative work of Hank Koehn and Roger Selbert of Security Pacific National Bank's Futures Research Division in Los Angeles. I was appointed by LHS as its first futurist, to manage the Futures Program, and subsequently I headed LHS's unique research and development unit, the Center for Health Management Research.

Much of the research and preparation of *The New Hospital* was conducted while I was manager of the Futures Program, and the book is a joint effort of the Lutheran Hospital Society of Southern California with my own firm, the Health Forecasting Group. The Futures Program has flourished under the leadership of Mr. Tibbitts and expanded with the guidance of Dennis W. Strum, PhD, vice president for planning and development, and Lois Green, my successor as director of the Center for Health Management Research. With the support of Charles Ewell, PhD, president of American Healthcare Systems, the Futures Program has expanded to serve more than 25 AHS multihospital system members on a national basis.

Rick Norling, Len Labella, Duffy Watson, and Terry Belmont, chief executive officers (CEOs) of hospitals in the LHS system, are the innovators who have actively tested a number of the ideas against the realities of their environments. They seek to be the high-performance organizations of Chapter 20, and the relevance of my ideas owes much to them and their excellent staff.

A considerable debt of inspiration for my work is due Leland R. Kaiser, PhD, of the University of Colorado, who has been a pathfinder for futurism in health care. Special thanks are owed to Alex Cloner, PhD, of the University of Southern California School of Public Administration, and to Ferd Mitchell, DPA, and Bob Myrtle, DPA. Many of the concepts reflected in Part I were tested in Alex's doctoral seminar on managing tomorrow's health care organizations.

Several colleagues merit special mention. Jan Ney, PhD, worked as senior research analyst and assistant futurist with me at LHS and is responsible for much of the research and ideas in Chapter 4. Ira Studin, PhD, former assistant director of the Center for Health Management Research, lent his expertise in medical sociology to Chapter 11.

Chapter 12 owes a debt to Dennis Pointer, PhD, of UCLA's Program in Health Services Administration, and to Kathryn Johnson and Susan Anthony, publisher and editor, respectively, of *Healthcare Forum,* who published an early version of this chapter and continue to champion innovation in health care management.

Sam Tibbitts is the prototype for the new age CEO and architect of many of the concepts outlined in Chapter 13. This book, and the organizations he has helped to build, the Lutheran Hospital Society and American Healthcare Systems, are a reflection of his vision.

Dennis W. Strum, PhD, was the driving force in the Innovations in Health Care Management project funded by the W.K. Kellogg Foundation, which provided much of the inspiration for Chapter 18. Dennis likewise provided conceptual building blocks for Chapter 20, ''High-Performance Organizations.'' It has been a professional and personal pleasure to work with Sam, Dennis, and the LHS family. They exemplify much of what is hopeful about the future of the health industry.

This work would not have been possible without the able assistance of Judy Owens of the Center for Health Management Research, who coordinated the manuscript preparation, and the clear-eyed editing of many early chapters by Carole Sacora. I am especially grateful for the patient support of Mary Butler and her capable staff through the numerous manuscript revisions.

My thanks to Montague Brown, DPH, who provided critical early support to advance this book from the conceptual stage to reality, and to all those at Aspen Publishers, Inc. who have made the book possible, especially Mike Brown; Sandy Cannon; Barbara Tansill, health care editor; and Marsha Davies for her editorial assistance. The contributions of all those cited were substantial and appreciated, but only I deserve criticism for the final content.

Finally, there is a tendency now by some in our industry to yearn for the past, with its predictable patterns (and revenues). The past is gone, and the golden age of cost-reimbursement is over. The road to the future will not be found in the rear-view mirror. There is no such thing as destiny or fate. The New Hospital will not just cope with environmental change but will master it. Conceding its threats but anticipating its opportunities, I share a belief that the new age of the health industry lies ahead, and I wish each of the New Hospitals well with theirs.

Russell C. Coile, Jr.
Health Forecasting Group
Alameda, California

Part I

Managing Tomorrow's Health Care Organization

On Becoming the New Hospital

1

Tomorrow is the near side of the future. The decisions of today will drive the organization's success tomorrow. The future is neither remote nor mysterious. Threads of its design are visible today. Tomorrow's health care managers must look for patterns of change and act strategically.

If there is a single concept by which tomorrow's hospitals must be designed and directed, it is futures management. The future is a resource to be managed. Think of the future as a set of opportunities to be strategically managed in the same sense as capital and human resources. There will be many opportunities. Most of our dreams about the future—laser surgery, space travel, satellite communication—are no longer science fiction. For the New Hospital, the future is here.

BREAKING WITH THE PAST

The health care environment of tomorrow will be more hostile and competitive than today. The hospital industry is in transition. By the year 2000, market failure and takeover of some hospitals is likely. Third party insurers and government will refuse to provide a safety net for overpriced services and mismanaged hospitals. Management mistakes may be fatal. The margin for strategic error is shrinking. Paul Starr's chronicle of health care in the twentieth century, *The Social Transformation of American Medicine* (1982) should be instructive. Leland Kaiser (1980, 1981) warns that a critical mistake would be to assume that the future will be like the past.

Managers of tomorrow's health care organizations will need a long-range, global perspective as health care becomes an international enterprise in a highly interdependent world economy. The health industry may be dominated by large multinational companies. Between now and the year 2000, the U.S. health

5

industry will reach the $1 trillion level. Health is big business. Managers of the New Hospital in tomorrow's health industry should raise and broaden their perspective, to avoid aiming too low or too short.

TOMORROW'S ENVIRONMENT: TEN DRIVING FORCES

There is no consensus on the future. Futures watchers have positioned themselves all along the optimistic/pessimistic continuum from the survivalist Howard Ruff to relentless optimist Herman Kahn. Economic turbulence characterized the 1970s, and has continued. Wild card events such as the Arab oil embargo of 1974 and sky-high interest rates of the early 1980s have played an unexpectedly dominant role. Inflation in the health sector has continued 50 to 100 percent above the Consumer Price Index, and experts predict an imminent recession that could push many hospitals and other health care organizations into economic catastrophe.

Powerful forces will reshape the hospital industry in the near to midrange future by the year 2000. Here are ten of these megatrends that may have the greatest impact on the future of the New Hospital.

Aging. In 1980 one of nine Americans was over 85; in the year 2010 it will be one of five. Today's elderly are heavy health care users; they are three times as likely to be hospitalized than those below age 65. Tomorrow's elderly will be different. A new generation, the young elders (age 50–70) will be healthier, more fit, better educated, more affluent, and better informed about their health than any previous generation of elderly. The New Hospital can build a solid consumer base by marketing to the young elders.

Competition. The door to competition in health care has been opened, and there is no closing it. Hospitals will compete on price. Blue Cross, Aetna, and other major carriers are forming national preferred provider organizations to contract selectively. Not all hospitals will be preferred. Blue Cross of California has signed selected provider contracts with a preferred minority of the state's nearly 700 hospitals and 40,000 physicians. Jeff Goldsmith (1981) warns that hundreds of hospitals may close in the 1990s due to competitive pressures.

Integrated Health Plans. The distinction between those who pay for health care and those who provide it is blurring rapidly. In 1985 fewer than 15 percent of all Americans were enrolled in health maintenance organizations (HMOs), preferred provider organizations (PPOs), and other integrated health plans (IHPs). By 1995 these new financing-service organizations are forecast to gain a 40 to 50 percent market share. As the federal government encourages the Medicare population to enroll in HMOs, this trend will accelerate.

The growth of integrated health plans has tremendous implications for tomorrow's hospitals. HMOs utilize only half the hospital days now commonly required in traditional health insurance plans and government health programs. The life-blood of the New Hospital will be contracts that provide patient referrals from the HMOs and PPOs. Since most of these contracts will include a prenegotiated price for hospital services, it will put a premium on cost-effective management in the New Hospital. Those nonpreferred providers locked out of HMO and PPO contracts will wither without substantial private-pay patients or government subsidy.

Conglomerates. The multihealth corporation (MHC) is a conglomerate. Today one of three hospitals is affiliated with a multiinstitutional system. By 1990 it will be one of two hospitals. Yesterday's multi-hospital systems were small; in 1980 only one owned more than 100 hospitals. By 1990 at least three multihealth corporations will own or manage more than 500 hospitals, and 30 percent of total health care expenditures will go to multihealth corporations. MHCs will have the capacity to be large vendors to major corporations and insurance carriers buying health care in volume and at discount prices. Having the needed service capacity, location, and financial strength to compete on a volume and price basis will accelerate the growth of multihealth corporations and leave the free-standing hospital in a precarious position.

Corporate Practice. The health care industry is about to be totally restructured, and medical practice will change fundamentally before the turn of the century. One of 2 physicians practices in a group setting today; in the year 2000 it will be 9 of 10. Physicians will work with hospitals, not for them, through professional medical corporations. Hospitals and physicians will share financial risks and rewards, as reimbursement shifts from fee-for-service to capitation and prospective payment. Some hospitals and MHCs will own or manage medical groups, but most will have negotiated relationships with professional corporations that are independent. Case management systems will incorporate the philosophy and style of practice of the hospital or MHC.

The New Consumer. National opinion polls indicate consumer attitudes are shifting. Consumers have traditionally wanted quality care regardless of cost. Today's consumer is more price-sensitive. In Houston, for example, there are more urgent care clinics than hospitals because urgent care clinics typically charge half of what a hospital emergency room visit would cost. The Rand research (Phelps 1982) on consumers and health insurance underscores the lesson that consumers are cost-conscious. Where deductibles and coinsurance were high, health care utilization was reduced as much as 50 percent. Employers and insurance carriers are reinstating front-end deductibles in health plans across the country. This shift in health benefits will have the short-term effect of reducing hospital and physician use. In the long term these employer policies will drive consumers into health maintenance organizations, which minimize coinsurance and deductibles.

Information and Telecommunication. Think of health as information. Reconceptualizing the health care business as providing information puts a new light on the use of cable television, video discs and tapes, and even the telephone as ways of providing information therapies to consumers. Almost all of these information technologies are more cost-efficient than the physician-patient encounter. Leading-edge hospitals that invest the capital and expertise to utilize information technologies will gain the fullest advantage. In the information society multihealth corporations will be linked on a national and global scale by telecommunications. The American Hospital Supply Corporation is a model of a multinational company that makes extensive use of computer systems and video conferencing to link a worldwide network of facilities and services. Its computer-based customer network provides a model for the health industry.

Shifting Dollars. Health care dollars are shifting from inpatient to outpatient, from fee-for-service to capitation, from public to private, and from acute care to long-term care and health promotion. The New Hospital will need to establish effective case management systems and exercise the necessary discipline to effectively keep costs down. Hospitals will have real market advantages in being selected as lowest price preferred providers. As low-cost producers, they will have preferred access to large-volume purchasers.

Bionic Age. Six revolutions in technology will continue to be major driving factors in health care: (1) computerization, (2) artificial intelligence, (3) office automation, (4) genetic engineering, (5) super drugs, and (6) bioreplacement technology. There is an estimated demand for 35,000 to 50,000 artificial hearts each year. The bioreplacement organs and joints—hip replacements, knees, livers—will similarly provide new market opportunities for hospitals. On the other hand, as technology gets cheaper and more portable, many procedures will be done out of the hospital, with sophisticated new technology, such as laser surgery. New superdrugs may eliminate procedures such as kidney stones and cardiac bypass surgery.

Values. Today's board rooms are dominated by financial issues. The issues agenda of the New Hospital will be broader. Management values will play a key role in shaping the corporate culture of the hospital. The leading companies in tomorrow's health industry will have a distinctive set of values at the core of their management approaches. The hospital will have to deal with new bioethical issues raised by technologies such as inuterosurgery. Issues of life and death will be highly complex. The hospital may need an in-house ethicist and ethics committee to provide guidance for boards and medical staff. As a major corporate citizen, the New Hospital may also need an issues management program to identify emerging social and environmental issues, as well as to distinguish issues that serve the public interest.

THE NEW PARADIGM OF HEALTH

Illness has been the base business of the health care industry. The New Hospital must reconceptualize its business as health. The new generation of health care organizations should begin to reorient their planning toward the emerging paradigm of health. Society's attitude toward the concepts of health and health care is changing. The New Hospital must reposition itself to take a leadership role in the evolution of the health industry.

The old paradigm of curative medicine is gradually being superseded by a new orientation toward health. As individual and community values shift toward health enhancement, the health care organization of tomorrow must get out of the illness business and become an institution whose purpose is to keep its customers healthy. Borrowing heavily from Marilyn Ferguson, Table 1–1 compares the assumptions of the old paradigm of medicine with the new paradigm of health.

The central themes of the new paradigm are personal responsibility and wellness. The health care system is decentralized and deemphasized. Professional services are broadened from medical care to a wide range of human development and support functions. The contribution to health of the environment, the workplace, and the home is emphasized. For example, under the new paradigm the following may occur:

- Many hospitals will become health organizations—some with no beds at all, providing only ambulatory services instead.
- Only a few hospitals will possess the financial resources and expertise to provide high-technology acute medical care.
- The chronically ill will be cared for at home or in low-cost personal care homes, and dying will be at home, assisted by hospice programs.
- Health care organizations will share financial incentives with their customers to stay well; health maintenance organizations, which link prepayment and healthy life styles, will prosper.
- Changes in diet and life style will reduce chronic and acute illness, and there will be a declining demand for curative services and facilities.
- The leader of the health team of tomorrow may be the psychologist or health educator who calls in physicians and other therapists as consultants when needed.

Signals of the change are evident today, from the fitness movement to self-health groups. This shift is likely to have a profound effect on the health industry in the medium-term, as well as in the long-range.

Table 1–1 The Old Paradigm of Medicine vs the New Paradigm of Health

Old Paradigm of Medicine	New Paradigm of Health
Treatment of symptoms	Search for patterns and causes
Specialization by disease	Integrated, concerned with the whole patient; emphasis on customer satisfaction
Emphasis on efficiency	
Intervention with all drugs and therapies available until death	Intervention with the minimum appropriate therapies
Body as a machine in good or bad repair	Body as process, field or energy, context, dynamic system
Goal to eliminate disease	Goal to promote maximum health and well-being
Patient as dependent; professional as the authority	Patient independent; professional as a therapeutic partner
Body and mind separate; psychosomatic illness mental, treated separately	Body and mind connection recognized and utilized in therapeutic approach
Primary reliance on quantitative data; defensive medicine, batteries of tests	Major reliance on subjective data from patient and professional intuition to comprehend test data
Centralized regional health facilities and services	Widely decentralized services with many types of care providers
Isolation of the patient from home and family in a hospital for treatment	Treatment of the patient in the context of home and family
Physician's total control over the patient's care	Patients' assumption of responsibility for their own health

Source: Adapted from *The Aquarian Conspiracy* by Marilyn Ferguson, pp. 246–248, with permission of Jeremy P. Tarcher, Inc., © 1980.

NETWORKS: DESIGNING TOMORROW'S HEALTH CARE ORGANIZATIONS

Critics of today's health care industry have frequently characterized it as a nonsystem, with many fragmented and unconnected components. The remedy, they believe, is to impose a large, formal structure on the industry. Public-sector advocates argue for imposing a national health system. Private-sector defenders want deregulation to permit the growth of a variety of competing corporate configurations.

The critics miss the point. Far from a nonsystem, the health system today is a highly complex arrangement of providers, payers, and consumers. It may appear to lack a grand design, but it is neither unintentional nor irrational. An alternative way of looking at the health care system is to conceive of it as a network, a complex arrangement of interrelated organizations, shown in Figure 1–1.

As an organizational concept, the hospital is obsolete. The New Hospital of tomorrow is a corporation. The hospitals of today are real estate—assets to be employed by their corporations to gain the highest value and best use. The health care corporation is not a captive of its physical asset base. Health care corporations are networks of facilities, product lines, and operational units. Their pattern changes constantly. The New Hospital may own no beds in the same way a shipping company owns no ships. Beds are owned or leased as needed. The all-ambulatory hospital would have no overnight accommodations.

The organizational concept that ties all this together is the network. Some components in this corporate network are more tightly coupled and interdependent, such as the hospital members of a regional multihospital chain. Alliances are a network model, especially popular with nonprofit hospitals. The American Healthcare System (AHS) and Voluntary Hospitals of America (VHA) are well-developed alliance models. AHS has 35 members, all multihospital systems, with nearly 1,500 hospitals across the nation and annual revenues exceeding $14 billion in 1985. Other network components are support groups, such as group purchasing, HMOs or PPOs, capital corporations, and related businesses, such as durable medical equipment and ambulatory care centers. These are more loosely coupled and less interdependent.

Investor-owned health corporations are more centrally managed, extending their dominance through corporate ownership and standardized policies across their network. Both nonprofit and investor-owned health care organizations within

Figure 1–1 The Health Care Network

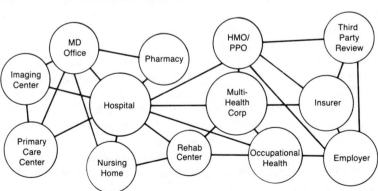

a network may act collaterally, as a unit, using the market cluster strategy to gain a dominant market share in a regional or local market.

The network concept provides a way to operationalize the more abstract systems model of organizational behavior. Social systems theorists have advanced the analogy from biology of the natural system, extending it into the corporate world. From this perspective the organization functions like an organism in nature interacting with and interdependent on its environment—the health care marketplace.

Like a natural system, the health industry is constantly adapting. Disturbances, new demands, and changes in the environment create disequilibrium, which is countered by a natural tendency to create a new balance. In extending the systems analogy to health care, rising prices stimulate resentment by major employers. Big businesses form political action committees and generate countervailing pressures through their insurers. Hospitals are forced into competition for preferred provider status. Some hospitals cut prices as others resist. A dynamic tension—the need for survival—permeates the system. As the environment changes, so must the successful organizations.

The Intentional Organization

If this discussion has a Darwinian flavor, it is deliberate. The successful health care organization of tomorrow is one that creates a vision of its future and builds toward it. This is the intentional organization. To rephrase Santayana, those who neglect the future risk losing it.

The intentional organization is committed to futures management: developing organizational strategies to offset or promote certain aspects of the future. The long-range perspective of futures management contrasts with contingency management, an adaptive model of organizational strategy that focuses on surviving the immediate present. Both futures management and contingency management are grounded in environmental theory, but with important differences that are illustrated in Table 1–2.

Fundamental to successful application of the concept of futures management is the link between intentionality and values. Corporate analysts in this country are increasingly referring to this link as essential to the long-term success of any business or industry. Tom Peters argues in *A Passion For Exellence* (1985) that an important organizational value must be a commitment to excellence. Organizational humanist John Brozovich (1984) calls for value-based management, in which the organizational values and culture are constructed on the highest social principles.

The point of departure for becoming an intentional organization is the value base of the New Hospital. First of all, health care is a social institution. Meeting that social commitment is the primary obligation of all health organizations,

Table 1–2 Futures Management versus Contingency Management

Organizational Characteristics	Contingency Management	Future Management
Time frame	Short-range	Long-range
Orientation	Reactive	Initiating
Strategy	Adaptation	Coalignment
Planning mode	Marketing	Corporate development
Motivators	Market forces	Social values and needs
Style	Entrepreneurial	Institution builder

regardless of their ownership or control. Each organization must balance its responsibility to community service with its need for survival and net return on equity.

The economic success of Japan in the post-war years has inspired envy and attention from corporate analysts. Western companies have tended to favor the three S's: strategy, structure, and systems, according to Japan watchers Richard Pascale and Anthony Athos in *The Art of Japanese Management* (1981). Japan has been more successful than the United States using its four S's: staff, skills, style, and superordinate goals. The Japanese secret is the amalgam of organization values and corporate cultures in a mutually reinforcing pattern.

The Japanese experience offers an alternative to Western patterns. Their secret is not unlike Blake and Mouton's (1964) 9.9 managerial grid—a management style that blends a concern for people with an equal priority for production. In Japan the corporate commitment to its employees on a long-term basis offers an alternative Theory Z to Douglas MacGregor's Theory X and Theory Y. Zen Buddhism and its concept of the tao (the way) permeates Japanese life. An openness to life and experience—the process—is as or more important than the product in the Japanese corporation, as Albert Low instructs in *Zen and the Art of Creative Management* (1976).

In American companies the pattern of job rotation and career mobility is changing slowly to the Japanese direction. Organizations have enormous investments in their human resources, which need the same level of careful management as their financial resources. American managers have been inspired by the Japanese experience to refashion the corporate culture and to align it with human-centered goals and values, with practices James O'Toole (1985) calls vanguard management.

There is no one best way to the intentional future of the New Hospital. In tomorrow's health care marketplace the organization may have a variety of roles and product lines. Each market will be unique. No single organizational approach may be appropriate to all enterprises. Primary care and long-term care may require very different organizational structures and managerial philosophies. Flexibility, open organizational systems, and a sense of core values will infuse the management of the New Hospital.

PURPOSE OF THE BOOK

The purpose of this book is to open a window on the future and to suggest managerial implications and strategies from the coming changes for the managers of the New Hospitals. The challenge for managers of tomorrow's hospitals and large health care organizations will be to create their desired future through foresight and strategic management. The New Hospital can be an intentional organization with a vision of its preferred future—not an accidental organization, which is pushed around by payers, competitors, and market forces.

The challenge of futures management is to bring four dimensions into coalignment toward the New Hospital's preferred future:

1. future environment
2. organizational structure
3. management strategy
4. values

There is no question that health will continually evolve as an industry. Part II of this book spotlights critical dimensions of the changing environment in which hospitals will operate. Change is a constant that underlies them. Each of these selected factors—social, technology, economic, environmental, and political—will be driving forces in the market of tomorrow's hospitals.

That is why tomorrow's hospitals need futures management. Futures management means estimating the likelihood of future conditions and developing organizational strategies to offset or promote certain aspects of the future. No one organizational model will be future-proof—capable of surviving all environmental shifts and dislocations. Tomorrow's organizations must be dynamic and continuously innovative.

In a turbulent and uncertain present it is essential to manage for tomorrow. In response to change, the New Hospital will adapt and innovate. Part III identifies critical areas in which the health industry will break with the past. The New Hospital and all of tomorrow's health care organizations must be value-based as well as market-oriented. Not all hospitals will survive. Successful adaptation will require skillful alignment of social and organizational goals with the personal goals of managers and their work force. The task of instilling motivation in an uncertain market will be a continuing challenge for management.

There are many futures ahead. Four scenarios—high technology, conglomerates, national health system, and wellness—are sketched in Part IV to provide a sense of alternative possibilities. Each health care organization should design and implement its future ideal. The ones that do so successfully—intentionally—will have thrived because they understood and practiced futures management. They will be the New Hospitals.

REFERENCES AND SUGGESTED READINGS

Athos, Anthony, and Pascale, Richard. *The Art of Japanese Management.* New York: Bantam Books, 1981.

Blake, Robert R., and Mouton, Jane S. *The Managerial Grid.* Houston: Gulf Publishing Co., 1964.

*Boland, Peter, ed. *The New Healthcare Marketplace: A Guide to PPOs for Purchasers, Payers and Providers.* Homewood, Ill.: Dow Jones-Irwin, 1985.

Brozovich, John P., and Shortell, Stephen M. "How to Create More Humane and Productive Health Care Environments." *Health Care Management Review,* Fall 1984, pp. 43–53.

*Cavanaugh, Richard E., and Clifford, Donald K. *The Winning Performance: How America's Midsize Companies Succeed.* New York: Bantam Books, 1985.

*Ehrenreich, Barbara and Ehrenreich, John. *The American Health Empire: Power, Profits and Politics.* New York: Random House, 1970.

Ferguson, Marilyn. *The Aquarian Conspiracy: Personal and Social Transformation in the 1980's.* Los Angeles: J.P. Tarcher, Inc., 1980.

Goldsmith, Jeff. *Can Hospitals Survive?* New York: Dow-Jones Irwin, 1981.

*Johnson, Richard L. "Old Memories and New Dreams: Economics for Nonprofit Hospitals." *Health Matrix* 3, no 1. (Spring, 1985): 15–21.

*Kahn, Herman, Brown, William, and Martel, Leon. *The Next 200 Years: A Scenario for America and the World.* New York: William Morrow & Co., 1976.

Kaiser, Leland R. "Futurism," Parts I–III. *Hospital Forum,* November-December 1980, March-April 1981, May-June 1981.

Low, Albert. *Zen and the Art of Creative Management.* New York: Playboy Paperbacks, 1976.

*Naisbitt, John. *Megatrends.* New York: Warner Books, 1982.

O'Toole, James. *Vanguard Management.* New York: Doubleday & Co., 1985.

*Ouchi, William G. *Theory Z.* New York: Addison-Wesley, 1981.

*Perrow, Charles. *Complex Organizations: A Critical Essay.* 2nd. ed. Glenview, Ill.: Scott, Foresman and Co., 1979.

*Peters, Joe, and Tseng, Simone. *Managing Strategic Change in Hospitals: Ten Success Stories.* Chicago: American Hospital Association, 1983.

Peters, Tom, and Austin, Nancy. *A Passion for Excellence.* New York: Random House, 1985.

Phelps, Charles. "Health Care Costs: The Consequences of Increased Cost-Sharing." Rand Corp., R-2970-RC, November 1982.

Starr, Paul. *The Social Transformation of American Medicine.* New York: Basic Books, 1982.

*Tibbitts, Samuel J. "Future Belongs to New Multihealth Corporations; Hospitals Should Join Now." *Modern Healthcare,* September 1984.

*Timmel, Ned, and Brozovich, John. "Managing through Values." *Hospital Forum,* May/June 1984, pp. 31–39.

*Suggested reading.

Part II

The Changing Health Care Marketplace

Chapter 2
Shifting Dollars

2

Health is a growth industry. From 1975 to 1985 it has consistently outperformed other industries including communications (15.1 percent) and diversified services companies (15.8 percent). The popular perception is that health is a mature industry whose decline is just ahead. That perception is wrong. The hospital industry is mature, and its decline is already beginning, but the health industry is young. It is a broad-gauged, diversified services industry. Many components are experiencing rapid growth. Industrywide the trends are for a period of sustained growth that will not peak until the year 2000 or beyond, as indicated in Figure 2-1.

TWELVE FINANCIAL MEGATRENDS

While attention has focused on the decline of the hospital sector, other more fundamental shifts are occurring across the breadth of the health industry. These long-wave changes will have a major impact on the payment and the pricing of services by the new hospital.

From Institutionalization to Noninstitutionalization

To put it simply, fewer people will be admitted to hospitals in the future and they will go home sooner. California is a bellwether state. Its residents in 1982 used an average of 845 patient days per 1,000 population per year. For the nation the comparable figure is more than 1,200 patient days per year. In some health maintenance organizations subscribers use fewer than 500 hospital days per year. These differences reflect more than simply variations in medical philosophy. Length of stay in the Kaiser-Permanente Health System, for example, is 5.3 days

21

Figure 2–1 National Health Care Expenditures, 1970–2020

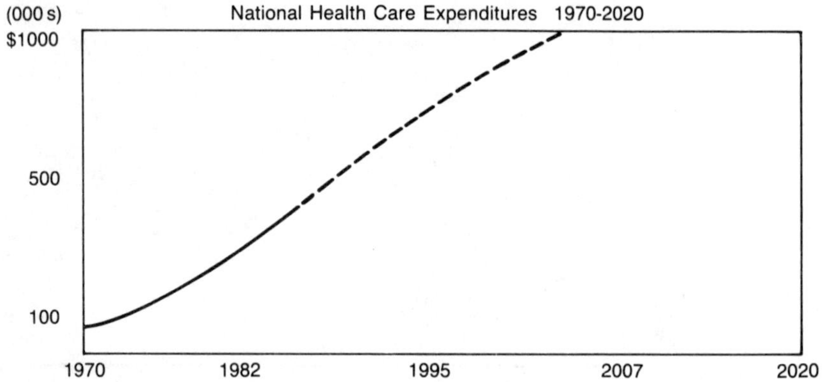

Source: Futures Program, Lutheran Hospital Society of Southern California, July 1984.

per admission. For all California hospitals it is 6.5 days per admission (1983). The difference is that Kaiser admits fewer patients.

Two key factors are at work: (1) financial incentives and (2) control. In the short term there will be some benefit for nursing homes and other institutional arrangements. In the long run all incentives will favor noninstitutional care. Nationwide the average length of stay for Medicare patients declined from 10.2 to 8.8 days in hospitals using diagnostic related groups (DRGs) in the first two years of the program (1982–1984). The California Hospital Association (Arstein-Kerslake 1984) reported that patient days fell more than 30 percent in 1981–1983, the first two years of operation for the new Medi-Cal Selective Provider Contracting Program. A 1983 study by the Institute for the Future (Schmid and Poulin 1983) forecasts an 8 percent drop-off in patient days by 1995 under the most hopeful scenario with up to a 25 percent reduction possible. Jeff Goldsmith, author of *Can Hospitals Survive?* (1981), has predicted that a substantial share of the nation's 1.4 million hospital beds may be converted or closed by 1995.

From Acute to Ambulatory

Two factors underscore the shift from acute to chronic illness as the principal business of the health industry of tomorrow: (1) changing disease patterns and (2) demographics. Heart disease, the number 1 cause of death for the past generation, has declined absolutely since 1975. Cancer and chronic lung disease will overtake it by the year 2000. While some of this reduction in heart disease is due to the success of high-tech coronary care units, many experts attribute the overall decline to improvements in life style.

Changes in age patterns—the graying of America—are powerful forces for the future. Today one of nine Americans is over 65; by the year 2010 it will be one of five. Older persons experience more chronic illness. More than 80 percent of those over 65 have at least one chronic illness. Tomorrow's older Americans are the young elders. They will be more fit, more active, more affluent, better educated, and healthier than any preceding generation. They will live longer and enjoy better health levels, despite one or more chronic conditions; because they are healthier, they will need fewer acute institutional health services.

From Invasive to Noninvasive Procedures

Tomorrow's patients and payers will prefer noninvasive technology. The number of surgical procedures of all types can be expected to decline 20 percent by the year 2000. Noninvasive techniques use fewer hospital days—or none at all. They are safer, with less danger of complications to the patient than raised by invasive technologies. Particularly hard hit will be high-cost procedures like coronary bypass surgery. The lithotrypter dissolves kidney stones and eliminates gall bladder surgery, one of today's most frequent procedures. New drugs to prevent coronary artery blockage may make it obsolete. If super drugs do not eliminate their surgical competition, payers may.

From Third Party Payment to Direct Contracting

In tomorrow's health care marketplace, as already in the retail industry, the only middlemen who will survive are those who add value to the process. The fastest growing competitor in the health insurance market today is self-insurance. As major employers cut out their middlemen, they are contracting for administrative services only or managing their own health programs and claims directly. Instead of using fiscal intermediaries, major employers and local and state governments are contracting directly with providers.

Purchasing decisions are made primarily on the basis of price and the provider's willingness to follow the policies of the purchaser. Much of this business is at a discount, below market prices. In 1984 more than 80 percent of the Fortune 500 companies were self-insured. By the year 1990 more than half may also administer their own health benefits. Mid-size and smaller employers will coattail this trend, through purchasing consortia arranged by brokers.

From Health Insurance to Integrated Health Plan

The insurance concept in health is dead. The companies that have relied on the insurance principle are experiencing runaway costs and rapid market erosion. In 1975 Blue Cross held a 45 percent national market share, and the indemnity companies 41 percent. By 1983 the market shares for Blue Cross and Indemnity companies had declined 10 percent.

The integrated health plan (IHP) will be the dominant form of health plan in the future. The barriers between insurance, financing, and service delivery are disappearing. Enrollment in health maintenance organizations has quadrupled since 1970, rising to 14 million subscribers in 1984 and a 12 percent share of the national market. In some metropolitan areas HMOs have achieved market penetration rates of 25 percent (Los Angeles, Minneapolis) and more than 30 percent (San Francisco, Alameda). By 1985 all Blue Cross plans had an IHP in the planning, development, or operational phase. They hope to siphon consumers out of traditional insurance plans and into these integrated health plans before the traditional plans go broke. Blue Cross of California prices its preferred provider organization, Health Net, at 25 percent below the price for its traditional insurance plan.

From the Insensitive Consumer to the Price-Conscious Buyer

One of the primary contributing factors to spiraling health cost in the past has been the consumer. Traditional insurance plans and generous employers buffered the consumer from paying out-of-pocket for health care services, especially higher-cost hospital care. So have Medicare and Medicaid. That is changing, and for two reasons. First, employers are revising health benefit plans to add deductibles and coinsurance. Second, consumers are demonstrating more price-sensitivity. The high cost of emergency room care has spawned a whole new industry: urgent care clinics.

The 1982 Rand study on consumer cost-sharing (Phelps 1982) demonstrated convincingly that deductibles and coinsurance could reduce health care utilization—and cost—by as much as 50 percent. This will hasten the reimposition of cost sharing by employees, as employers take away the generous health care benefits many companies bestowed in the 1970s, which are costing them dearly today. *Forbes* magazine reports that 34 percent of major employers now require employee deductibles for health care, up from 18 percent in 1984 (Teitelman 1984). By 1990, consumers will pay at least 30 percent of all health care expenditures.

From High-Margin to Low-Margin Pricing

The Byzantine world of health care prices has had little to do with cost and everything to do with the reimbursement policies of major payers. In tomorrow's marketplace health care services will be priced in a much more competitive way. In the past, high-profit services subsidized those whose cost could not be fully reimbursed under current reimbursement policies. Ancillary services were priced high, while many routine therapeutic services were underpriced.

As payers move to capitation or all-inclusive rates under selective contracting, health care services will be put to the market test. Fewer services will be sold a la carte. The pricing policies of the New Hospital will redivide the middle market. Premium services like intensive care and coronary bypass surgery will be charged premium prices. High-volume services such as cataract surgery will be discounted and subjected to heavy price competition.

From Local Markets to Global Markets

In today's marketplace there are enormous variations in health care utilization and expenditures, from Maine to California. Studies indicate these differences are primarily due to styles of medical practice that have become part of the health care culture of the region. Cost and charge-based reimbursement schemes allowed regional differences. In its new reimbursement policy based on DRGs, the federal government provides a structure for recognizing regional variations, particularly length of stay. The goal of federal policy is to level these differences, providing one national standard of reimbursement under Medicare.

At the state level, health insurance interests are seeking legislation to establish all-payer rates. Their intent is to reduce cost shifting from government-paid patients to insurance-coverage consumers. A third factor can be expected to reduce regional differences further—international competition. U.S. health care companies should expect foreign competition. There is substantial foreign investment in U.S. banking and real estate. Health care is ripe for foreign competitors. The success of U.S. multinational health care companies like American Medical International, National Medical Enterprises, and American Hospital Supply will encourage others. International business today is less than 5 percent of these companies' gross revenues; expect this to rise to 10 percent by 1995.

From Long-Term Debt to Equity Capital

The capital needs of the U.S. health care system have been estimated at $150 to 200 billion in the 1980s. This estimate is just for the redevelopment of hospitals and related equipment. Major amounts of capital will be needed for acquisitions, diversification, and new business ventures. The acquisition of Lifemark by American Medical International in 1983 was the first $1 billion deal. Health care is becoming a large industry, with commensurate capital needs.

Hospitals have traditionally relied on the long-term capital market and have taken advantage of federal and state loan underwriting programs. Investor-owned health care companies have made effective use of the equity market, as well as making aggressive use of the capital market. As a group, the for-profit hospitals are leveraged at 15 to 20 percent higher indebtedness than their not-for-profit competitors. Seeing that the for-profit hospitals can borrow safely at higher-asset–long-term debt ratios than once considered safe, nonprofit hospitals will borrow aggressively in the 1990s. Increasingly, nonprofits, too, will look to the equity market as a major new source of capital by creating new for-profit entities to attract investor funding.

Initial public offerings in biotechnology and home care were well received in 1982-84, although initial performance has been below expectations, which may dampen some venture capital enthusiasm. Nonprofit health care companies are converting existing activities to for-profit or creating new ones to take advantage of equity funding. Despite the roller-coaster unpredictability of investor interest in initial public offerings, dozens of new health care companies are likely to go public before 1990.

From Case Payment to Carload Purchase

The health care marketplace today is characterized by millions of individual transactions. The volume of these transactions is staggering. In 1982 there were 3.2 million hospital admissions and 381 million doctor visits. Although health care is the third largest industry in the United States, based on total revenues, virtually all these health care purchases are made on an individual basis.

Major employers are beginning to take advantage of their purchasing power in the health market. Given that employers spent more than $70 billion dollars directly on health care in 1984, their potential market clout is enormous. In the future the health care market place will be characterized by larger and larger deals. Health care will be purchased like styrofoam cups, based on price and volume. With their purchasing power, major employers and other big buyers such as state and local governments can achieve some substantial price discounts. Big buyers will need big vendors, giving impetus to the formation of national health care networks such as American Health Care Systems and Voluntary Hospitals of America, with 1,500 hospitals and locations in every region. Conglomerates will control 30 percent of the health care market by 1990.

The New Hospital must adjust its marketing and pricing policies. Nondifferentiated products like medical-surgical patient days will be considered commodities, sold on a large-volume, low-margin basis.

From Single Product to Diversified Portfolio

Today's hospitals are predominantly reliant on sales of a single product: inpatient care. For most hospitals, inpatient and related services account for 95 to 99 percent of all revenues. As inpatient care becomes a mature product its prices have risen to the point where many purchasers will seek lower-cost alternatives.

The rapid growth of ambulatory surgery and urgent care clinics since 1980 demonstrates how product innovation can occur. As the cost of inpatient care continues to rise, it will stimulate the development of new products and services along the broad spectrum of health services. As competition intensifies and traditional revenues shrink, health care organizations will expand their definition of health products and services. Health testing and self-diagnostic equipment are product lines that could expand any health care company's portfolio.

Diversified health care companies will seek revenues from unrelated businesses as well. Information systems, staff leasing, and real estate development are but a few examples of nonhealth activities that may provide a broader revenue base for tomorrow's health care organizations. By 1990 the combination of related and unrelated new business will reduce the average hospital's dependency on inpatient care from 95 + percent to 85 percent. For larger multihealth corporations, non–inpatient revenues could account for 25 to 40 percent or more of all revenues by 1990.

From Public Relations to Marketing

In a growing number of hospitals the public relations function is being superseded by marketing, often managed at the vice-president level. In an increasingly competitive marketplace, hospitals are using paid advertising to tell their story. Health will be one of the fastest-growing industries for advertising. Hospital billings are rising rapidly. Early hospital advertising efforts were low-key image builders. Now health care advertising is product-specific, using local newspapers to sell health-related programs such as sports medicine. Regional and national magazines are now being utilized for full-color ads prepared by the premier Madison Avenue firms.

Television is the next media resource for hospitals. Brand-name advertising has been initiated by the for-profit hospital chains. National Medical Enterprise has bought air time during the "Johnny Carson Show" in Los Angeles, and Humana's HMO ads appear coast-to-coast. Initial advertising focused on image creation, but price competition, at least in print advertising, began in early 1986. The merchandizing of health care has entered a new era in which health products will be sold like soap.

STRATEGIES FOR THE NEW HOSPITAL

Plan for a recession. The core business of most hospitals, inpatient services, will continue to decline into the 1990s. On the product life cycle, hospital inpatient services have reached the top of the curve and can be expected to decline. Experts disagree on how fast and how far the decline will go. Plan now for the recession in strategic business planning; there are three classic solutions to this problem:

(1) sell (divestiture), (2) harvest—cash cow—without new investment, and (3) innovate (product diversification).

Anticipate new competitors and new settings. New types of competitors will provide many of the new treatments in ambulatory care settings. Hospitals that diversify into these new service areas will therefore be competing with both traditional partners—physicians—and new health care entrepreneurs. Hospitals will be picked apart by other competitors, beginning with the most profitable product lines. Competitors can be expected to undercut on price and offer amenities hospitals cannot provide. To fight them, hospitals need to create low-overhead subsidiaries that can play competitively under the new rules.

Start retailing health care. The merchandising of health care is just beginning. Health care is not a product like soap, but it can be sold to customers—to individual consumers in the community and to major purchasers. These big buyers need a specialized sales approach. Effective retailing to the mass market of consumers requires market research, marketing expertise, advertising, and public relations. Few hospitals spend more than 1 percent of budget on marketing; more realistically it should be 2 to 5 percent of expenditures. It will take money to make money. Medical staff and hospital interests are converging—to keep their customer base and expand it. The medical staff is still the hospital's primary sales force. The medical staff needs to be integrally involved in the hospital's marketing approach, for their mutual advantage.

Develop contingency plans for price wars. Price competition can be expected. Major purchasers are already fomenting bidding wars between hospitals for preferred provider status. For-profit chains are repositioning themselves to be low-cost producers and low-price competitors. Discounting and price-specific advertising in all media, including television, should be expected. Hospitals should prepare contingency plans in anticipation that competitors may initiate price wars. Hospital boards should begin to address the issues of discounting and advertising on price now, instead of having to react under pressure for a competitor's initiative.

Cut losses. This is the time for tough-minded management. Product elimination can be as important to financial success as product development. In many businesses 80 percent of the revenue comes from 20 percent of the product lines. Hospitals are spread too thin across too many programs and services—too many to be effectively developed and marketed. Programs should be carefully culled to protect those that have the best profitability and most advance the mission of the organization. This pruning process is essential to maintain a healthy enterprise.

REFERENCES AND SUGGESTED READINGS

Ardell, Donald B. *High Level Wellness*. Emmaus, PA: Rodale Press, 1977.

Arstein-Kerslake, Cindy. "Medi-Cal Utilization Starts to Stabilize." *CHA Insight*, 8, no. 27. (September 17, 1984).

*Gibson, Robert M. et al. "National Health Expenditures 1983," *Health Care Financing Review* 6, no. 2 (Winter, 1984).

Goldsmith, Jeff. *Can Hospitals Survive?* New York: Dow Jones Irwin, 1981.

*Goldsmith, Jeff. "Capital Strategies in an Era of Changing Ground Rules." *Trustee,* January 1983, pp. 31–35.

*Hastings, Arthur C., Fadiman, James, and Gordon, James S. *Health For The Whole Person.* New York, NY: Bantam, 1981.

*Kouri, Mary E. "From Retirement to Re-Engagement: Young Elders Forge New Futures." *The Futurist,* June 1984, pp. 35–42.

*Mistarz, Jo Ellen. "The Changing Economic Profile of U.S. Hospitals." *Hospitals,* May 16, 1984, pp. 83–88.

*Moxley, John H., III, and Roeder, Penelope C. "New Opportunities for Out-of-Hospital Health Services," *New England Journal of Medicine,* January 19, 1984, pp. 193–196.

Phelps, Charles, "Health Care Costs: The Consequences of Increased Cost Sharing," The Rand Corp., R-2970-RC, November, 1982.

*Potzmann, Mary Ann. *Environmental Assessment: Moving Forward—An Integration of Interests.* Minneapolis, MN; Health Central, 1985., p. 88.

Schmid, Gregory and Poulin, Mary. "Health Care Services Environment: Hospital Utilization to 1995," Final Report, Year Two, Institute for the Future. Menlo Park, CA, June 1983.

*Skretnny, Roger, "The High Cost of Staying Healthy," *California Business,* June 1984, pp. 47–51.

Source Book of Health Insurance, 1982-83. New York: Health Insurance Association of America, 1984.

*Stano, Miron. "Financing an Alternative for Group Health Insurance." *Health Care Financial Management,* February 1984, pp. 36–39.

Teitelman, Robert. "Taking the Cure," *Forbes,* June 4, 1984, pp. 84–91.

*Trauner, Joan B. "The California Health Care Market—Where Is It Headed?" *Frontiers,* May 1985.

---

*Suggested reading.

Chapter 3

The New Medicine

3

From the pages of *Business Week* magazine, the headline shrieked: "Health Care Costs: The Fever Breaks. Fierce competition has set in—but will quality suffer?" (Cahan, Deveney, and Hamilton, 1985). The headline is a signal of change: a watershed has been reached in American medicine.

Administrators of the federal Health Care Financing Administration (HCFA) should be pleased. In the fiscal year ending September 30, 1984, Medicare spending rose only 5.6 percent. For the first time in a decade public payments for health care increased less than 10 percent. America's hospitals know why— hospital revenues increased only 4.6 percent in 1984. According to the American Hospital Association, hospital utilization has fallen 3 to 10 percent in every region of the nation since 1983. Some hospitals have held their own, but others have seen admissions and revenues slip badly. Who or what is to blame? The root cause is the new medicine that hospitals and physicians must practice under the federal government's DRG-based payment system.

WINNERS AND LOSERS

The new medicine reflects fundamental changes sweeping across the health industry. The shift to prospective payment for hospitals is only one of a number of key factors driving the apparent recession in revenues. Hospitals are the most visibly affected but only because they are the biggest target of cost cutting by government and major employers. The decline touches physicians, pharmaceuticals, and hospital supplies. Physician earnings, in real terms, fell 10 percent in the 1980s. Suppliers were hit harder yet. American Hospital Supply, which boasted it had never had a layoff, cut 600 employees in the wake of falling sales. Even Baxter Travenol, one of America's most high-performance com-

33

panies, saw revenues and earnings drop more than 20 percent in 1984. Both companies merged in 1985, to reduce their competition and increase market share in the face of a dwindling demand for hospital supplies and pharmaceuticals.

They are not alone. The entire health industry is in a transition period. The more fundamental questions are: Is the health industry's recession a temporary phenomenon or the start of a permanent decline? Will growth return, and how soon? And who will be the winners and losers under the new medicine?

SHIFTING PIE

The pie of American health economies is shifting. Economists are rewriting the textbooks of health care economics to calculate the impacts of the new medicine on the industry. It is clear that the old rules are no longer holding—it is much less obvious what will replace them. Here are ten of the most fundamental megashifts which will transform health economics in the next 10 years, with implications for which segments of the health care pie will shrink or grow:

Fee-For-Service to Integrated Health Plans

Like Mark Twain's death, reports of the demise of the fee-for-service medical system are still premature. Fee-for-service is still the dominant pattern of health care financing, but the end is near. The alternative delivery systems (ADS)—including the health maintenance organizations (HMOs), preferred provider organizations (PPOs), and other integrated health care financing/delivery plans—will gain the dominant market share into the 1990s.

The Health Insurance Association of America estimates that 15 percent of all 191 million Americans covered by some form of health plan are members of alternative delivery systems. More difficult to pin down is the growth of new and experimental forms of health care companies, which are hybrids of health financing and delivery. By one description these are the OWAs—other weird arrangements—organizational forms so new they don't have names yet.

The future is promising for HMOs, PPOs, and OWAs. Lutheran Hospital Society President Sam Tibbitts (1985) predicts when the dust settles in 1995, the market shares will be reversed: fee-for-service will hold on to 25 percent, with 75 percent won by the upstart integrated health plans.

From Health Insurance to Health Maintenace

Among the alternative delivery systems HMO growth has been most dramatic. Membership increases since 1980 in the nation's health maintenance organizations have averaged 12 percent per year and should reach 15 to 20 percent growth by 1990, predicts Dr. Paul Ellwood of Interstudy. In 1970 there were 33 HMO plans; today they number 311. New HMOs are rushing to gain federal qualification. In the first five months of 1985, the Office of Health Maintenance Organizations in the Department of Health and Human Services received 51 applications; 27 won quick approval, approaching the numbers for all of the previous year.

Nearly a third (85) of the nation's HMOs are for-profit. Wall Street is bullish on publicly held HMOs. Their price-earnings multiples are defying market norms with stock prices ranging from 15 to as much as 30 times earnings. HMOs are projected to increase their enrollment to 30 percent of the population by 1995. And for-profit HMOs will control 50 percent of the HMO market, up from 20 percent now. Preferred provider organizations (PPOs) are coattailing on the success of HMOs. By the end of 1984, 141 PPOs were in operation.

In contrast, only 4 of the top 10 commercial insurance companies reportedly made a profit on their health insurance business in 1984. Most of the commercial carriers and traditional Blue Cross/Blue Shield plans are scrambling to siphon members out of traditional insurance plans and into their new HMO and PPO plans—before costs under the old indemnity plans bankrupt the companies. Aetna, for example, is involved in a joint-venture HMO with Kaiser in Texas and has launched a new national health insurance venture with 400-member Voluntary Hospitals of America. Equitable has done likewise with the Hospital Corporation of America.

From Medi-Gap Insurance to Competitive Medical Plans

The nation's biggest customers of health services may be switching health plans. Medicare enrollees, who use health care at 350 percent of the rate of their under-65 counterparts, are finally being offered a bona fide HMO option: federal competitive medical plans (CMPs) to provide HMO-like comprehensive plans to Medicare enrollees. Only two CMPs had been certified by mid-1985, but more than 20 were anticipated in the first year of the program, growing to 100 or more by 1990.

When Family Health Plan of Long Beach announced open enrollment into its HMO plan for Medicare eligibles in Southern California in late 1984, it signed up a record 30,000 enrollees in three weeks. The reason was simple—virtually no out-of-pocket costs or front-end deductibles. That had enormous appeal to Medicare beneficiaries, who are paying more today out-of-pocket, as a percentage of their income, than were the aged 20 years ago, when the original Medicare bill was enacted. Today an estimated 80 percent of all Medicare enrollees have Medi-gap policies to insure against the uncovered costs of the federal program. With new federal regulations that pay HMOs at 95 percent of Medicare's adjusted average per capita cost (AAPCC), the Department of Health and Human Services estimates that half of the nation's 311 HMOs will enter the Medicare market.

Motivated by lower out-of-pocket costs, 40 to 50 percent of all Medicare enrollees could shift to HMOs and CMPs by 1990. Where would that leave the commercial insurance carriers like Prudential and Metropolitan, who write Medi-gap policies today? Likewise, where would such a major shift leave the average community hospital? Out in the cold, unless they join the HMO and CMP movement.

From Inpatient to Ambulatory Care

The biggest losers in tomorrow's health care marketplace will be hospital acute inpatient services. A forecast of hospital bed demand in 1995 by the Institute for the Future, under a grant from the Robert Wood Johnson Foundation, predicted an 8 percent decline of inpatient days in 10 years under the best-case scenario. The institute forecasts a possible drop of more than 25 percent, if all major factors—HMO growth, shifts in payer policies, and growth of ambulatory care—occurred at once. Signs of the transition are becoming evident. For the first time the rise of consumer expenditures for physicians' services (9.6 percent) outpaced hospital costs (5.6 percent) in 1985. Most potent in its chilling effect on hospital bed demand is the 12 percent annual growth of HMOs, which encourage ambulatory care and utilize hospital days at a rate only half the national average.

From Cottage Industry to Megacorps

The hospital pie may be shrinking, but the slices are getting larger. The hospital industry is consolidating into a smaller number of large companies. The era of the free-standing community hospital is ending. In 1984 the number of multi-hospital systems increased slightly, to 250 systems, up from 243 in 1983. Hospitals connected to systems rose to 2,052 in 1984, from 1,958 in 1983. The multis now own, lease, or control 30 percent of U.S. hospitals, and manage an additional 6 percent.

A Delphi survey of the future of the health industry conducted in 1984 by Arthur Anderson & Co. with the American College of Hospital Administrators forecasts the coming dominance of multis. By 1995, industry experts polled predicted that multihospital systems will own or manage 53 percent of all acute hospitals. The alliance model for nonprofit hospital system development is growing rapidly. American Healthcare Systems of San Diego added 5 systems to its membership in the first year, to include 35 multihospital systems with almost 1,500 hospitals. Voluntary Hospitals of America of Irving, Texas, is growing by the cluster concept on a regional level, projecting development of 20 of these groups by the end of 1985.

Looking ahead to 1990, health care market analysts predict that for-profit hospital chains may own or manage one-third of all U.S. hospitals. Antitrust is a coming issue. Already some for-profit multis are running up against the Federal

Trade Commission. American Medical International of Beverly Hills was forced to divest itself of at least one hospital in a market where AMI controlled more than 75 percent of local hospital facilities. Until 1993 AMI will have to seek FTC approval to buy any hospital individually valued at more than $1 million.

From Urgency Care to Primary Care

A major shift in marketing strategy is taking place in the urgent care industry. Urgent care centers originally targeted hospital emergency rooms as the major source of customers, where an estimated 80 percent of patients are nonemergent. Industry observers first thought the ambulatory care centers would attract about 40 percent of their business from hospital emergency rooms (ER). In reality they pulled only 10 percent from the ER. The wider market now being targeted is the mobile population without an established relationship with physicians.

In a quiet change of tactics, *urgent* is being dropped from the name of many of the ambulatory care facilities. They now emphasize routine health care and return visits. PrimaCare, Inc., of Dallas, began to expand services beyond episodic care in response to consumer demand. Continuing patients are billed; walk-in patients must pay all charges at the time of visit. An estimated 2,500 ambulatory care centers had been opened by the end of 1984, according to the National Association for Ambulatory Care (NAFAC), representing a growth of 1,400 facilities over 1983.

Interest in primary care centers is growing among hospitals, which comprise only 10 percent of the ambulatory care market today. The hospital-sponsored centers are increasingly becoming involved in HMO and PPO networking. Humana's network of more than 200 MedPlus centers are designed as feeders for its hospitals, as satellites of its new national HMO. The strategy is beginning to pay off. Humana's insurance plan—Humana Care Plus—grew from 40,000 members in 1984 to 360,000 enrollees in a single year, an increase of 900 percent.

From Warehouses for the Aged to Subacute Facilities

The long-term care industry, isolated from many of the changes in the health industry, is about to undergo a period of tremendous change, which will blow the lid off this heretofore placid sector. Experts predict the shortage of nursing home beds will become critical by 1987, as demand rises to the point where supply will no longer be restricted by state governments.

Under the DRG prospective payment system, hospitals need to move patients quickly in and, more importantly, out of the hospital as efficiently as possible. But not all patients are sufficiently recovered or capable of meeting their posthospital needs at home. Demand for nursing home beds under prospective payment systems (PPS) is predicted to grow 15 to 25 percent by 1995.

Nursing homes will be used as extensions of the hospital, as subacute facilities, for a short stay until the patient is ready for home care or self-care. Nursing-home stays still average more than 100 days per patient; 80 percent of those admitted to nursing homes never leave. That will change with shorter lengths of stay and more intensive treatment. In recognition of this expanded use of the nursing home, some industry experts recommend that Medicare restore to hospitals a higher payment level for extended care facilities for this type of subacute care and extend that higher level of reimbursement to specially certified nursing homes when they treat patients with higher levels of acuity.

Rapid growth of the 85 + population, from 2.2 million in 1980 to a projected 5.1 million in the year 2000, is putting tremendous pressure on the supply of long-term-care beds. A study conducted for the National Center for Health Statistics predicts one of five in this age group will require nursing home care at some point.

From Acute Care to Life Care

Investor interest in life-care facilities is returning, after financial troubles plaguing the industry in the early 1980s have eased. The life-care industry has been dominated by church-owned, not-for-profit organizations, many of which underestimated the cost of providing long-term care to their members. More than half of the 550 life-care facilities nationwide were built before 1976.

Today, as entrepreneurs enter the life-care market, the newer projects offer refundable entry fees, rentals with no entry fees and health care benefits on a fee-for-service basis—all counter to the traditional life-care pattern. In many cases the depreciable property is owned by a taxable entity. The latest trend is rental adult congregate living facilities, with no entrance or endowment fee. Limited use of a nursing home is sometimes included.

New life-care facilities are being developed by partnerships between not-for-profit institutions—hospitals, universities, churches—and investor groups that finance the projects. The not-for-profit operators have options to purchase the properties for fair market value about 10 years after they open, at a point when tax benefits are substantially diminished. With predictions that one in five Americans will be over 65 by the year 2010, the boom in Life-care facilities is building.

From Institutional Care to Home Care

A fourfold growth in home care revenues is forecast by Predicast, a Cleveland market research firm (Riffer 1984). In a study of 330 home care markets, revenues for home health services and products are predicted to reach $12.2 billion by 1988 and $24.8 by 1995, compared with the $6.3 billion market share they garnered in 1983. The major reasons for growth will be the rapid increase in the over-65 population and the concurrent increased reliance on home health care by major payers.

In a recent survey of Fortune 1,000 companies, 75 percent of the firms reported they had increased home health benefits for their employees in the past two years (Teitelman 1984). The real spur to growth of home health should come from DRG-based prospective payment, which emphasizes quick-turnover hospital stays and early discharge.

New for-profit competitors are entering the home care market. Home Health Care of America, based in Newport Beach, has boomed with an annual sales growth of 25 percent for the 1983–85 period, based strongly on its enteral feeding therapy product line. The field is not without risk. In 1985 the company wrote off $4 million in bad debts from enteral therapy that the Medicare program would not cover.

From Institutional Dependence to Self-Care

Hospitals have good reason to be anxious about the future. Like schools and government, hospitals are losing the confidence of the public. Social observers like John Naisbitt (1982) and Daniel Yankelovich (1981) find a growing distrust of large institutions.

Instead Americans are taking more responsibility for their own health. This interest is reflected in growing sales of home testing products and over-the-counter drugs. Health books have always sold well, averaging more than 25 percent of best sellers in the past decade, but they are joined by a proliferation of new self-health and fitness magazines, like *Shape* and *Medical Self-Care*.

The Stanford Research Institute estimates that 20 to 25 percent of all Americans are living a voluntary simple life style, which emphasizes self-help and self-health (Mitchell 1983). Thousands have joined self-help groups formed in the 1970s, many involved in health promotion and adjusting to chronic illness. These local groups are free-standing, seldom aligned or supported by health care providers. They represent a set of consumer demands that is being met largely outside of the mainstream of health care delivery today.

PRODUCT LIFE CYCLE

Since the Boston Consulting Group developed the concept of the product life cycle, it has been applied widely by business analysts to a variety of industries. On the product life-cycle curve (Figure 3–1), inpatient care is ranked a mature industry. If the analysts are right, hospitals will slide inexorably into decline. According to Harvard Business School guru, Michael Porter (1980), once a company reaches this final—and potentially fatal—phase, there are three escapes:

Figure 3–1 Product Life Cycle

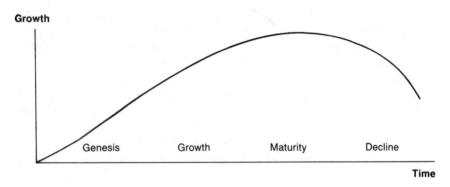

1. Harvest. Sell now, while the assets still have value. Hospitals like St. Joseph of Omaha and Presbyterian/St. Luke of Denver have done just that, selling at prices 20 to 40 times earnings.
2. Hold. Drive costs down to rock bottom, investing no additional capital, and maximize profits for as long as possible (the cash cow strategy). Hospital Affiliates pioneered the successful application of this strategy with marginal hospitals, setting a path now followed by Republic and Summit, with excellent financial results (14 to 20 percent growth and net earnings).
3. Innovate. Break the cycle through diversification and product development, finding new markets for old products and new products for old markets, and start the cycle all over again. A recent study of America's mid-sized companies ($25 million–$1 billion revenues) by McKinsey and Company revealed that the most successful firms innovate constantly, through product enhancement and product-line extension (Cavanagh and Clifford 1983).

U-Shaped Curve

From a different perspective, the health care dollar is being analyzed on the wrong curve. Rather than the product life-cycle curve, the health industry may be on the U-shaped curve (Figure 3–2). This cycle is more typical of boom-and-bust sectors like metals and agricultural products, which go through periodic cycles of high and low prices for their commodities. Over time, these U-shaped troughs average into waves, sometimes (but not always) predictable but usually survivable.

Free-market economists welcome such competitive markets. Fluctuations in prices and revenues shift with changes in demand and supply. When prices rise too high, new suppliers rush into the market. A glut of supply causes prices to drop, forcing all suppliers to cut costs and accept lower margins. When marginal

Figure 3–2 U-Shaped Curve

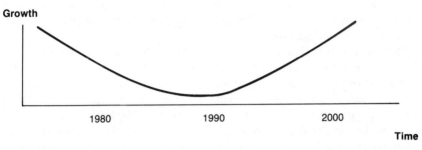

suppliers have been shaken out of the market, prices come back up to acceptable rates of return.

Or so goes the theory. In reality the crunch of falling prices, overinvestment, and a high-credit burden can leave an industry badly weakened, as American farmers can bear witness. Some declines are so decimating to an industry that it never recovers its former vitality. Steel, copper, and aluminum have been permanently weakened. On the other hand auto manufacturing has regained its former growth rates and profitability. The health industry is not used to the rough-and-tumble practices of competitive markets, but it is learning quickly.

SUNSET TO SUNRISE

The golden age of hospitals is over. The U-shaped curve may simply be the intersection of two lines—the decline of the hospital industry coinciding with the rise of the health industry, comprising a wide array of diversified health products and services. Each has its own dynamics, just as the decline of the railroads has not limited the growth of the transportation industry.

The growth of the health industry as yet has few boundaries and enormous potential. The proof is in the numbers: the hospital sector grew less than 6 percent in 1985, while the health industry broke through the 12 percent level in its share of the nation's gross national product.

American consumers today are more concerned and involved with their own health than ever before. That is no cause for alarm. Instead it is the promising base for growth of the health industry well through the turn of the next century. The new age of health is just dawning.

STRATEGIES FOR THE NEW HOSPITALS

Take a lesson from deregulated industries. From industries that have recently undergone extensive deregulation and increased competition, several lessons are instructive. One of the most important is that when change occurred, its speed and impact were often underestimated. Time to plan was a luxury. Those with a bias for action took industry leadership positions, invaded new markets, and established customer recognition.

Initiate product elimination. Hospitals and health care companies should act now to retreat from shrinking markets. They should adopt hold tactics, driving operating costs down and taking profits out to use for diversification and product development. Those product lines with low profit potential should be sold (harvested) or closed before losses cut into margins of healthy products and services.

Move into high-growth segments. Which segments of the shifting market should be targeted for diversification and investment? It's simple—those products and services that can be sold to business. A recent analysis by Slater (1985) of the U.S. Census Bureau's economic census for 1977–82 demonstrated that business services grew faster (123 percent increase) than personal services (91 percent). From this perspective HMOs and PPOs are prime targets for investments; ambulatory centers and home care will take longer for break-even and will yield lower profit margins.

Find the silver linings. In every crisis there is also opportunity. This may be the time to acquire hospitals or programs in financial distress. Consider making approaches to hospitals with losers—especially not-for-profit hospitals—that need to shed services and products. Hospitals with a charitable mission may prefer to give losers away to another institution that would carry them on, in preference to abandoning the service and its customers. The additional program volume can strengthen the market share of the recipient hospital and at minimal cost of acquisition.

Who will be market followers or leaders? When change occurs, it is said there are three types of people and organizations: (1) those who make it happen, (2) those who watch it happen, and (3) those who wonder what happened.

REFERENCES AND SUGGESTED READINGS

*Baldwin, Mark F. "HMOs, Other Prepaid Plans Rushing to Get Federal Medicare Qualification." *Modern Healthcare*, April 12, 1985.

Cahan, Vicky, Deveney, Kathleen, and Hamilton, Joan. "Health Care Costs: The Fever Breaks." *Business Week*, no. 2917 (October 21, 1985): 86–94.

Cavanagh, Richard E., and Clifford, Donald K., Jr. "Lessons from America's Midsized Growth Companies." *McKinsey Quarterly*, Autumn 1983.

*Fackelmann, Kathy A. "Hospitals Must Consider Expansion into Long-Term Care Market: Experts." *Modern Healthcare*, November 15, 1984.

*Fackelmann, Kathy A. "Nursing Home Crunch to Hit Hospitals Soon." *Modern Healthcare*, November 15, 1984.

*Gibson, Robert M., Levit, Katherine R., Lazenby, Helen, and Waldo, Daniel R. "National Health Expenditures, 1983." *Healthcare Financing Review*, Winter 1984.

"Health Care in the 1990's: Trends and Strategies." Chicago: Arthur Anderson and American College of Hospital Administrators, 1984.

*Health Insurance Association of America. "Source Book of Health Insurance Data, 1984 Update." Washington, D.C.: Health Insurance Association of America, 1984.

Herzlinger, Regina E., and Calkins, David. "How Companies Tackle Health Care Costs, Parts I–III." *Harvard Business Review*, September/October, November/December 1985, January/February 1986.

"Home Care Market Revenues Seen to Soar." *Hospitals*, December 1, 1984.

*Jackson, Bill, and Jensen, Joyce. "Home Care Leads Rising Trend of New Services." *Modern Healthcare*, December, 1984.

*Lovic, Robert H., and Gentry, Joanne. "Health Maintenance Organization (HMOs)—A 15-Year Perspective." *Dimensions in Healthcare*. Peat, Marwick, Mitchell & Co., November 1984.

*Mistarz, Jo Ellen. "Multis' 1984 Growth: Small in Numbers, Large in Impact." *Modern Healthcare*, December 16, 1984.

Mitchell, Arnold. *The Nine American Lifestyles*. New York: Macmillan, 1983.

Naisbitt, John. *Megatrends*. New York: Warner Books, 1982.

Porter, Michael C. *Competitive Strategy: Techniques For Analyzing Industries and Competitors*. New York: Free Press, 1980.

*Punch, Linda. "Ambulatory Centers Try to Broaden Appeal by Shifting to Primary Care." *Modern Healthcare*, December 1984.

*Punch, Linda, and Johnson, Donald E.L. "HMOs Predict Rapid Enrollee Growth as Consumers' Cost Concerns Mount." *Modern Healthcare*, January 1984.

Riffer, Joyce. "Freestanding Emergency and Surgery Centers Proliferate." *Hospitals*, December 16, 1984.

*Rose, Aaron M. "Entrepreneurs Reshaping Lifecare." *Modern Healthcare*, July 1984.

Slater, Courtenay. "The (Business) Service Economy." *American Demographics*, May 1985.

Teitelman, Robert. "Taking the Cure." *Forbes*, June 4, 1984, pp. 84–101.

Tibbitts, Samuel, J. and Strum, Dennis W. "Looking Forward: The Future of PPOs." *The New Healthcare Market*, Peter Boland, Ed. Homewood, IL: Dow Jones-Irwin, 1985, pp. 934–946.

*Wallace, Cynthia. "HMOs Can Seek Medicare Business, but Will Reimbursement Be Sufficient?" *Modern Healthcare*, July 1984.

*Wallace, Cynthia. "Investor-Owned Hospital Systems Tap into Growing HMO, PPO Markets." *Modern Healthcare*, June 1984.

*Wallace, Cynthia. "Investors Cool on Hospital Companies While Interest in Alternatives Heats Up." *Modern Healthcare*, July 1984.

*Wessel, David. "As HMOs Increasingly Become Big Businesses, Many of Them Convert to Profit-Making Status." *Wall Street Journal*, March 26, 1985.

Yankelovich, Daniel. *New Rules*. New York: Random, 1981.

---

*Suggested reading.

Chapter 4

The New Consumer

4

Americans believe they have the best health care in the world but are willing to consider tradeoffs to reduce its cost. Three-quarters of the respondents to a 1983 Harris poll believed that the U.S. health care system needs major changes. Consumers rated these cost containment options most acceptable:

- alternatives to hospitalization for minor surgery, tests, and care of the chronically ill
- higher deductibles and copayments
- requiring second opinions for nonemergency surgery
- insurance rate incentives for preventive care
- alternative delivery systems, such as HMOs and PPOs that limit choice of provider
- alternatives to physician care, such as clinics and other health providers

One of the most striking findings of the Harris poll was the discrepancy between physicians' and consumers' responses. Even more marked was the difference between responses made by physician leaders and consumers. While 44 percent of the public believed that lack of price competition has contributed very much to health care costs, only 8 percent of practicing physicians and 4 percent of leaders agreed. Sixty-one percent of consumers versus 13 percent of practicing physicians and 7 percent of physician leaders favored government price controls on doctor and hospital fees; 76 percent of consumers, 37 percent of practitioners, and 32 percent of physician leaders favored prospective reimbursement and standardized fees.

THE MARKET-DRIVEN HOSPITAL

Successful organizations are customer-driven, as opposed to product-driven. Product-driven marketing emphasizes the features of the product, not the needs of the customer. In contrast, customer-driven marketing matches the organization's resources and capabilities to the identified needs and preferences of consumers. Xerox has developed one of the most successful sales training programs used by Fortune 500 companies and health care conglomerates like Humana and Republic. The Xerox sales approach is based on a simple concept. What do customers need and want (needs)? How can the product meet these needs and wants (benefits)? How can the firm let present and future customers know it can serve them—and do it better than the competition (product differentiation)?

Redefining the Customer Base

There are three tiers of customers for the New Hospital: (1) major purchasers—employers, insurers, and third party payers; (2) physicians—traditionally, the real consumers of health care—those who made the purchasing decision; and (3) individual consumers—the new mass market for health care. Hospitals have and will continue to gain most of their customers for inpatient services through physicians. However, other factors are increasingly influencing consumers' choices about where and from which providers they will obtain health care, such as selected provider contracting.

Today's consumers are exercising a broader range of choices not just among physicians but among many different types of health service delivery systems and health care organizations. In a recent market survey consumers indicated that they made the hospital selection decision 30 percent of the time.

Employers and insurers have taken an increasingly active role to contain health care costs. Large self-insured corporations and third party payers have capitalized on the volume of business they bring to a community's health care system to negotiate discounted or prospective payments with preferred providers. Many of the agreements include cost control mechanisms, such as requirements that referrals to a specialist be made by the primary care provider and mandatory second opinions for elective surgery. As employers and insurers tighten their coverage and reimbursement policies, individuals will of necessity become more aware and discriminating health care consumers.

Taking Aim at the Mass Market

Getting close to the customer necessitates looking at population demographics across the nation and in the health care organization's service area. America has traditionally been a mobile society; the Westward movement of the nineteenth century continues, with a southern tilt. By 2000 the Census Bureau estimates that the Northeast and Midwest will lose 8 million people, while the South will gain 15.6 million and the West 12.3 million. By 1990 the population of the 10 Sunbelt states will increase at least 20 percent. Economic growth in this region will come from new companies and industries, not corporate relocations. People will migrate from other states and foreign countries.

John Naisbitt, author of *Megatrends* (1982), identifies Florida, Texas, and California as bellwether states. Florida is notable for its high percentage of elderly, Texas for its tradition-busting politics, and California as the originator of many consumer trends. The combined population (and purchasing power) of these three states is nearly 25 percent of the entire nation.

Targeting Ethnic and Regional Markets

Fully 83 percent of Americans identify with at least one ancestry group, but none is a clear majority. The Pacific coast, in particular, is becoming the new melting pot. In the 1980 census California's population included 38 percent of the nation's Armenians, 19 percent of the Yugoslavs, 13 percent of the Swiss, 11 percent of the Lebanese, and 35 percent of the Iranians. In southern California both the Hispanic and Asian markets are growing rapidly. Los Angeles is home to more people of Mexican descent than anywhere except Mexico City. There are more Samoans in Los Angeles than in Samoa and more Cubans in Miami than in Havana. Ethnic shifts are influencing every market and region. For health care providers the ethnic mix is important because of cross-cultural barriers to seeking or delivering care and different ethnic groups with disproportionately high incidences of selected diseases or disabilities.

Joel Garreau argues that the United States, far from being one nation, indivisible, actually contains nine distinct nations. Each differs widely, as profiled in *The Nine Nations of North America* (1982). They range from Yankee in New England to Mexamerica, which comprises southwest Texas, New Mexico, Arizona, southern Colorado, southern and central California, and all of Mexico. Each has its own population dynamics. Garreau notes predictions that by 1990 Hispanics, the majority from Mexico, will become the nation's largest minority group. In Mexamerica they are already a potent political, economic, and cultural force, only recently discovered by marketers. Oregon is in the middle of Ecotopia, which runs along the Pacific coast from northern California to Southern Alaska. The name is drawn from the contraction of ecological utopia to emphasize the values and life style of the nation's residents. Ecology in this nation is not a passing fad but a way of life.

Each region has a distinct cultural identity, which drives its economy, consumption patterns, and growth. National health care companies will have to be sensitive to the regional differences, and regional firms like Intermountain Health Systems and Sun Health Alliance may find a strong regional niche.

Impact of the Baby Boomers

By 1990 more than half of the American work force will be in the 25 to 44 age range, prime time in terms of earnings and productivity. The population explosion of the 1950s will be concentrated in the 35 to 44 age bracket; this age group will become the principal growth sector of the consumer market, with the number of family units expanding by 50 percent.

The baby boomers are significantly better educated than their depression-era parents: 22.7 percent of people aged 25–39 are college graduates versus 13.9 percent of those 40–64. Growing up during the Vietnam conflict fostered a distrust of government, manifested by declining political participation and traditional party affiliation. The activism of the 1960s has waned, but small consumer watchdog groups still flourish. One such consumer organization, the Health Research Group, operates a clearinghouse for attorneys researching product liability claims against drug companies. Its investigation of liver and kidney damage to Oraflex users led to a successful petition to the Food and Drug Administration to take this drug off the market.

As baby boomers age, social scientists worry about the strain this huge generation will place upon Medicare and social security. Beginning in the year 2010 more than 1 million will turn age 65, a phenomenon that will continue for 20 years. Phillip Longman (1986) predicts age wars in the future between the boomers and the baby-bust generation that will have to support their health and retirement burden.

Segmenting the Elder Market

Our concept of old age is obsolete. Today's older Americans are healthier, more fit, and more affluent than most appreciate. There are about 37 million households headed by a person 50 or older—44 percent of the current U.S. population. They are about evenly divided into four demographically distinct household subgroups headed by persons aged 50–69, 70–85, 85–100, and 100+.

Young elders of 50–59 are the largest and most affluent segment. Most of its members, especially heads of household and increasing numbers of married women, are still in the work force. Their $28,814 average annual household income (1981) was only slightly larger than that of the 35–49 cohort, but per capita income was about 20 percent higher. These empty nesters enjoy reduced living expenses as their children leave home, and most have purchased homes before prices skyrocketed. The 50–59 age group received almost half of all the money available to the older population, with an aggregate disposable income of $550 billion annually.

In the 60–69 preretirement years, people start leaving the labor force, and average household income drops slightly (about 10 percent) below the national level. Since household size is small, per capita income is still above the national average, by about 17 percent. Slightly more than 30 percent of the total revenues accruing to the older population were accounted for by this group.

Seventy will become the new retirement age. This is the most mobile population group in the United States—most likely to change their residence. The golden years 70–85 cohort contains few actively employed people. While household income is 56 percent of the national figure, per capita income is 93 percent of the national average.

The number of the new aged 85–100 is projected to double by the turn of the century, reaching 3.5 million by 2000, 1 million more than in 1986. The Census Bureau in 1984 made additional population forecasts for cohorts older than the 85+ group that indicate that the oldest of the old are the fastest growing population group of all. By 2000, the number of people 85–89 will increase 85 percent; 90–94, 119 percent; 95–99, 183 percent. Centenarians are the fastest-growing segment of the population today. The 100+ population will rise 238 percent by 2000. In 1982 there were 32,000 centenarians; by 2000 the figure is projected at 75,000.

Upscale: The Growing Affluent Population

Thanks to 30 years of economic growth and the spread of the two-paycheck family, Americans are prospering. Median household income is projected to grow about 20 percent by 1995, reflecting a rising level of affluence. Households with incomes of $50,000 or more (in constant 1982 dollars) will show the greatest growth. Eight percent of households in 1980 were officially affluent; by 1995 the number is expected to reach 18 percent. The upscale affluent are especially valued customers, willing and able to pay for products and services that meet their needs. They are less price-sensitive and more concerned with quality, amenities, and convenience.

While it is true that many of the higher-paid blue-collar jobs in smokestack industries are disappearing, the middle class (those earning roughly between $15,000 and $35,000 a year) is still growing. The new high-technology industries, where most new jobs are created, have a slightly higher share of middle-class jobs than heavy industries, according to several recent economic studies. In 1983, according to U.S. Census Bureau data, 40 percent of households had annual incomes between $16,500 and $38,354.

The Changing Family

No small part of the growth in the number of affluent families is due to an increase in the number of families in which both spouses work. The media have reported widely that over half of all adult women are now in the labor force. A more surprising and relevant statistic is that when women 65 + are excluded, the percentage of adult women in the labor force rises to 62.5 percent. Only 6.2 percent of women aged 16–64 are in school. The number of adult homemakers (not working nor attending school) increases with age, from 18 percent for women aged 20–24 to 47 percent for those aged 55–64. Women now constitute 52 percent of the undergraduate college population, up from 30 percent in 1950.

The Census Bureau found in its 1980 census the highest proportion ever of couples with two workers—62 percent. Seventy percent of dual-income couples have household incomes above $20,000 a year, versus 50 percent of single-income households. Dual-income families have more money and less time to spend on health care. Convenience and extended hours are likely to be prime attractions for them as health care consumers.

Redefining the Household

Household formation grew dramatically during the 1970s, as younger people moved out of their parents' homes and more households split up due to divorce. The number of households is expected to increase less during the 1980s and in different ways. Newly married couples will account for only 6 percent of the 12.7 million new households formed between 1980 and 1990.

Households headed by females alone will increase 26 percent; male household heads with no woman present will rise 35 percent. One-person households will increase by 30 percent. Forty percent of one-person households are headed by a person 65 +, but the fastest growth has been and will continue to occur among persons under 35 never married or divorced. Unmarried couples living together are still a small percentage of the population, likely to account for only 3 percent of all households by 1990.

The Diverse Single

About 40 percent of Americans 15 or older are often lumped together into a generic "single" category. This figure includes 45.7 million who have never married, 11.5 divorced, and 12.7 million widowed. The Census Bureau distinguishes between these categories and demographers urge businesses to do the same, since the life styles, needs, and preferences of each group are quite distinct.

Delaying Marriage

The median age at first marriage in 1982 was 25.2 years for men and 22.5 for women. This reverses a trend toward early marriages, which peaked in 1955, when the median ages were 22.6 for men and 20.2 for women. In the 20–34 age group in 1982, 42 percent of the men and 29 percent of the women had never been married. Rates of nonmarriage increase with education, particularly for women. Men have been more likely than women to remain single throughout life, but one population demographer projects that 10 percent of men and 12 percent of women now aged 25–29 may never marry.

Those who do take the plunge into matrimony have fewer children and start their families later, continuing a trend begun in the 1970s. Households with two earners are generally smaller than those with one. Only 10 percent of one-paycheck couples are childless, compared with 20 to 24 percent of two-paycheck couples. A tripling of the number of children born to unmarried women—from 5 percent in 1960 to 18 percent in 1980—is one of the most significant aspects of the decline in marriage.

Close to the Customer

Hospital executives indicated high interest in customer relations in a recent survey reported by *Modern Healthcare* (Gent 1984). Two-thirds of CEOs feel or were perceived to be close to patients, in contrast to 45 percent of senior managers. The survey revealed a major commitment by both not-for-profit and investor-owned hospitals to employ patient representatives as the CEO's ears. The patient representative, by listening to customers, physicians, and employees, senses trends in patient satisfaction. Many CEOs are also practicing walkaround management, spending up to 10 percent of their time talking to patients.

Expanding emphasis on customers is widening the use of product line management among hospitals. Product lines have long been used by manufacturing industries and are just starting to be adopted by the health care industry. Ed LaGasse, vice president of marketing for California Hospital Medical Center, is a prototype of the hospital marketing executive. Using LaGasse's experience at Baxter Travenol Laboratories, CMC has implemented product line marketing and management services. A full-time market manager is responsible for creating and capturing demand for pricing and for cost-effective promoting of the product to the internal and external target markets. Market managers work closely with their counterparts in nursing, who are responsible for developing and delivering the product on the operational side. A full-time market research manager challenges and supports the market managers with primary and secondary market research data used to make information-based decisions.

Table 4-1 Nine Publics for Hospital Market Research

Internal Publics	External Publics
Medical staff	Former patients
Residents (CMC is a teaching hospital)	General public
Nurses	Area employers
Employees of other departments	Referral sources (insurers, ambulance
Ancillary services	services, police and fire departments,
	highway patrol)

Source: Ed LaGasse, California Medical Center, 1984.

Taking the Pulse of the Market

As a 1984 survey (Sturm 1984) by *Modern Healthcare* magazine showed, few U.S. hospitals had conducted any type of attitudinal market research. Hospital marketing strategies are often based on instinct, rather than empirical data. A baseline market assessment done for the California Medical Center identified nine publics: five internal and four external (Table 4-1).

The purpose of the market research project was to provide a snapshot of the prevailing level of awareness for CMC and its principal products among each of these target publics. It revealed that the hospital did not have a negative impact to overcome but that it needed to create more visibility and a more positive, clearly defined image. Market research is a critical first step to identify the hospital's multiple publics so that appropriate product lines can be marketed to meet their needs and purchasing abilities.

While outside consultants can be helpful for special studies and to begin a marketing program, all hospitals need to develop an internal marketing capability. Insufficient resource commitment is a prime reason for the failure or ineffectiveness of many hospital marketing programs. Norman McMillan, author of *Marketing Your Hospital* (1981), recommends that 1.5 percent of a hospital's annual operating budget be devoted to marketing. This figure encompasses market planning and audits, research, program design, graphics, and advertising and public relations.

That's still on the low side compared to other businesses, where marketing expenditures range from 1 to 10 percent of a company's annual operating budget. It is also low for developing a new marketing function within the organization or for development of new products in a highly competitive environment.

Consumers Agreeing to Hospital Ads

More than half the respondents to a public opinion survey (Jackson and Jensen, 1984) by *Modern Healthcare* magazine said that hospitals should advertise their services—and the younger the respondent, the higher the rate of agreement. Two-thirds felt that advertising influenced the consumer's choice of a particular hospital, and 75 percent named a specific hospital where they would seek care. Most important factors affecting customer choice were the medical staff, emergency care, new equipment, and complete services.

America's foremost consumer-product corporations like Procter & Gamble have learned there is no such thing as a mass market. Demographic and life style changes have splintered the mass market into many different consumer groups—each with special needs and preferences. Marketing efforts directed at these better educated, more sophisticated, and more diverse consumers must be aligned with market research on consumers' ability to pay for specific products and services, on where and what types of services they will purchase, and on the most appropriate communications media through which they can be reached.

BECOMING CUSTOMER-DRIVEN

For the New Hospital to become a customer-driven organization, it must know who and where its customers are and how to reach them with appropriate marketing strategies. Marketing is not only acceptable but vital for health care organizations to know and serve the new health care consumer. A fully integrated marketing function uses up-to-date information about the organization's current and targeted consumers to shape program initiatives into new products and services. The critical activity is listening to consumers and finding out what they want. Marketing the hospitals products and services is a communication process, to let customers know that you have what they want.

Not all hospitals have willingly embraced marketing, but there will be no escaping it. Those hospitals that first master the new rules of a customer-driven marketplace will definitely have a competitive edge in the future.

STRATEGIES FOR THE NEW HOSPITAL

Recognize consumer savvy. The new health care consumer is better educated in general, and more knowledgeable about health care in particular, than previous generations. Baby boomers who have been exposed to television advertising since early childhood are sensitive to their rights as consumers and quick to question advertising claims. Marketing approaches and advertising must be as sophisticated as today's consumers.

Focus on segmented markets. The new consumers' divergent life styles mean that there is no such thing as a typical consumer. Rather, there are distinct health care market segments, with clearly defined needs and preferences. Hospitals need to use sophisticated research and planning methods to identify and reach the market segments they can serve best, balancing targeted marketing objectives with community service obligations.

Practice nichemanship. Find a need and fill it is a fundamental business adage. This is particularly important for hospitals in a time of declining inpatient services. In tomorrow's competitive marketplace excellent companies will find ways to differentiate their product or service from the competition, so that they are perceived as special by both their employees and their customers. They also will find ways to do what the competition didn't think or bother to do. Identifying new market populations and products means not following the herd. In a time of intense competition, market segments generally considered less desirable may become more attractive. Veterans are an example of a potential new market segment. Veterans Administration hospitals in many areas are overloaded, the World War II and Korean veteran population is aging, and Congress is disinclined to build more facilities and expand the federal work force if the private sector can provide the services.

Take a lesson from the private sector. Health care organizations have much to learn from America's businesses, which have created the world's most successful consumer economy. Hospital board members are an invaluable resource for this purpose. Their experience in the community is particularly relevant for marketing planning purposes. Many also have knowledge and experience in product line development, manufacturing, sales, and distribution that can be helpful in health care product marketing and management.

Revision the hospital through a marketing perspective. For health care organizations to become "customer-driven," the view of patients, physicians, and employees as consumers must permeate the organization and be reflected in all of its activities. Listening to consumers is the first step. Treating them as valued patrons and partners in the business of health is the operating principle. Every aspect of the operations of the New Hospital should be revisioned from a marketing perspective—that means through the eyes of your customers.

REFERENCES AND SUGGESTED READINGS

*American Council of Life Insurance. "The Prime Life Generation." Washington, D.C., 1985.

*Beckman, Dan. "Some Marketing Moves Unique: Others Borrowed from Industry." *Modern Healthcare*, April 1984, pp. 104–106.

*"Challenge to Business: America's Changing Face." *Nation's Business,* July 1984, pp. 18–25.

*Cherlin, Andrew, and Furstenberg, Frank F. "The Shape of the American Family in the Year 2000." TAP #22, Washington, D.C.: American Council of Life Insurance, 1982.

"Demographic Forecasts: Growing Old." *American Demographics*, January 1985.

"Demographic Forecasts: The Affluent Years." *American Demographics,* September 1984.

Garreau, Joel. *The Nine Nations of North America.* New York: Avon Books, 1972.

Gent, Donald I. "Hospitals Embrace Customer Relations." *Modern Healthcare,* February 1, 1984, pp. 134–35.

Lou Harris and Associates. *The Equitable Healthcare Survey—Options for Controlling Costs: A Survey of the American Public and Selected Professionals in the Health Care Field.* Washington, D.C., August 1983.

*Hauser, Les. J. "Ten Reasons Hospital Marketing Programs Fail." *Hospitals,* September 1, 1984, pp. 74–77.

Jackson, Bill, and Jensen, Joyce. "Majority of Consumers Support Advertising of Hospital Services." *Modern Healthcare,* April 1984, pp. 93–97.

*Lazer, William. "Inside the Mature Market." *American Demographics,* March 1985.

*Lehrer, Linda. "More Marketers Seek To Target People Over 50." *Wall Street Journal,* February 18, 1986.

*Marketing: The New Priority." *Business Week,* November 21, 1983, pp. 96–106.

McMillan, Norman H. *Marketing Your Hospital: A Strategy for Survival.* Chicago: American Hospital Association, 1981.

*Mitchell, Arnold. *The Nine American Lifestyles.* New York: Macmillan, 1983.

Naisbitt, John. *Megatrends: Ten New Directions Transforming Our Lives.* New York: Warner Books, 1982.

*Nelton, Sharon. "Adapting to a New Era in Marketing Strategy." *Nation's Business,* August 1984, pp. 18–24.

*Otten, Allen. "Decision-Makers Often Fail To Spot Key Changes Behind the Statistics." *Wall Street Journal,* December 6, 1985.

*Ralston, Richard M., and Jelen, Syma. "Hospitals in the News." *Hospitals,* April 1984, pp. 104–106.

Sturm, Arthur C., Jr. "Who's Your Target? The Answer Will Help Trigger Effective Ads." *Modern Healthcare,* April 1984, pp. 98–102.

*"Ten Forces Reshaping America." *U.S. News & World Report,* March 19, 1984, pp. 40–54.

*Suggested reading.

Chapter 5

Working Smart: The Intellectual Technologies

5

The key to increased productivity in the future will be working smart. The essence of the concept is to rethink the processes of producing goods and services to increase efficiency and output. American productivity has been widely criticized for not keeping pace with Japan and Germany despite higher pay for American workers. Working smart is an attitude, not a magic bullet solution, for enhancing productivity. The United States holds a worldwide edge in information systems technology that may help close the productivity gap.

The intellectual technologies will provide new strategies for productivity improvement. In contrast to the industrial technologies, these computer-based techniques improve the thought processes involved in the production of a good or service. They include word processing, data processing, decision support systems, robotics, expert systems, and artificial intelligence. Intellectual technologies do not achieve their most powerful effects by mechanizing what people are doing. Instead they simplify tasks and eliminate unnecessary job steps.

OFFICE AUTOMATION

Office automation may be one of the techniques of the future for increasing white-collar productivity. According to a major study by management consultants Booz Allen and Hamilton (Curley and Pyburn 1982), appropriate information technology could reclaim 15 percent of managerial and professional time. Sixty percent of the American work force today is classified as white collar, a sizable target for productivity improvement through office automation. The target is bigger in hospitals: 75 percent of hospital staff can be classified as "knowledge of workers."

61

These knowledge workers could work more efficiently utilizing word processors, decision support systems, and telecommunications. Office automation consultants have suggested that offices are unproductive because business has invested only $2,500 per white-collar employee versus about 10 times that amount of capital investment for each factory worker.

Office automation has been slow to take hold. In 1984 only 60 major corporations had systems with more than 100 work stations. Problems of linking equipment from different manufacturers may soon be overcome by local area networks (LAN) now coming to market. Lack of standardization, incompatibility between different manufacturers, and rapidly changing technology have kept buyers skeptical. New LAN systems from Apple, IBM, and independent vendors are overcoming the compatibility problem. Hewlett-Packard's experimental pocket computer for nurses links bedside computer work stations with a shared host computer.

Computer-Assisted Work

The new world of computer-assisted work will change not just the tasks and process of work but the work itself. Newspapers are the most highly automated industry in the nation. When a reporter types an article on the computer terminal, it goes into a central processing unit, where it is edited and then utilized to prepare the printing face from which the newspaper will be directly printed. This efficiency is made possible by a radical change in the entire process in which paper is eliminated from all but the final phase of production, printing the newspaper itself.

By 1990 an estimated 40 to 50 percent of all American workers will be making daily use of electronic terminal equipment, using some 38 million terminal-based work stations in offices, factories, and schools. There will be 34 million home computers and another 7 million portable terminals, most of them quite inexpensive.

Work Stations

In the information era the work station will replace the assembly line as the work site of the majority of American workers. Advanced circuitry will make possible fully integrated work stations operating under standard protocols requiring the minimum of user computer literacy. Smarter work stations can be used by lesser-skilled workers at lower cost without compromising productivity or quality. As the price of hardware falls, work stations will become increasingly specialized. Work stations with unique hardware and software, data bases, and lexicons will satisfy the demands of a work force segmented by function and occupation, for example, physician, nurse, accountant, and manager.

The physician's office is becoming a highly automated work station in tomorrow's decentralized remote practice networks (RPNs) linked to PPOs and HMOs. Computerization and miniaturization of diagnostic equipment for physicians' offices by companies like Electro-Nucleonics and Clay-Adams give doctors the capacity to conduct sophisticated office testing using equipment costing only 10 to 20 percent of hospital-based equipment.

Increases in the data storage capacity of microsized personal computers will decentralize many tasks and functions. A new mainframe computer introduced by NCR in 1985 takes up only 2 cubic feet. Work stations can be located anywhere—in the office, nursing unit, factory floor, or home. The Internal Revenue Service ordered 18,000 Lap-top Zenith microcomputers in 1986 for its field agents. Telecommunications makes location a minimal factor for many work activities. Portable computers—even hand-held models—add mobility to the work station. With pocket-sized computers as the medical chart of the future, nurses and physicians can access the hospital's clinical data base and medical decision-support software directly from the bedside.

CAD/CAM

Computer-aided design and manufacturing (CAD/CAM) is working to change the face of American industry. Computer miniaturization has made possible new control systems, decentralized deeply into the processes of production. This has reduced dependence on large, centralized, computer-based management systems. Automation drove the development of the sophisticated hospital laboratory, but a new generation of testing equipment will allow a number of procedures to be conducted by small, highly efficient devices backed by personal computers. These will be located on the hospital unit, at bedside, and even directly on the patient. Similar devices in physicians' offices will link office-based practitioners to the shared data bases of the hospital or even the health care corporation. In health care CAD/CAM will mean computer-assisted diagnosis/computer-aided medicine.

Robots

Robots are the ultimate in computer-aided manufacturing systems. Japan has established world leadership in robotics. One fully automated factory in Japan produces robots capable of building themselves. The concept of artificial life may need redefinition. Robots will change the work place, not simply by replacing people but by changing the way in which goods and services are produced. Robots are already capable of a wide range of functions, including assembly, materials handling, testing, and manufacturing.

The robotics industry is estimated to grow 35 percent per year through the 1980s stimulated in part by the market entry of IBM. Only 10,000 robots were at work in U.S. industries in 1985, but the number is expected to mushroom to 150,000 by 1990. Materials-handling robots are already at work in hospital supply systems, and patient-lifting robots are making an entry. In health care jobs with high repetition, robotics solutions will be developed. Domestic robots will provide home support for the chronically ill, under guidance from the Home Health Agency and the physician.

Software

Software transforms the computer from a massive abacus into a many-faceted instrument. In the early generations of computers, programming the devices required highly specialized technicians who could work in complex mathematical languages. The term *software* describes the programs that have been created to manage everyday tasks as well as complex routines. The information industry is already beginning to shift from a hardware to a software orientation. There are commercially available software programs for many industrial, business, and personal needs.

Decision software programs utilize computing power to search, array, compare, display, and analyze data. Wordstar and Lotus's 1-2-3, for word processing and quantitative analysis, are two of the most popular software programs available for personal computers. Framework and Symphony bundle software for an electronic spreadsheet, data base manager, text processor, and graphing module into one integrated analysis tool for managers. The MacIntosh personal computer from Apple provides built-in software to facilitate its use by symbols and an electronic pointer called a mouse. If users want to get rid of something, they just point to the trashcan symbol and push the button. Software will make the computer a user-friendly device for many business and personal uses.

The new software of medicine is being written today. More than 4,000 software programs with health care applications were available in 1985, most to support physicians' office practice. Clinical practice software will come to market before 1990. Already more than 50 expert systems in medicine are in development and testing.

Distributed Data Systems

Distributed data systems will decentralize information processing. It will allow individual users at their work stations to define their needs and solve their own problems using simple commands, even with large data bases. Eliminating channels and levels in multitiered organizations has enormous potential to increase efficiency. Reducing the distance between the product and the user can increase the likelihood of successfully satisfying consumer expectations.

Keeping close to the customer—a classic principle for marketing excellence—can be facilitated by decentralization of data resources, analysis tools, and information. Hospitals and health care companies are linking physicians' offices, home health agencies, and other decentralized providers into large-scale integrated remote practice networks, to share software and common data bases.

Executive Work Station

The executive work station is intended to provide a supportive environment for the managers of the future. Not all executives are eager to join the information society. At least 1 of 10 managers confesses to acute computer-phobia. Executive reluctance to be seen at a keyboard, a status problem, and limited typing skills pose real barriers to acceptance of the new armament of intellectual technologies. The executive work station will include a computer terminal as a standard feature. It's simply a matter of time.

Office automation experts predict that one of two managers will work at a terminal by 1990. One office furniture manufacturer offers up to 40 different components attached to a central power-wired beam, providing a wide array of electronic decision-support and communications systems for the future executive. For those concerned about being seen with their computer, terminals can be stored behind hidden panels, and detached keyboards can be operated from the executive lap.

The executive university of the future may be the home computer terminal. A two-year postgraduate course for executives in strategic management, costing $25,000, is being conducted via computer by the Western Behavioral Institute in La Jolla, California.

Artificial Intelligence

Artificial intelligence (AI) may be a commercial reality by the twenty-first century. It is an ambitious attempt to duplicate human intelligence in a machine. In the practical application of artificial intelligence, experts suggest it will first come to market in the field of medicine.

The deductive reasoning process of medicine is highly compatible with the computer logic process. Computerization of diagnostic routines is well underway, with dozens of extensively developed programs in various specialties. Knowledge-based systems such as INTERNIST-1 and MYCIN have been developed by AI centers such as the Decisions-Systems Laboratory at the University of Pittsburgh. As INTERNIST may become the standard diagnostic tool of internal medicine, more than 50 expert systems are being refined and tested in oncology, mental health, and other specialties. Dr. Lawrence Reed, inventor of the Problem-Oriented Medical Record, is developing a new series of clinical decision support software packages. Priced at $100 per module, each is designed to diagnose and treat a specific medical problem.

Supercomputers

A handful of supercomputers now make enormous computational power available. While personal computers are capable of a few hundred arithmetic operations per second, these powerful machines have peak computing speeds of more than 100 million operations per second. The speed of large-scale scientific computers has doubled every two years since 1950. The latest supercomputers are the Cray-1, built by Cray Research, and CYBER 205, from the Control Data Corporation.

The kinds of problems for which these computers are designed are found on the frontiers of fields like aerodynamics, seismology, meteorology, and atomic, nuclear, and plasma physics. Japan is investing $10 billion in a five-year research and development (R&D) effort to build the next generation of supercomputers in an effort to surpass U.S. leadership.

INTELLIGENT BUILDINGS = INTELLIGENT HOSPITALS

Real estate developers are building "smart" office buildings and computerized homes in California, Texas, New York, and Florida. The hospital of the future will be designed as an intelligent system. Integrated voice and data communications will be hard-wired into the facility using fiber optic cable linking work station plug-in locations at bedside and in all clinical and administrative locations. Electronic environmental sensors will continuously monitor the indoor climate, adjusting heat and air-conditioning automatically. Built-in computers will run the elevators, monitor fire and security, and control video programming to patients and professionals.

STRATEGIES FOR THE NEW HOSPITAL

Productivity. Successful health care organizations of the future will be those that can deliver an integrated package of services at a prenegotiated price.

- Productivity is not a fad. In a marketplace where all purchasers will want discounts from their health care vendors, there will be a premium on cost effectiveness.

- Intellectual technologies can assist health organizations to reverse the trends toward greater intensity of staff and patients and declining productivity per employee.

- Many health workers are knowledge workers performing information-related tasks and are targets for adaptation of the intellectual technologies from the private sector.

- Health organizations are 24-hour operations with excellent potential for substitution of computer-based systems and robotics for personnel.

- Redesign of tasks and functions using CAD/CAM will produce even more productivity gains by changing the nature of work to take advantage of the new technologies.

- Planning the transition into the information era will need a blend of strategic planning and management science with real sensitivity to the human aspects. To avoid an antitechnology backlash, those who are closest to the tasks should be involved in rethinking and redesigning them.

Decentralization. The intellectual technologies will facilitate development of management systems for the decentralized health care conglomerates of tomorrow.

- Successful health organizations will invest in R&D for management and service programs that can be institutionalized through software and utilized systemwide.

- Control over decentralized organizations can be maintained through interlocking management software and information systems, promoting uniform quality and cost-efficiency.

- Decentralization of initiative and responsibility can be expanded through distributed data systems, which allow local users to interact with the large central data base in routines that meet their specific local needs (one solution to the problem of underutilized automated hospital information systems).

- Facilities and services need not be clustered in high-cost hospital space but can be located in high-access convenience locations, close to the customer. Support services can be located in low-cost space out of the hospital, even miles away.

- Health services and programs can be franchised on a regional, national, and multinational basis. Standardized software will provide control systems for finance, records, administration, and even marketing and customer relations.

Changing practice of medicine. Artificial intelligence will profoundly change the practice of medicine.

- Computerized medicine will become commonplace before the year 2000 in a growing number of fields of general and specialty practice. At first the computer will be utilized as a consultant, to generate second opinions and test physician judgments.

- Ultimately the computer may become the primary diagnostician and therapy director based on standard protocols for all major disease categories that will have been developed and sanctioned by the various specialty boards. Physicians will function as consultants for more complex cases, as well as therapy providers.

- The computer will backstop health workers in remote rural locations and relieve professional isolation.

- Nurses and other health workers will bypass the physician for many routine questions and functions. The computer will be more accessible and significantly lower cost.

- Health information data bases will become commercially available directly to consumers, at first as a luxury service through commercial computer service bureaus but then as a service from health care organizations to their subscribers.

- A corporate philosophy of care can be programmed into the computer medical programs, to promote delivery of standardized quality of care across many decentralized locations.

REFERENCES AND SUGGESTED READINGS

*Barrett, F.D. "The Robot Revolution." *The Futurist* XIX, no. 5:37–40.

*Burck, Charles G. "Working Smarter." *Fortune*, June 15, 1981.

*Clancy, William J., and Shortcliffe, Edward H. *Readings in Medical Artificial Intelligence: The First Decade*. Reading, MA: Addison-Wesley, 1984.

*Coates, Vary T. "The Potential Impact of Robotics." *Futurist*, February 1983.

*Cordell, Arthur J. "Work in the Information Age." *The Futurist* XIX, no. 6 (December 1985):12–14.

Curley, Kathleen F., and Pyburn, Philip J. "Intellectual Technologies: The Key to Improving White Collar Productivity." *Sloan Management Review*, Fall 1982.

*Forbes, Jim. "IRS Announcement Sparks New Interest in Portables." *Info World* 3, issue 9 (March 3, 1986).

*Giuliano, Vincent E. "The Mechanization of Office Work." *Scientific American*, September 1982.

*Krouse, John, L. "Engineering Without Paper." *High Technology* 6, no. 3 (March 1986):38–46.

*Lecht, Charles P. "Blueskying without Apology about the Future Office." *Administration Management*, August 1982.

*Levine, Ronald D. "Supercomputers." *Scientific American*, January 1982.

Longman, Phillip. "Age Wars: The Coming Battle Between Young and Old." *The Futurist* XX, no. 1: (January-February 1986):3–11.

*McCorduck, Pamela. *Machines Who Think*. San Francisco: W.H. Freeman & Co., 1979.

*Meyer, N. Dean. "The Office Automation Cookbook: Management Strategies for Getting Office Automation Moving." *Sloan Management Review*, Winter 1983.

*Miller, Randolph, Pople, Harry E., Jr., and Myers, Jack D. "INTERNIST-1, An Experimental Computer-Based Diagnostic Consultant for General Internal Medicine." *New England Journal of Medicine*, August 19, 1982.

*Rowan, Roy. "Executive Ed. at Computer U." *Fortune*, March 7, 1983.

*Sachs, Randi T. "Executive Workstations: From Mahogany to Mechanized." *Administrative Management*, October 1982.

*Uttal, Bro. "What's Detaining the Office of the Future?" *Fortune*, May 3, 1982.

*Zuboff, Shoshana. "New Worlds of Computer-Mediated Work." *Harvard Business Review*, September–October 1982.

———

*Suggested reading.

Chapter 6

Telecommunications

6

America today is in the postindustrial era. This is a change as significant as the shift from the agricultural to the industrial age, more than 150 years ago. The growing visibility of the computer is the sunrise of the information society. The economy has changed dramatically. More than 50 percent of the work force is employed in information-related industries. For comparison, information workers comprised 19 percent of the work force in 1920 and 50 percent in 1976.

Health is information, and the New Hospital is part of the information society. Much of health care involves the processing of information and the provision of information therapies—expert counsel for the treatment of the ill and reassurance for the worried well.

TELECOMMUNICATIONS REVOLUTION

Rapid-pace advancements in communications technology that began with the space program have led to the shift to the information society. These breakthrough technologies are coming to market at prices that will make telecommunications affordable for multihealth corporations, hospitals, and a growing home market. Satellite communication is already handling 80 percent of all long distance calls. More than 100 satellites now circle the planet. The majority of the nonmilitary satellites provide communication services. An international call in 1995 may cost 50¢ or 25¢ by the year 2000.

Telecommunications was the first commercial venture in space. As the cost of satellite use drops, telecommunications is widely used in long-distance data transfer in a growing number of commercial applications. Banking and retail will be two major users. Banking data can be relayed across country via satellite, facilitating development of national banking networks. Retail will use it for credit checks and point-of-sale (POS) debit of consumer accounts. The boundaries between computers and communications are breaking down rapidly. IBM is repositioning to become a communications company; AT&T is a new entrant in the computer industry.

Fiber Optic Cable

The telephone will continue to be the most frequently used mode of communications, but there will be something new: the wire. The familiar twisted-wire cable that links America's 162 million telephones (there are 257 million worldwide) will be replaced by fiber optic cable. Fibers as fine as a human hair are not only smaller, so more can be bunched in each cable, but have a much broader bandwidth. They can carry a number of messages simultaneously on radio-frequency carriers, a major advantage over twisted wire, which carries one message at a time directly. Fiber optic cable can transmit two-way messages simultaneously. It will be the medium by which the office of the future will connect the many telephones, videophones, computers, and automated equipment of all kinds.

Laser Communications

Lasers, utilizing fiber optic cables, will relay many communications. This is the solution to the capacity problem phone companies are experiencing in major urban areas. With lasers, telephone service can be expanded tenfold over short distances (10–20 miles). Then signals are processed back into the traditional telephone cables. A new development in laser applications may be in satellite relay. The end result will be quicker, cheaper communications on a global basis.

Picture Phone

The long-awaited picture phone is here but not yet for home or office. The Bell System has initiated a video conferencing service with locations in 18 major U.S. cities. Video is two-way but only between two points at a time, with audio from all other participating sites. Costs are approximately $1,000 per half hour for two-site meetings, with additional sites at $200 each. A handful of companies like ARCO and American Hospital Supply have actually installed their own direct video communications systems, but costs are substantial.

Video Conferencing

The next best thing to being there may be the video conference. Typically the conference has one-way video and two-way audio. Stimulated by rising travel costs and slumping hotel occupancies, Holiday Inn is offering a national service and making major investments to create video conference centers in 260 hotels across the country.

Video conferencing will be expensive but not prohibitively so. Video conferencing with one-way video has some limitations in its use. It is much better for disseminating a new corporate policy than creating one, since all the receiving sites can only transmit audio responses. It will have symbolic value, allowing a decentralized company to meet simultaneously in many different locations. Commercial video conferencing can be supplied by vendors in most major urban centers. Satellite communications receptor dishes can be rented so users can create their own instant video networks. Video conferencing has potential for continuing education and is being widely utilized by universities as well as professional associations.

Cable Television

Cable television (CATV) is growing very rapidly. In 1984 there were 14 million households (about 20 percent of the total) on cable systems, and it is predicted that 100 million households will be wired by the year 2000. Today's CATV systems typically offer 10 to 20 channels, plus amenity services like Home Box Office. Stock reports, financial news, and health education are other services being offered in some locations. The Hospital Satellite Network (HSN) provides 24-hour programming of health and professional education; patient entertainment is already reaching more than 400 hospitals. With broadcast-quality programming, HSN intends to reach 30 to 40 percent of its market by 1991.

CATV networks are moving to the use of fiber optic cable with two-way communications capacity into the home. The TV is called the electronic hearth because it is the center of the modern American household. There are now 73 million black-and-white sets and 54 million color sets, with virtually 100 percent saturation of American homes. With fiber optic cable in CATV hookups the range of stations can expand from 100 to 200. More importantly, it makes possible the dream triad of communications: a marriage of TV, telephone, and computer. Not unexpectedly, there is stiff competition for cable franchises, not simply for today's profit but because cable is the pathway into enormous potential home markets of tomorrow.

Videotex

Videotex is the umbrella term for electronic print displayed on a TV screen. It includes two types of services: teletext, a one-way service; and viewdata, with two-way communications for interactive service. The terms are all coming to mean two-way communication. Teletext, the one-way service broadcast, is being utilized for electronic newspapers. Viewdata offers the great range of potential services we associate with the electronic cottage: electronic mail, banking, travel reservations, information retrieval, electronic encyclopedia, marketing, bartering, and electronic publishing. An estimated 2 to 5 percent of American households will be served by viewdata services, via CATV, by 1985, and 30 to 40 percent by the year 2000.

Despite videotex's potential, it has been slow to catch on. By July 1985 some 600,000 subscribers bought multiple-service on-line videotex services. CompuServe (250,000 customers) and Dow-Jones (220,000) dominate the videotex market. There is a major confrontation coming between the telephone, computer service, and CATV companies, potentially joined by the giant of the information industry, IBM. While telephones could provide the keyboard for user participation, home computers offer a vastly superior mechanism. Prices of personal computers are coming down, and sales have increased 30 to 40 percent per year since 1983. By some projections more than half of all American households will own one or more personal computers by 1990.

Electronic Mail

Electronic mail has not replaced the postal service but may take away a major share of its market. Electronic mail will provide a more efficient and effective alternative to the mail, both for external and internal communications. Messages are prepared on a computer or word processor, sent via telephone or over an internal electronic network, and displayed or printed at the user's request on the other end.

Electronic mail offers an alternative to telephone tag, where busy people can spend an average of four telephone calls before making contact. Users send and receive messages when convenient for them. Electronic mail overcomes the problems of time, time zones, and distance. Using satellite communications, electronic mail could be virtually instantaneous (transmitted at the speed of light).

THE NETWORK NATION

The telecommunications revolution is facilitating development of widely decentralized networks of organizations and individuals. The web that will link them is the network of various electronic media, speeded by satellite and with two-way communications for simultaneous interaction.

Computer conferencing services like Infomedia of San Bruno, California, provide the medium by which the Bechtel Corporation manages its worldwide construction projects, and the world's 200-plus nuclear power plants operate an emergency network. Network Technologies (NETI) of Ann Arbor provides computer network access to a variety of extensive health data bases for even the most remote physician and hospital.

Data transmission is driving growth of telecommunications networks and expected to expand to 40 percent of all telecommunications traffic by 1990—up from 5 to 15 percent in 1985. With leased data lines costing $1,000 to $1,500 per month, some companies have purchased satellite space and created private data networks, and the trend to private networks is growing.

Electronic networks could be the mechanism for the board meeting of the future. Imagine its utility for national associations. The American Hospital Association is establishing its own private network, and so will many organizations whose members are widely dispersed. Telecommunications has enormous potential for individuals to form their own networks through national service bureaus like The Source and CompuServe. The personal computer, linked via telephone through national (and international) communications services like Tymnet, will be the CB radios of the future. Computer clubs are mushrooming, and special interest groups are forming with membership not limited by time or distance. The term *colleague* can be widely expanded via electronic communications networking. Research shows that up to 50 persons can effectively collaborate on the same project, and location is no barrier to participation.

Computer Phones

The barriers between computers and communications are breaking down. The technologies are converging, as AT&T and IBM invade each other's markets. The Federal Communications Commission is easing regulations that have separated the phone business from the computer industry. These rules have forbidden phone companies to mix the computers used in providing regular phone service with the other services they sell. Deregulation will make possible computerized telephone monitoring and point-of-sale electronic funds transfer.

Distinctions between computing and communications are blurring rapidly. The computer phone prototypes on the market combine a computer screen and key pad with telephone receiver, but these hybrids are costly and cumbersome to operate. Development of the computer phone will be spurred by a new kind of communications link: the Integrated Services Digital Network (ISDN) transmits not only voice and data communications but pictures and graphics as well.

Hospital on the Wrist

Futurist Clem Bezold (1982) of the Institute for Alternative Futures forecasts the advent of the hospital on the wrist, a miniature health-monitoring device that could also transmit and receive health information. This would vastly expand the Lifeline service some hospitals now provide to the chronically ill, using micro-transmitters worn about the neck to signal the hospital to summon emergency medical aid. Think of the potential of the hospital on the wrist to monitor high-risk and chronically ill enrollees of HMOs, to prevent high-cost acute illness by continuous telemonitoring.

STRATEGIES FOR THE NEW HOSPITAL

The information society. Health is an information industry. This is a simple concept but potentially powerful. Thinking of health as an information industry puts a number of aspects of health organization in a whole new perspective:

- The product is information for the consumer.
- Information can be packaged and delivered via a wide number of communications media—telephone, computer, videotex—and at low cost.
- Information on a variety of consumer needs can be prepackaged (canned), using video discs, audio-tapes, and videotex, and sold to the user in the home on user demand on a 24-hour basis.
- Information can be substituted for many more expensive resources, such as physician time.
- The computer will be the ultimate repository of health knowledge—this will break the medical monopoly and allow health organizations to substitute other, lower-cost information providers, for example, health educators, and even lower-cost machines.
- The health care organization—not the physician—will be the source of health information to the consumer.
- Invasive (and high-cost) therapies like surgery will be the last resort, after information therapies and other lower-cost modalities.

Networks. The building blocks of tomorrow's health organizations will be networks, linked by telecommunications:

- Work will be organized into projects that are conducted by teams of people, who may be located at dispersed sites and work for different corporations or subsidiaries.
- Large, decentralized health corporations—the new conglomerates—will be networks of largely autonomous subsidiaries that all work to achieve the goals of the supercorporation, but each in their own market and in their own way.
- Physicians will be linked to hospitals and health care organizations into remote practice networks via telecommunications.

- Cross-cutting functions like management policy, strategic planning, and finance will be conducted by teams operating under central policy direction but whose members may be widely decentralized.

Consumer-provider relationship. Telecommunications and reconceptualizing health as an information industry will reshape the consumer-provider relationship:

- The health marketplace is national and global.
- Telecommunications can be the on-line, on-demand link between consumers and their health care organization (HMO, PPO, etc.).
- The chronically ill and the homebound can be monitored at home, periodically or continuously, and interventions can be made when the system alerts the health organization that their condition has gone outside expected parameters.
- Easy access to information and reassurance via low-cost telecommunications can reduce emergency room (ER) and other urgency demands on hospitals and physicians and promote better health—implementing the health maintenance concept.

REFERENCES AND SUGGESTED READINGS

*Annison, Michael. "Telecommunications: The Big View." *Hospital Forum*, November/December, 1984, pp. 25–27.

*Bell, Daniel. *The Coming of the Post-Industrial Society*. New York: Basic Books, 1976.

Bezold, Clement. "Health Care in the U.S.: Four Alternative Futures." *The Futurist*, August 1982, pp. 14–18.

*Botkin, James W., et al., *Global Stakes: The Future of High Technology in America*. Cambridge, Mass.: Ballinger Press, 1982.

*Coile, Russell C., Jr., Longe, Mary E., and Dizon, John O. "Computer Conferencing: A Technology Ahead of Its Users." *Hospital Forum* 27, no. 6 (November/December 1984):20–22.

*Cornish, Edward, ed. *Communications Tomorrow*. Washington, D.C.: World Future Society 1982.

*Davis, Dwight B. "Making Sense of the Telecommunications Circus." *High Technology*, Vol. 5, No. 9, September 1985, pp. 20–29.

*Dunn, Donald H. "Push-Button Banking from Your Easy Chair." *Business Week*, October 7, 1985, pp. 125–26.

Harmon, Willis W. *An Incomplete Guide to the Future*. New York: W.W. Norton & Company, 1979.

Harris, Catherine L. "Information Power: How Companies Are Using New Technologies to Gain a Competitive Edge." *Business Week*, October 14, 1985, pp. 108–114.

Johansen, Robert, Valle, Jacques, and Spangler, Kathleen. *Electronic Meetings: Technical Alternatives and Social Choices*. Reading, Mass.: Addison-Wesley, 1979.

Petrosky, Mary. "Micros Take Over as Workstations." *Info World*, August 26, 1985, pp. 36–38.

Saddler, Jeanne. "AT&T and Regionals Are Ready to Step Up Computerized Services." *Wall Street Journal*, October 29, 1985.

Turoff, Murray, and Hiltz, Roxanne Starr. *The Network Nation.* New York: Basic Books, 1978.

Williams, Frederick. *The Communications Revolution*, rev. ed. New York: New American Library, 1983.

---

*Suggested reading.

Chapter 7

Diagnostic Medical Imaging

7

In the 15 years between 1986 and the year 2000, exciting new advances in medical imaging will radically change the diagnostic process. Diagnostic imaging is at the intersection of two important streams of technology development. First, computerization is supporting an increasingly sophisticated array of tools for imaging. Second, the imaging technology itself is undergoing considerable innovation and experimentation with new approaches. Both of these are accelerating the trend toward noninvasive technologies. Diagnostic imaging equipment is becoming smaller and more powerful, through computer miniaturization and more efficient computer central processing units. Diagnostic imaging will be safer, far more precise, capable of a wider array of uses, and perhaps in the far future less expensive as well. Tomorrow's diagnosticians will have a much broader range of techniques and approaches, with the capacity to simultaneously compare multiple images generated by alternative imaging modalities.

IMAGING IN TRANSITION

Diagnostic imaging in today's hospital is in a transition period. Diagnostic nuclear imaging and radiology are still located in separate departments in most hospitals. Newer, noninvasive approaches are beginning to predominate. During the transition period hospitals will be faced with the expense of duplicative testing, where both old and new approaches are used to confirm results.

Hospitals will face substantial capital demands, in the range of $2 to $5 million, to upgrade their diagnostic imaging equipment and facilities. Ancillary services have been profit centers in the past, subsidizing other hospital activities. All that is changed under the new medicine. New reimbursement schemes, like prospective payment for diagnostic related groups (DRGs), reimburse hospitals on a per diem or per case basis. Thus, lab and x-ray charges must be accommodated within these all-inclusive rates, which will certainly reduce their utilization and profitability in inpatient care.

Five Imaging Modalities for Tomorrow

There are five competing modalities of diagnostic imaging available today, or emerging, for the medical imaging department of the future.

1. *Conventional x-ray.* Conventional x-ray continues to dominate the business of hospital radiology. Improvements in cameras and film, a wider range of contrast media, and technical advances in invasive techniques have greatly extended the range of applications of this technology. Cameras and film are better, resolution is higher and cleaner, and conventional x-ray is being utilized in a number of innovative hybrid techniques. Computerization and microfiche are helping to manage the records storage problem. Because of its low cost and wide availability, conventional x-ray should continue to be the dominant mode of imaging until the twenty-first century. Two changes are likely. First, invasive imaging techniques such as angiography will gradually be supplanted by noninvasive techniques such as computerized tomography (CT), ultrasound, and magnetic resonance imaging (MRI). Second, conventional x-ray will be replaced over time by newer computer-based digital x-ray imaging. Concern about x-ray exposure, as a consumer issue and work place health issue, will hasten the transition to digital x-ray.
2. *Computerized tomography.* The acceptance of computerized tomography is widespread. Its range of applications is growing rapidly. Cost of equipment is declining. The new Toshiba whole-body CT scanner, for example, cost $600,000 in 1985, about half the price of conventional top-of-the-line scanners, but weighs almost 40 percent less, and requires about the same space as a head-only scanner. Through advances in CT technology, imaging speed is faster, scanning time shorter, and patient processing more efficient. Among diagnostic imaging tools, CT is unsurpassed for resolution and details. Once considered a sophisticated tool only for research and teaching facilities, CT will be found in every modern community hospital.
3. *Ultrasound.* Ultrasound is continuing to develop and, may be the fastest growing modality in the medical imaging field by 1990. The technique has found expanded uses beyond obstetrics and is being utilized in cardiology and a variety of other diagnostic as well as therapeutic applications. The technology is still undergoing considerable experimentation. Ultrasound is reportedly operator-dependent. This may cause problems for hospitals, both in keeping pace with the technology and in maintaining the needed expertise.

4. *Digital x-ray*. Digital imaging is a method that converts x-ray data so it can be processed by computer. CT is a digital imaging system. Digital x-ray imaging is associated primarily with digital video angiography (DVA), a technique that may replace intravenous arteriography. Tomorrow's imaging department may be totally digitalized. In 1986 only a limited number of hospitals have digital radiography. One industry forecast anticipates annual growth of 200 to 400 hospitals that will acquire this capacity by 1990.

5. *Magnetic resonance imaging (MRI)*. MRI is so new that its uses are still speculative. Enthusiasts believe that its potential is tremendous. MRI has the capacity to provide direct visualization of the cardiac chambers without contrast material. It can also be used spectroscopically to determine levels of various chemicals in the body. MRI has promise as an imaging technique that can identify disease before anatomical changes. Since MRI uses no ionizing radiation, it is less harmful for the patient than x-rays. The first MRI systems were delivered to an estimated 50 hospitals in late 1983 and 1984. By 1985, 300 units were in place. Costs of acquisition range from $1.5 up to $2 million per unit. The market anticipates growth of 200 to 300 units per year through the 1980s as MRI applications broaden.

Capital Investment

Keeping up with the state-of-the-art in diagnostic medical imaging will be expensive. The minimum cost of equipping a state-of-the-art imaging department is estimated at $3 to $5 million. There has been rapid obsolescence of imaging equipment since 1975, a trend expected to continue or accelerate into the twenty-first century. Diagnostic imaging was a $2 billion market in 1985 and will easily double by 1990.

Equipment planning is complicated by the rapidly advancing state of the technology. Generations of some equipment have been as brief as 18 to 24 months. Hospitals updating their imaging tools during a major construction project have sometimes discovered that their new imaging equipment was no longer state-of-the-art by the time it was delivered.

Changing Reimbursement

Radiology and imaging services have been substantial revenue generators for hospitals in the past under cost reimbursement, often subsidizing other hospital operations. Under new reimbursement schemes such as diagnostic related groups and per diem contracting, the cost of imaging services must be folded into the per-day of per-case cost of care. Potential impacts of reimbursement changes follow:

- imaging services cost the hospital more than they produce in net revenues
- increased need for controls over testing
- reduced numbers of tests per case
- substitution of lower-cost tests for patients with limited health care benefits
- price competition on tests, with competition from commercial imaging labs and outside physician groups
- dampening of capital expenditures by hospitals for imaging equipment in the future, as well as slowing the diffusion of new imaging technology

CENTRALIZED CONSULTATION SERVICE

The future diagnostic medical imaging department will consolidate technologies and staff that were dispersed across radiology, nuclear medicine, and other departments, providing a variety of imaging media to diagnosticians and therapists:

- conventional x-ray
- computerized tomography
- ultrasound
- digital x-ray
- magnetic resonance imaging
- new multimedia devices (hybrids)

The medical imaging department will provide a centralized consultation service for physicians from all specialties. This will eliminate the need for clinicians to wander from one department to another in order to obtain a comprehensive diagnostic workup. The consultation service will facilitate a new level of control over the diagnostic plan that is broader and more diagnostically specific than previously available.

Centralizing the imaging service should also reduce the inconvenience and cost of redundant examinations. Working with carefully constructed clinical problem lists, the imaging consultation service will be able to integrate the needs of the clinician with a diagnostic imaging plan. This should yield a much more satisfactory diagnostic imaging report. As the technology advances, consultants can assist clinicians to utilize the specialized capacities of each tool to most efficient advantage.

The Computer

The brain of tomorrow's diagnostic medical imaging department is the computer. The computer provides imaging, analysis, and record storage, as well as billing and accounting. Data are fed from microcomputers that support the diagnosing equipment, to be interpreted and filed by a central main-frame computer. Rapidly expanding storage capacities of microprocessors and minicomputers will make the diagnostic medical imaging department virtually self-sufficient, a node on a distributed data system based in the hospital's mainframe computer.

Images from multiple diagnostic imaging systems will be transmitted, processed, and stored in a centralized diagnostic imaging center computer. Results are presented on computer screens with high-resolution capacity, and the results compared side-by-side. Because all images are digitalized, they can be manipulated for contrast and level. Data from the original scans are maintained in the computer, with the enhanced scans as well, for future analysis. Imaging equipment can be decentralized around the hospital or in multiple remote sites away from the hospital campus. The imaging network could be regional, even national and international. This would facilitate remote consultation and make possible remote quality control by tomorrow's large multihealth corporations and HMOs.

RTAS

The Rapid Telephone Access System (RTAS) may revolutionize communications and records storage in the diagnostic medical imaging department. This new apparatus converts voice into digital data. Diagnostic interpretation of images is dictated conventionally, but the voice data are transformed into digital form and stored in the computer. Only selected reports need be typed. The digital voice data will be capable of being transformed into print.

For now, physicians can call the RTAS system, dial the patient identifier number, and hear the voice data directly from the computer. Cost of the RTAS prototypes is $45,000, but their expense is recovered in staff savings from eliminating much of the typed dictation. There is already the potential for remote viewing of diagnostic imaging studies through transmission of digital images, with voice reports (RTAS) from the diagnostic medical imaging central computer.

Telecommunication

Telecommunications will provide the linkages to physicians in their offices, to patient units, and even to the physician's home. Slow-scan TV services are available to transmit x-rays, ultrasound, and CT data.

When all imaging data are computerized, they will be batched and transmitted to other locations by satellite at high rates of speeds without distortion. Telecommunications will facilitate remote diagnosis and consultation, for example, to determine the need to evacuate a patient from a remote location to a centrally located service. National and international teleconferences among specialists are possible. This may promote development of a national consultation service, perhaps established by the American Medical Association. A number of the speciality professional associations could provide a similar teleconsultation service, as well as several of the best-known teaching medical centers, and the market could be competitive.

Falling Costs

Cost of medical imaging will drop dramatically. Computerization is reducing cost by improving the speed of imaging procedures, as well as lowering storage and data maintenance costs. The imaging department of tomorrow will be paperless, with no film archives to maintain. In a recent study of nuclear imaging (Barhard and Lane 1982), cost of a digital x-ray study averaged $1.19, compared with $3.46 per study recorded on film. The cost of silver-based film has continued to rise, while magnetic media costs are falling. Filing, accounting, and billing will be handled automatically.

A significant feature of this integrated imaging data system is its potential as a management information system for administrative control. The system has the potential to optimize patient scheduling, using software available today, and optimize staffing as well. Patient flow will be increased, resulting in higher possible volumes of patients that can be handled by the hospital's facilities and equipment. Need for additional facilities and equipment should be reduced as efficiency is increased.

Artificial Medical Intelligence

Computer software for diagnostic analysis will become commonplace. Researchers in teaching settings are developing software for analysis of many common diagnostic problems. Computer images will fit predefined diagnostic patterns, and decision trees will be provided to physicians to aid diagnosis and treatment.

The market potential for this artificial intelligence (AI) and expert systems in medicine will almost certainly attract nonmedical competition, perhaps from pharmaceutical companies, from the manufacturers of imaging equipment like GE, Picker, or Siemens, and from computer companies with a significant interest in health like IBM.

Customer Service

New imaging technologies mean that patient comfort and safety will be much improved. When digital x-ray replaces conventional x-ray, patients will no longer be exposed to ionizing x-rays. Length of procedures and processing time will be reduced. Without the need to wait for film processing, diagnoses will be made in real time. Diagnostic imaging and surgery, for example, are already becoming closely linked.

Redundancy of tests will be largely eliminated. As diagnostic imaging technology improves, the need for defensive medicine will decline. Digitalization of imaging data will allow patients to carry their medical records with them on a smart card with an imbedded computer chip for records storage.

Imaging Consulting Boutiques

The centralized diagnostic medical imaging department will provide services to a variety of specialty imaging consultants. Consulting practices may be housed in boutique suites that are located around the imaging department. All will utilize the imaging facility and central computer through time sharing. Off-site physicians can access the imaging data directly via telecommunications and their home or office-based computer.

The medical imaging department may be a for-profit subsidiary of the hospital. Physicians' offices adjacent to the department could be made available as condominiums. Both facilities and equipment would be depreciable. Although imaging reimbursements per procedure are expected to decline, the medical imaging department should continue to have a highly profitable bottom line, thanks to improved efficiency, higher productivity, and lower per-procedure labor and equipment costs.

STRATEGIES FOR THE NEW HOSPITAL

The future is here. Diagnostic medical imaging is continuously evolving, on the near side of the future. Hospitals and physicians don't have to wait until the twenty-first century for most of the advances discussed here. The technology will be available. The more difficult problem for today's hospitals—and tomorrow's—will be whether to continue to be technology-driven. Can, or should, every hospital acquire the latest imaging technology as soon as it can afford it? The cost of keeping up with the technopush of advances in equipment is not limited to capital investment. Each advance requires new medical, technical, and support staff. The human resource cost is a significant component of the technology investment equation.

Strategic imaging planning. Strategic planning for diagnostic medical imaging will be essential. Given the advances in technology, each hospital should plan which imaging tools will be needed in its case mix and marketplace. Investments in imaging technology should be given a solid business analysis and plan. Assessment of the competition is an important component of that business analysis. Which competitors will acquire new imaging technology (not just hospital competitors)? Likewise, what is the potential for competition from office-based medical groups or commercial imaging services? State-of-the-art diagnostic medical imaging can provide a marketing advantage, and capital investment should be strategically planned, if the new hospital is to maintain its technology advantage over competitors.

Reimbursement changes. The impact of reimbursement changes on diagnostic medical imaging will be sweeping. DRGs are just the first wave of changing patterns of health care reimbursement that will end a la carte billing for lab and x-ray. As these costs must be accommodated into per-diem or per-case reimbursement, utilization of imaging services will be much more controlled. Hospitals will need to establish processes and control mechanisms for assuring that imaging studies are necessary and appropriate. This will probably mean establishing a prior authorization process to control use of high-cost tests. Requirement of a diagnostic imaging plan before testing is one potential mechanism a hospital could install, through a centralized imaging consultation service.

Hospital-physician relations. Diagnostic medical imaging may be a symbolic battleground for redefining hospital-physician relations in the 1980s. Hospitals that must live within preestablished per-diem and per-case rates must be able to control expensive resource inputs like imaging studies. Physicians do not at present share the financial risk with the hospital for living within a budget for each patient. MDs are still paid on a fee-for-service basis. This conflict in reimbursement formats will place a real stress on hospital-medical staff relations. Anticipating these problems, hospitals will need to establish a process of reconciling the demands of physicians for the highest quality medical care with the reimbursement cost limits imposed on hospitals.

Telecommunications and the computer. Telecommunications and computer-based hospital information systems are revolutionizing diagnostic medical imaging services. Telecommunications offers the potential for multiinstitutional systems to share high-cost imaging capital equipment like MRIs. It can also link remote hospitals and office-based practitioners with a remote practice network to a centralized imaging service. This may create new business opportunities for hospitals and health care systems. RTAS will advance the day when the hospital becomes paperless. RTAS is an example of working smart, using information technology to reduce costs and improve productivity.

REFERENCES AND SUGGESTED READINGS

*Atkins, L. "Hospitals Face Challenge Keeping Pace with New Advances in Imaging." *Review of the Federation of American Hospitals* 15, no. 3 (May-June 1982):43–44,49.

*Baker, Steven R. "The Operation of a Radiology Consultation Service in an Acute Care Hospital." *Journal of the American Medical Association* 248, no. 17 (November 5, 1982):2152–154.

Barhard, Howard J., and Lane, Gloria B. "The Computerized Diagnostic Radiology Dept: Update 1982." *Radiology* 145(2):551–558.

*Carter, Kim. "MRI, Ultrasound Seen as Leaders." *Modern Healthcare* 15, no. 26 (December 20, 1985).

*Conway, J.B. "Radiology Management: Some Thoughts for the Future." *Radiology Management* 4, no. 3 (September 1981):11–16.

*Craddock, T.D., et al. "Expanding Horizons." Editorial. *Applied Radiology* 10, no. 3 May-June 1981 :99,120.

*Crooks, L.E., et al. "Clinical Efficiency of NMR." *Radiology* 146, no. 1 (January 1983):123–128.

De Brusk, R.T. "Digital X-Ray Imaging: The Basics." *Radiologic Technology* 54, no. 4 (March 1983):280–286.

*Evans, R.G. "Reflections on the Future for Radiology." "Can History Predict the Future?" *American Journal of Radiology* 139, no. 2 (August 1982):408–410.

*Gilday, D.L. "Nuclear Medicine and Computers in the 1980's." Editorial *Applied Radiology* 10, no. 1 (January–February 1981):104,117.

*Heilman, R.S. "What's Wrong with Radiology." Editorial. *New England Journal of Medicine* 307, no. 7 (August 12, 1982):445–447.

*Hidalgo, J.U., et al. "Acquisition Planning for Nuclear Medicine Imaging Equipment." *Clinical Nuclear Medicine* 6, no. 11 (November 1981):541–543.

*Johnson, J. Lloyd, and Abernathy, David L. "Diagnostic Imaging Procedure Volume in the U.S." *Radiology* A6, no. 3 (March 1983):851–853.

*Merz, Beverly. "Let Your Fingers Do Walking to Get Radiologists' Reports." *Journal of the American Medical Association* 248, no. 8 (August 27, 1982):919.

*Neuhauser, D. "Thinking about the Future" *Radiology Management* 4, no. 3 (June 1982):10.

*Oldendorf, W.H. "NMR Imaging: Its Potential Clinical Impact." *Hospital Practice* 17, no. 9 (September 1982):114–128.

*Parker, John A., et al. "An All-Digital Nuclear Medicine Department." *Radiology* 147, no. 1 (April 1983):237–240.

*Poundstone, W. "Reader Survey: Radiology Administrators—Future Shock in the Radiology Department" *Applied Radiology* 4, no. 3 (June 1982):10.

*Riederer, Steven J., and Kruger, Robert A. "Intravenous Digital Subtraction: A Summary of Recent Developments." *Radiology* 147, no. 3 (April 1983):663–638.

*Scanning the Field of Neuroradiology." *Journal of the American Medical Association* no. 8 (February 25, 1983):994–996.

*Weiss, Sholom M., Kulikowski, Casimir, A., and Galen, Robert S. "Developing Microprocessor-Based Expert Models for Instrument Interpretation." *Readings in Medical Artificial Intelligence: The First Decade,* William J. Clancey and Edward H. Shortcliffe, Eds., Reading, MA: Addison-Wesley, 1984, pp. 456–462.

---

*Suggested reading

Chapter 8

Office Automation

8

Imagine a paperless hospital. There would be no written orders, lab results, progress notes, or financial information—none of the estimated 400 to 500 forms used in the average hospital. The average hospital inpatient chart has more than 200 pages and forms. All of this information may be essential, but none of the paper is—not, that is, when the automation of tomorrow's hospital is complete.

The pace of office and factory automation is picking up. Nowhere is it further advanced than in Japan. In a Japanese factory, robots assemble and package robots. There are no humans working on the assembly line, and only a few oversee the operations. Because the factory is completely automated, even the few technicians are simply a gesture to tradition. The factory is basically self-monitoring and self-sufficient.

The American work place is being revolutionized by computer assisted design (CAD), computer assisted manufacturing (CAM), and robotization. General Motors is investing heavily in high-tech automation—$33 billion over five years. In its new Buick City plant, the assembly line was redesigned to make maximum use of automation and robotics. Workers from the old factory assisted the new systems designers to engineer the new work flows. Jobs were reduced 40 percent. Deeper cuts were possible, but GM promised the union not to pass a certain point in eliminating workers.

The challenge to automation is white-collar work. Already computerization, systems engineering, and new technology are making deep impacts on pink-collar secretarial jobs, as well as blue-collar assembly-line manufacturing. The next targets will be white-collar managers and professionals.

Andrew Grove, president of Intel and author of *High-Output Management* (1983), believes a 30 percent improvement in white-collar productivity is possible. Since 50 percent of the work force is white-collar and it accounts for

95

75 percent of the average payroll, office automation is widely predicted. Today the office is the work place of 53 percent of all employed Americans. That could rise to 70 percent by 1995.

Who are the early adaptors who are not waiting for office automation to become commonplace? In suburban Denver, Direct Sales Tire Company has computerized almost every aspect of its business, including sales at each of its stores. Its new data system is based on the powerful IBM System/38. With 19 terminals in the headquarters and four in regional offices, the cost was about $400,000. In 1985, the company added IBM PC-XTs in each of the 55 retail outlets. Corporate managers and store managers now have ready access to the same central pool of information on inventory, sales, shipping, and finance. The system provides a detailed daily picture of cash flow. A daily report is telecommunicated automatically to the stores' computers at midnight. Now the company is experimenting with computerized sales assistance. Customers will be queried about auto use and mileage, and the computer will recommend tires to purchase. With an investment of $700,000 in computer hardware and five people to find new uses for it, Direct Sales has staked its future on automation.

ROADBLOCKS TO THE AUTOMATED OFFICE

If much of the technology is available, why is office automation so limited? The reasons are that businessmen are still unsure how to use it—or what the payoffs are. These suspicions are confirmed by a study of the Stanford Research Institute (Uttal 1982). After surveying 4,000 offices to find out which activities could be automated at a profit, SRI concluded that in all but special cases, such as legal departments, there are few direct cost savings from any current form of office automation, including word processing.

The problem has been in fitting a highly structured technology to highly unstructured white-collar work. Xerox seems furthest along in understanding professionals and reports significant time savings in four common sets of professional tasks: communication of data and ideas among work groups, creation of documents, filing and retrieval of documents and distribution of written work. Acceptance will be slow. By 1990 only 25 percent of managers and professionals are likely to be using sophisticated work stations.

Technophobia

A genuine problem that has slowed acceptance is that today's senior business executives have no computer experience. This problem is compounded by an executive bias against being seen at a keyboard, which is associated with lower-status tasks. Even among executives with a computer in their offices, only

5 percent use it. Computerization of the executive suite should accelerate through 1995 as computer-trained college graduates rise in the management ranks.

For today's technophobic managers there are training programs, such as those offered by the American Management Association and Peat Marwick, and even computer camps in resort settings. Vendors are assisting to make computers user-friendly. Forthright Systems of San Jose offers the management connection, a simplified keypad that calls up sales and other preprogrammed reports without ever dealing with the computer directly.

PC Proliferation

Even in 1980 few businesses had more than a handful of microcomputers. Most had been smuggled in by technophiles, who were using homemade programs on Radio Shack or Apple computers to assist in office tasks. Then in 1981 IBM introduced the PC personal computer. Microcomputer sales have soared, as has business confidence in the PC investment. The micro market was $9 billion in 1983, rose to $15 billion in 1984, and may grow to $55 billion by 1990.

Now users are complaining there are too many computers—at least there are too many unattached, incompatible, mismatched small computers in today's office. The result is a hodgepodge of automation that hardly begins to achieve the potential of the new information technology.

Local Area Networks

Throughout the 1960s and 1970s most large organizations installed central office-based PBX Centrex telephone systems. During the same period these organizations also were installing data networks consisting of 3270-type terminals connected to the data center by coaxial cable; the terminals were used principally by the programmers and data-entry staff. Neither of those functions—data and voice communications—had much overlap.

As a result of the proliferation of traditional computer terminals and the new personal computers, there is a need to connect these systems in a local area network (LAN)—easier said than done. A new technique is emerging in the form of third- and fourth-generation PBX systems that can address handling of all corporate data and voice information on one cable network. Unfortunately the existing coaxial telephone cable in older Centrex systems could not be used by the new local area networks. Vendors are now converging on IBM's Token Ring network as the LAN standard to begin to bring integration to the problem of mismatched equipment.

Integrating Voice-Data Communications

The technology that today holds most promise for improving white-collar output is already on virtually every office desk: the telephone. Big stakes lie in the replacement for the telephone. Today there are 257 million telephones in use worldwide. That is the potential market for tomorrow's integrated communications instrument. Prototypes of computer-phones are coming to market now.

The display-phone, manufactured by Northern Telecom Limited, combines a traditional telephone with a computer screen and numeric and typewriter-type alphabetic keyboards. Retail price is nearly $5,000 per instrument. With cut-rate standard phones available today for $4.99, manufacturers will have to cut prices dramatically to make integrated voice-data communications a widespread consumer phenomenon. Business users are waiting for the technology to stabilize and come down in price.

Technodisplacement

The information revolution is not universally welcomed. Unions fear that new technology will result in job displacement. That fear is supported by an unpublished study (Diebold 1985) prepared by Nobel laureate Vasily Leontief and Faye Duchin of New York University, which projects that office computers will cost as many as 2 million management jobs and 8 million clerical positions by the year 2000. The Federal Bureau of Labor Statistics is more optimistic, predicting that office employment will keep pace with the growth of the work force at least until 1995.

TOMORROW'S OFFICE TECHNOLOGY TODAY

American industry does not have to wait for the year 2000 for the office of tomorrow. Much of the technology is already here, and second-generation equipment in many areas is coming to market now. Vendor competition is improving features and beginning to drive down costs. Surprisingly the Japanese are not a major competitor, at least not yet. Most of the office automation technology is homegrown.

The first function most likely to be automated is mail—the communication on a daily basis of messages, memos, reports, and the myriad of business information. Electronic mail started as a secondary function to large-scale data systems. Today it is a primary function for a variety of information-rich industries like insurance, travel, and publishing.

Electronic mail systems like Digital's All-in-1 system have four classes of delivery priority: express, first class, second class, and deferred. Incoming mail can be forwarded automatically to another user, and the sender can receive an automatic reply. Documents or messages go into a filing system that allows easy refiling and cross-filing. Users can print a hard copy or simply utilize the electronic file capacity of the system. Periodically larger systems purge outdated communications, transferring them to another storage file such as a computer tape for archiving.

Computer-Speak

When computer technologists made the breakthrough to digitalized voices, little did they realize how far and fast this technology would come. Synthetic speech is now providing many routine messages, from giving the time of day to computerized sales pitches (known as junk calls). One day health information may be provided interactively between patient and computer.

The ability to recreate voices has many potentials. One is message forwarding. Voice messages can be digitalized, stored in the computer, and retrieved later or forwarded electronically to another telephone number. Now users can call into their office electronic message center from any touch-tone telephone to retrieve messages. Digital's second-generation electronic mail system allows callers to hear their messages and have documents read aloud by the computer. Users have a choice of standard replies that can be sent immediately, making even a roadside telephone a remote terminal.

Software Symphony

The greatest automation advances since 1980 have been made in software. WordStar is today's most popular word processing software, and Lotus 1-2-3 the most-used spreadsheet software. Integrating these two specialized programs had been left to the users. Now the software companies are creating integrated software systems that combine word processing, spreadsheet analysis, and graphics in one program. Lotus's new Symphony and Jazz are designed for the IBM-PC and Apple MacIntosh, with prices double the cost of the single-function programs ($700 versus $350 to $395).

In the work place PCs can share software when linked to a mini-computer or mainframe that hosts the base programs that any user can access. Thus managers across a region, or across the globe, can access the same data base of information and prepare reports and analyses using these popular programs.

Prototypes of medical software, like Caduceus and Internist, are mainframe based. Innovative software developers like Lawrence Reed, MD, believe medical management software can be made to fit into microcomputers. His PKC software modules are problem-oriented and run on an IBM PC. The new medical work stations can be widely decentralized, inside and outside the hospital.

Global Communications

The latest information systems are literally global in their range. Electronic mail can be forwarded to the office down the hall or the office in Caracas. Using satellite technology, a growing number of businesses have established private information and communications systems, serviced by companies like Vitalink, which provide satellite earth stations. New satellite technology is expected to reduce the total cost of satellite communications 80 percent in the 1980s, so even medium-size companies will be able to afford satellite facilities (Williams 1983).

Citicorp and American Hospital Supply have made a significant capital investment in video conferencing. Both have state-of-the-art systems that can communicate two-way pictures as well as data facsimile transmission, so copies of documents can be exchanged across thousands of miles.

AT&T's Picture-phone network of a dozen locations makes cross-country video conferences possible for users who don't need or can't afford their own systems; the cost is about $1,500 per hour per site. Technologists predict that holographic video technology will give users the feeling they are in the same room. That technology reportedly will not be usable until 1995.

Lasers

Laser technology is being brought to bear on office automation in several areas. As a medium for electronic communications, lasers are being used by the telephone companies to transmit large batches of messages in downtown heavy-use areas. Ranges of 10 to 20 miles limit lasers at this point; that will expand.

Laser printers are beginning to make their mark in business. Early versions were large and expensive ($15,000–$20,000). Table-top models now coming to market provide finished pieces with letter-quality output and fast turnaround time, and at a substantially lower cost, perhaps as low as $1,000 to $1,500. Laser printing uses electrophotographic imaging and xerographic printing technology. No instrument ever touches the page; thus laser printing is nonimpact. At a speed of 333 letter-quality characters per second, one of the new tabletop printers can print eight 2,500 character lines per minute. That's about 10 times faster than most letter-quality printers. Laser printers can use a variety of typestyles, generate graphics, and integrate text and graphics on the same page. They interface with mini- and microcomputers and can be shared by a network of users.

Intelligent Buildings

Private sector developers are putting up smart buildings oriented toward high-tech companies. These buildings have been wired with fiber optic cable, which has a broad-band capacity for carrying both voice and data. Computers control the office environment and climate, run the elevators, and even provide electronic advertising messages in the elevators.

Some smart buildings provide computer services like electronic message forwarding to tenants. Satellite earth stations located on the roof link tenants into satellite-based communications systems. Developers in New York and California are building teleports: office and industrial parks with telecommunications.

Medical office buildings (MOB) are a natural fit as intelligent buildings. Clinical and financial data support can be provided by the hospital's mainframe computer, services through a minicomputer in the MOB. Smart MOBs need not be located on the hospital campus but can be sited in R&D industrial parks or well-trafficked commercial locations.

At the other extreme some workers will work at home and telecommute to work. By 1990, 2 to 3 percent of the employed population is expected to be working from home-based computers. Home-based consumers will be able to obtain health care information electronically, just as they can get the Dow-Jones averages online today.

Silicon Valley Fever

In the information era, information is the capital for the redevelopment of American business. In the Silicon Valley near San Jose, California, technologists, entrepreneurs, and venture capitalists are creating today's office automation tools out of tomorrow's technology.

A directory listed 59 venture capital firms located in and around Silicon Valley in 1985, with $80 to $100 million to invest in new technology. This infusion of capital is giving America worldwide leadership in the information era and providing the funding to bring a dazzling array of technologies and products to the marketplace. Here are just a few of the technical advances that will soon be ready for commercial applications:

- superchips holding millions of bytes of information on a single chip
- high-resolution screens with three times the image clarity of today's CRT computer displays
- voice recognition leap-frogging the keyboard as the primary data input mode so that users can simply speak into their computers—and naturally the computer will use synthetic speech capabilities to speak back
- new storage media like Tallgrass' 80-megabyte hard disk, putting enormous storage capacity into microcomputers
- miniaturization to make everything smaller, more compact, easier to carry and to use, like the electronic chartpad for nurses

- integrated networks to provide the linkages between equipment that has frustrated so many users (and vendors)

And best of all many of tomorrow's office automation technologies will be cheaper than today's. Indeed technology and the future are converging in ways that will transform the hospital into the high-tech factory of the future.

STRATEGIES FOR THE NEW HOSPITAL

Integrated data systems. Today there are well-developed financial systems and clinical information systems—but they do not work that well with each other. Tomorrow's health information systems will routinely bring together clinical and financial information for case mix management. In a related development the various members of the health team—physician, nurse, and financial officer—will share the same data base from their respective locations without ever leaving their offices. All information, such as lab results, will be available more quickly to speed up the throughput process. If DRGs are widely used by payers, that speed will be worth money to hospitals.

Linkages to MDs. To link physicians with their hospitals it makes sense to put computer terminals in physicians' offices linked to the hospital's mainframe computer. Some hospitals now provide terminals for high-volume admitting physicians. Sharing a common base of data has much real and symbolic value. Realistically it brings together the physician's out-of-hospital data with the hospital's inpatient data. Physicians could use the large computer for accounting and billing, as well as for patient record storage. It would also provide electronic mail linkage among the medical staff, facilitating consultation and information transfer. Symbolically it provides a hard link between the physician and hospital, underscoring the collaborative relationship between the individual practitioners and the larger organization.

Interface with payers. Building an electronic linkage between providers and payers should have benefits for both. For providers, it should speed up payment and reduce receivables. For payers, it can provide a level of information and data retrieval that would improve their efficiency and effectiveness. Parenthetically it could also reduce the need for so many human information workers on both ends of the transaction, cutting labor costs for both. Expect to see this as an increasingly prevalent feature of PPO and HMO contracts.

Concurrent utilization review. Tomorrow's integrated clinical and financial data bases will facilitate concurrent utilization review on both the therapeutic impacts and costs of care. As these better data bases become available, payers—or their third party intermediaries—will seek direct access to them. The payoff for this (perhaps unwanted) intrusion by payers would be faster claims processing and payment. The hospital's own computer, or the central computer or the multi-hospital system, will do concurrent review against preset standards written in by the organization. This application of artificial intelligence in medicine will build in a continuous process of quality control for the business of caring.

Holistic medicine. Health organizations can actually practice holistic medicine when they have an adequately comprehensive financial and clinical data base. An integrated data base is the key to effective patient case management by the New Hospital. The computer will provide the link between the patient's needs and selection of the appropriate service from the health services spectrum. An integrated data base of clinical and financial information on its customers will be a major asset to vertically organized health care companies that want to sell a wide range of services to their customers. The flip side of holistic medicine will be holistic marketing.

REFERENCES AND SUGGESTED READINGS

*Burke, Stephen. "Specialized Packages Help Increase Profits." *Info World*, July 15, 1985, pp. 30–33.

Diebold, John. "New Challenges for the Information Age." *The Futurist*, June 1985.

*Dunn, Robert J. "Expandable Expertise for Everyday Users: Quantum Leaps in Artificial Intelligence." *Info World*, September 30, 1985, pp. 29–31.

Grove, Andrew S. *High Output Management*. New York: Random House, 1983.

*Kaltoff, Robert J. "Future Shock: Office Automation Circa 1994." *Information Management*, July 1984.

*Knerle, Dennis, and Smith, Randall. "IBM Introduces Office Network for Computers." *Wall Street Journal*, October 25, 1985.

*Lewis, Mike. "Cutting the Automation Giant Down to Your Office Size." *Nation's Business*, September 1984.

*"Micros at Work: A Special Report." *High Technology* 5, no. 11 (November 1985).

*Rogers, Everett M., and Larson, Judith K. *Silicon Valley Fever: Growth of High-Technology Culture*. New York: Basic Books, 1984.

*Siegel, Art H. "The Telephone System as a Local Area Network." *Telecommunications*, April 1984.

*Stewart, Bob, Hawe, Bill, and Kirby, Alan. "Local Area Network Connection." *Telecommunications*, April 1984.

Uttal, Bro. "What's Detaining the Office of the Future?" *Fortune*, May 3, 1982.

Williams, Frederick. *The Communications Revolution, Revised Edition*. New York: New American Library, 1983.

---

*Suggested reading.

Chapter 9

New Diagnostics

9

Think of the hospital as a factory. The objective is to process the patient through the hospital as quickly and cheaply as possible. That is the impact of the new medicine in which hospitals are paid on a per-case basis predetermined by Medicare computers in Washington. Each diagnostic related group (DRG) in the hospital factory is a product. The factories of the hospital industry are taking on a level of precision akin to producing optical lenses—high output but zero defects.

Once in the hospital, the prospective payment system (PPS) incentives favor speedy treatment (throughput) and discharge. Diagnosis is the key to maximum payment and efficient patient management. Service volume management entails monitoring and controlling how productively the hospital combines its resources to produce discharged patients, the final products. To become more efficient, hospitals must adopt industrial engineering and systems analysis techniques from private sector industries. Fine-tuning the throughput process is the management challenge for hospitals and physicians. Otherwise, Medicare prospective payment may be the tip of an iceberg that could sink a lot of hospitals.

Futurist Hermann Kahn (1976) was endlessly optimistic about the promise of technology. Kahn believed there was a technological solution for every problem, from energy (synthetic fuels) to diplomacy (limited nuclear war). Kahn's confidence in technology's potential in medicine is well warranted. Today's new diagnostics—pharmaceuticals and equipment—are full of promise. If the twentieth century is remembered as the age of electronics, the next 100 years may become the golden age of biology. Indeed in the twenty-first century man may finally conquer death, with antiaging drugs to slow or reverse the aging process. Already scientists are creating man-made life, in the lab and in the wombs of natural and surrogate mothers. This breakthough technology was made possible by unraveling DNA, which has spun out a new $100 billion industry: biotechnology.

IMMUNODIAGNOSTICS

Today companies like Hybritech, Genetech, and Cetus are bringing to market the first new genetically engineered products for diagnosis and treatment of a growing array of diseases. The building blocks of these new biomedical diagnostics are antibodies. Natural antibodies are protein molecules produced by human and other animal white blood cells to protect against foreign entities such as bacteria, virus, cancer cells, or poisons. Antibodies are an important part of the immune system, and scientists have found new uses for antibodies in medical diagnosis. New immunodiagnostic tests may offer a level of precision not previously possible, for example, pinpointing tumors before they are even large enough to be operable.

Monoclonal antibodies are specific pure antibodies. The early problem with producing antibodies in the lab had been obtaining a purity and consistency on which scientists could rely. Then in 1975 two British researchers discovered how to fuse an antibody-producing cell with a cancer cell. The resulting phyridoma produces a single type of antibody in virtually unlimited quantity. These monoclonal antibodies both improve the accuracy of diagnostic tests and for the first time make possible many therapeutic uses.

Turning Genes into Gold

The science lesson is over; back to business. The diagnostic market using conventional antibodies has grown to almost $2 billion annually. This is accelerating now that products based on monoclonal technology are beginning to come to market. The use of monoclonal antibodies in pregnancy tests illustrates how the market is developing. In 1982 Hybritech introduced a test to determine pregnancy. Selling into a strong market with a higher price, Hybritech became the leader, competing against established pharmaceutical giants Baxter Travenol, Becton Dickinson, Warner Lambert, and Abbott. Hybritech established this market position despite a small sales force. The next big step in pregnancy testing will be a further simplification of the test itself, expanding the home and doctor's office market. The purity of monoclonal antibodies makes existing tests more accurate and promises to make it possible to identify substances that could not be identified before.

Much of the research by biotechnology firms today is going into cancer diagnostics. Experts believe it likely that important breakthroughs in the early diagnosis of cancer will be hitting the market in the next few years. Pinpointing cancerous tumors with new levels of precision will be accomplished by linking the antibody with a radioisotope and injecting it into the body. The monoclonal antibody will seek out the cancer and bind with the cancer cells. The concentration of radioactivity can then be detected with a conventional gamma camera, targeting tumors for treatment and monitoring the progress of therapy.

A number of companies are working on this imaging technique, with Centocor conducting clinical trials in Europe and Hybritech conducting a number of trials in the United States. Hybritech's most advanced project—to image melanoma—is in phase 3 clinical trials. Hybritech is accelerating its development in this area, using funds from a $70 million R&D partnership. Another company with an active program in this area is Cetus.

Targeting Cancer

One reason within-the-body diagnostics are getting so much attention is that the same monoclonals can be used to diagnose as well as to deliver therapeutic agents to the site pinpointed. The biotechnology industry is designing cancer-killing systems, substituting a toxin, chemotherapy drug, or killing isotope for the radioisotope used in diagnosis. This turns a diagnostic system into a therapeutic system for killing the cancer. In most kinds of cancer, treatment will be accomplished by linking a killing substance to the antibody so that when it bonds with the surface of the cancer cell, it will kill the cell. There has not been sufficient research to determine which therapeutic agents will work best with various tumors; the companies with the biggest R&D efforts are exploring all three possibilities.

At Boston's Sidney Farber Cancer Institute monoclonals are being tested against leukemia. Removing the bone marrow is the first step in a new method for diagnosing and treating this often-fatal form of cancer. Normal cells would ordinarily be destroyed with conventional radiation therapy or chemotherapy. Using monoclonals to identify and bind the therapeutic agent only to the cancer cells leaves normal cells unharmed. The antibodies developed at Farber have shown promising results: of seven initial patients on which the drugs were tested, only one relapsed. The others were cancer-free for up to 18 months. Immunologists at Seattle's Hutchinson Center are targeting antibodies against the body's natural defenses but in a good cause: preventing the rejection of transplanted organs. In leukemia, marrow transplants from healthy donors have been rejected when the donor marrow attacks the new host's body, an often fatal illness known as graft-versus-host (GVH) disease. In experiments using antibodies against T cells, the part of the marrow that attacks the host, Hutchinson Center physicians have had success in 3 of 12 cases, after conventional therapies had failed. It is not yet a dramatic success, but the potential is encouraging.

Imaging Heart Disease

Imaging with monoclonals combines nuclear diagnostic technology with antibodies to determine if a heart attack has recently occurred, as well as determining the affected part of the heart muscle and the extent of the damage. In a new procedure developed at Boston's Massachusetts General Hospital, patients suspected of suffering myocardial infarction are injected with a monoclonal antibody that recognizes and binds to the protein myosin. When an infarction occurs, large amounts of myosin are released into the body for a few days. Using the monoclonal, linked to radioactive technitium-99m, the patient is screened with a conventional gamma camera. The damage appears on film as white on a black background. The greater the damage, the larger and more intense are the white spots.

The value of this method is that it is a specific marker of cell death. Heart specialists using traditional imaging technology are often unsure whether chest pains are the result of cell death or of nonfatal ischemia. If it is ischemia, a local and temporary deficiency of blood due to the contracting of a blood vessel, there is no image—and no damage. Knowing whether specific damage has occurred, cardiologists can select the most appropriate treatment from a growing array of cardiac therapies.

Investing in Biotechnology

Monoclonal therapy, while a breakthrough technology, is slow in coming to market. Initial investor enthusiasm in 1982-85 cooled, as few biotechnology companies showed a profit. This is still a future market whose real potential lies ahead. Only a few monoclonal products have been commercialized, producing less than $30 million in sales in 1984 (Lancaster 1984). In 1985 monoclonal revenues topped $130 million. Sales may explode to $2 billion by 1990 (DeYoung 1986).

As yet, investor caution is understandable. Landmark patents are being litigated, and hordes of patent applications have been filed. The technology is so new and so flexible that entry barriers are low. The field is filled with more than 200 new, predominantly small firms. Giants of the industry—Eli Lilly, Baxter Travenol, and others—are joint venturing with some of the new biotech companies and conducting their own R&D. The first real market success will probably be in diagnostics, potentially a $5 billion market by 1995, market researchers predict.

Biosensors

Sometime before 1990 a physician will insert a centimeter of platinum wire into the bloodstream of a diabetic patient. At its tip will be a barely visible membrane containing a bit of enzyme. Hair-thin wires will lead from the other end of the platinum probe to an insulin reservoir—a titanium device about the size and shape of a hockey puck. An implantable glucose sensor is just one of several experimental biosensors, the promising but still premature offspring of the marriage between biology and electronics.

Several new biosensors are being readied for market in the United States, Japan, and Britain that will monitor not just one or two but up to eight variables at the same time. Virtually all of today's experimental biosensors are based on a biologically sensitive material—an enzyme, cell, or monoclonal antibody—immobilized on or near a transducer (a device for relaying electrical signals). The transducer relays this information to an interfacing detector that records or displays the data. The biosensor will be capable of triggering an implanted drug sensor. Such an implanted insulin pump is being worn by a California triathlete on a pilot basis; he has successfully completed the grueling Hawaii triathlon three times.

An intriguing area for research is the brain. A brain sensor could monitor chemical or electrical levels and stimulate release of a drug or electrical impulse to alter mental states. Does this sound far-fetched? Closer to market are new clinical biosensors for monitoring blood pH and the partial pressure of carbon dioxide. Japan's Kuraray Co. introduced one in 1985; several British companies are reportedly close to production as well.

The Far Side: Biochips

Can molecules compute? The groundwork is being laid for twenty-first century computers based on carbon rather than silicon. Interest is growing in this futuristic technology, now that advances in biotechnology and polymer research seem to offer the basic tools and materials for such devices. No prototypes have yet been built or even designed. So far the biochip exists only in the imagination. An enormous R&D effort will be needed before practical development can begin.

Two basic concepts for biochips have been suggested. One idea is to develop digital biochips in which synthetic organic molecules would serve as the wires and binary switches, imitating the function of silicon components by turning the flow of electrons on and off. The second and more radical approach is to develop analog biochip devices that would employ protein molecules, such as enzymes, as the computing elements. Since enzymes have a large number of possible conformational states, they would theoretically be capable of graded responses and entirely new forms of computation.

A government-sponsored conference on chemically based computing was held in October 1984 in Santa Barbara. Says Michael Gold, assistant director of UCLA's Crump Institute for Medical Engineering, "The National Science Foundation told us that this was the most controversial meeting it has ever supported, and one of the most exciting" (Tucker 1984). The consensus of the experts is that a good deal of work is needed at a fundamental level before practical development can begin. Even if actual devices never prove commercially feasible, biochip research may yield useful spinoffs, including microfabrication techniques with numerous applications in new materials, methods, and products. If biochips do materialize in the twenty-first century, they could provide sight for the blind or perhaps boosters to the brain in specialized applications such as mathematical reasoning.

STRATEGIES FOR THE NEW HOSPITAL

Fine-tuning DRG case management. New diagnostics will assist hospitals and physicians to pinpoint diagnoses and expedite the therapeutic process. These new diagnostics will reduce length of stay by shortening the search for the problem. This should assist throughput management by hospital and physician, to make the best use of the limited time and resources Medicare will pay under DRGs. If other payers—Blue Cross, private insurers, employers—go to DRG-based reimbursement systems, the impact will be broader. Hospitals' ability to manage under capitation would be similarly affected.

Noninvasive diagnosis. The new diagnostics using monoclonal antibodies are part of a wider industry trend away from invasive procedures toward noninvasive substitutes. The new diagnostics will be useful across a growing range of conditions, especially cancer and heart disease, the leading causes of death in the United States.

Cheaper diagnoses. The cost of diagnosing illness may be reduced by the growing array of new monoclonal-based diagnostics for two reasons. First, monoclonals may be substitutes for more extensive and expensive procedures. Second, with their higher level of precision they should reduce the time (and expense) of diagnosis.

Revival of physician's office practice. The new diagnostics will assist physicians to conduct more diagnostic work away from the hospital, taking it back to their offices. Monoclonal pregnancy testing, for example, does not require a hospital laboratory. Cancer screening using monoclonals linked to radioactive isotopes can be filmed with conventional gamma camera equipment. This procedure can be done on an ambulatory basis and does not require a hospital. In the long run the new diagnostics may even pull work away from the physician's office and into the home.

Investment opportunity. This may be the opportunity to buy stock in the IBM of the future in the biotechnology industry. Hospital Corporation of America has purchased a 20 percent share of one biotech company. Biotechnology may be an appropriate long-term investment for the diversified health care organization.

REFERENCES AND SUGGESTED READINGS

*Bylinsky, Gene. "Biotech Breakthroughs in Detecting Disease." *Fortune*, July 9, 1984.

*Davies, Owen. "Clones vs. Cancer." In *Omni Book of Medicine*, edited by Owen Davies. New York: Zebra Books, 1983.

DeYoung, H. Garrett. "Biosensors: The Mating of Biology and Electronics." *High Technology*, November 1985.

DeYoung, H. Garrett. "Monoclonal Antibodies: Promises Fulfilled." *High Technology*, 6, 2:32–41.

*"Gene Splicers Go to War over Who Owns What." *Business Week*, July 30, 1984.

*Hall, Allan, et al., "The Race for Miracle Drugs." *Business Week*, July 22, 1985, pp. 92–97.

Kahn, Hermann; Brown, William, and Martin, Leon. *The Next 200 Years: A Scenario for America and the World*. New York: William Morrow and Company, Inc., 1976.

*Kuntz, Esther Fritz. "Task Forces Scour Diagnosis, Therapy Methods for Cost-Cutting Procedures." *Modern Healthcare*, February 15, 1984.

Lancaster, Hal. "Efforts to Develop Monoclonal Antibodies Are Moving More Slowly Than Expected." *Wall Street Journal*, May 1, 1984.

*McCamant, Jim; Kellogg, Meg, and Murphy, Michael. "Monoclonal Antibodies." *Medical Technology Stock Letter*, no. 14 (November 8, 1984).

*Nathanson, Michael. "Monoclonals May Shave Hospitals' Costs, and Expand Outpatient Service," *Modern Healthcare*, December 1982.

*"State of the Heart," *High Technology*, May 1984.

Tucker, Jonathan B. "Biochips: Can Molecules Compute?" *High Technology*, February 1984.

––––––––––

*Suggested reading.

Chapter 10
Noncompliance

10

When patients are unwilling or unable to follow medical advice, the additional expense of their treatment boosts everyone's health care bills. Dr. Raymond Ulmer, associate research professor at UCLA Medical Center and director of the Noncompliance Institute of Los Angeles, has studied patient noncompliance extensively and finds it a significant, though largely unrecognized, factor in medical expenses for the chronic diseases that account for an increasingly large proportion of today's health care costs (Stockwell 1982).

Noncompliant patients are time bombs waiting to erupt into acute episodes, often leading to hospitalization. It is a growing concern to hospitals and physicians and a major cost to HMOs, insurance companies, and government.

Compliance is generally defined as the extent to which a person's behavior conforms to or deviates from medical advice. For a given treatment regime to be effective, a patient must achieve a compliance level of about 80 percent of these specific behaviors:

- keeping physician's appointments
- reporting for medical examinations, treatments, hospitalizations, and operations
- taking medications as prescribed
- avoiding alcohol and drug abuse
- following smoking recommendations
- adhering to dietary suggestions
- conforming to work recommendations
- following exercise suggestions
- obtaining proper rest

Research indicates that half of all patients with chronic diseases—cancer, heart disease, emphysema, ulcers, diabetes, hypertension, and end-stage renal disease—fail to cooperate with medical advice, starting about six months after diagnosis. The longer a person has a given disease, the more likely that individual is to be noncompliant. These noncompliant patients require twice the treatment time, have double the number of complications, and the cost of their care is four times greater than compliant patients.

ROOTS OF THE PROBLEM

Noncompliance is epidemic. It is not a simple problem. The causes baffle experts. For example, more than 3 million Americans suffer from cancer. Treatment costs exceed $10 billion annually. Between 20 to 25 percent of cancer patients either refuse medically recommended treatment or seek unproven methods. The reasons why patients don't comply are as complex as the reasons why people get cancer in the first place and why there are differences in the progress of their disease. There is great anxiety attached to the diagnosis of cancer. To many people it is tantamount to a death sentence and they ask, "Why comply if I'm going to die anyway?" While some cancer patients will be immobilized by their fear of death, others deny anxiety and engage in reckless, self-destructive behavior.

Heart disease is widespread, and so is noncompliance by those who bear this diagnosis. Heart diseases are the leading cause of death in America. Their treatment costs more than $18 billion each year. Uncontrolled hypertension is a major contributing factor. By some estimates 50 to 75 percent of patients with diagnosed hypertension are noncompliant (Haynes et al. 1976). Noncompliant hypertensives are time bombs waiting to experience costly—and potentially fatal—heart attacks. If Americans understood the basic process of atherosclerosis, it could result in a reduction of cardiovascular disease similar to the reduction of infectious disease that besieged this country earlier this century.

Bypass Surgery versus Prevention of Hypertension

One of the most popular—and most expensive—hospital procedures is cardiac bypass surgery. On a national basis approximately 159,000 coronary bypass operations were performed in the United States in 1981. Each operation cost $15,000 to $20,000, for a total cost of $2.5 to $3 billion. In 70 percent of these patients the grafted vessels closed or narrowed within 10 years. Tremendous cost savings would be achieved by controlling more heart disease with diet and medication instead of treating it by surgery. But for this to happen, patients must reduce their intake of high-cholesterol foods and take medication when it is prescribed.

A major contributing factor to the high cost of heart disease is noncompliance by hypertensive Americans. Known as the silent killer, hypertension affects more than 45 million Americans. One in three Americans is either hypertensive or borderline hypertensive, but only half of them know it. Weinstein and Stason's 1980 study estimated the annual national cost of treating clinically defined hypertension (diastolic blood pressure greater than 95 mm Hg) at $2.9 million. Considering the cost effectiveness of antihypertensive treatment from a public policy perspective, they concluded that medical costs saved by prevention of deaths due to heart disease and strokes pay for less than 22 percent of gross hypertension treatment costs. They recommend more emphasis on treatment of already diagnosed hypertension and screening at sources of regular medical care, rather than special screening programs.

Because 75 percent of hypertensive patients are noncompliant, these programs are seldom as effective as they could be. One study of worksite control programs estimated that each patient generates about $250 in annual medical costs and $794 in lost wages due to avoidable illness and premature death. However, the $222 cost per year of the treatment program was of questionable cost effectiveness because so many patients failed to follow the treatment regime. A Canadian study found that employees newly diagnosed as hypertensive who did not control the condition were subsequently absent due to illness 80 percent more than before they were advised of their illness.

Smoking: The Leading Compliance Problem

Since the U.S. surgeon general published the first report on smoking and health in 1964, smokers have known they have a 70 percent greater chance of developing heart disease than nonsmokers and an even greater risk of developing lung cancer—yet smoking continues to be a common habit. The surgeon general in 1980 attributed 630,000 deaths annually to smoking. It is a contributing factor in about 10 percent of all deaths in this country each year. Smoking may be the most difficult addiction to reduce, and especially to eliminate entirely, which is why so many patients continue to smoke even when the consequences are so severe. In Reynaud's disease, for example, noncompliant patients with extreme circulatory problems continue to smoke even after undergoing amputations. Emphysema patients die from burns when a cigarette spark ignites their oxygen equipment. Such noncompliant behavior seems incomprehensible.

Diabetes remains an underestimated health problem. It is responsible, as an underlying or contributory cause, for the third largest number of American deaths after heart disease and cancer. Annual treatment costs exceed $10 billion. Diabetes is also estimated to cause 5,000 new cases of blindness, 17,000 to 20,000 amputations of lower extremities, and 2,000 new cases of end-stage renal disease annually in the United States. Coronary artery disease among diabetics is two to three times more prevalent than in the general population, and approximately 1,000 babies are born each year with defects attributed to maternal diabetes. In addition to controlling the level of insulin, it is critical for the diabetic to control hypertension, hyperlipidemia (cholesterol), obesity, and smoking in order to lower the increased risk of cardiovascular complications. All are associated with heart disease, and all but smoking are more prevalent in the diabetic population.

LIFE STYLE VERSUS HEALTH

Medical treatment that interferes with basic life style pleasures—eating, drinking, smoking, or sex—increases the problem of compliance. Many of the immediate consequences of health care regimens are unpleasant and difficult. Diets are restrictive, there are physical and psychological withdrawal problems involved in quitting smoking or drinking, and sexual practices that involve a high health risk (e.g., herpes and AIDS) are hard to give up.

Noncompliance is often misunderstood as an education or attitude problem, but informing patients about the benefits of treatment or the risks of noncompliance is no guarantee they will follow it. Reasons given by patients for noncompliance vary greatly and may be irrational. Cancer patients have refused chemotherapy because they didn't want to lose their hair.

Noncompliance can be encouraged by the treatment itself. Medications and treatments can have disagreeable side effects. Antihypertensive drugs have caused skin rash, diarrhea, nausea, impotence, and depression. The cost of $100 to $500 per year for these drugs is a strain for some patients. Noncompliant glaucoma patients describe taking their eye drops as unpleasant. Radiotherapy can cause hair loss, nausea, and loss of salivary functions in oral cancer patients.

Patients experiencing severe pain usually comply with a treatment recommendation to seek relief. However, most treatments are designed to improve the patient's health over time. The tradeoff, then, is between the initial discomfort and inconvenience of the life style change weighted against long-term gains. Often the gains are not tangible. The avoidance of a more serious health problem may not seem real to a patient in the early stages of the disease. The present life style disruption is real and often difficult to balance against the intangible benefit of avoiding (or postponing) future illness.

The Highly Vulnerables

Elderly patients pose special problems with compliance. They may be confused by physician instructions and taking a variety of incompatible medications. Giving up old habits, altering eating patterns, and changing a sedentary life style get harder with advancing age.

Children are another group of patients for whom compliance can present special challenges to parents and providers. Handicapped children or those with special health problems often make compliance a battle of wills between themselves and their parents. This is a recurring theme with adolescent diabetics and epileptics.

Language and cultural differences make compliance a special problem for minority and disadvantaged populations. Dietary modifications are difficult for ethnic groups, especially the older members for whom food has a strong emotional meaning as a reminder of home in a strange land. Health beliefs and folk medicine practices exert a continuing influence as well.

Just getting to the health care provider creates compliance problems. A California study of Medicaid Prepaid Health Plan (PHP) enrollees found that many of the health maintenance organizations considered these patients uncooperative because of their higher failed-appointment rate (California Dept of Health 1980). People who are marginally employed fear the loss of their jobs if they take time off from work and also miss the income from the time lost—even if they have insurance to cover the costs of treatment. Transportation may be unreliable or unavailable; parents may have difficulty finding and paying for child care.

PHYSICIANS AND COMPLIANCE MANAGEMENT

Physicians discover the problems of noncompliance in practice; few physicians are given formal training in either the classroom or their clinical studies to deal with noncompliant patients. Nurses receive more training but it is limited. Physicians need to understand that when a patient is noncompliant, the doctor's time, effort, and training are wasted. Sociologist Milton Davis (1968) studied patient compliance in terms of physician-patient interactions. He found that compliance was higher when patients' and physicians' communication styles were similar: aggressive patients tended to ignore the advice of passive physicians, as did more diffident patients with more assertive doctors.

The role of the physician is critical to successful compliance. Most patients will comply if their doctors will spend some time to plan therapeutic programs which are realistic for the particular patient. To enhance patient compliance:

- Physicians should communicate their belief in the effectiveness of the therapy to the patient in a positive, encouraging manner.
- Whenever possible, the simplest possible program should be followed (i.e., taking medicines once or twice a day instead of four times daily). If the patient is taking several medications, the primary physician should be aware of them all and coordinate a timetable.

- Noncompliance should be checked and physicians should modify the treatment regime if necessary.
- Physicians should consider cost for all patients without hesitating to ask the patient if it will be a problem.

Getting Tougher on Compliance

Compliance can be a key factor in malpractice litigation. If a patient fails to follow treatment recommendations, the physician's responsibility for treatment is necessarily altered. Routine documentation of noncompliance, in terms of the specific behaviors noted, is a safeguard for today's physician in an increasingly litigious society.

Large employers and health maintenance organizations that are at financial risk for the consequences of their consumers' noncompliance may find it worthwhile to use an internal or external compliance consultant as a trouble-shooter to help staff work with difficult patients and for general training. Behavior modification techniques can be effective if they are geared to the patient's culture, educational level, and life style. Employee assistance programs can aggressively encourage compliance.

Physicians and health professionals can promote compliance in a variety of ways. First, they can take more responsibility for compliance monitoring, that is, calling a patient who fails to keep an appointment or follow a treatment recommendation. Encouraging patients to reward themselves for behavioral changes and making a fuss over them when they succeed are effective techniques to strengthen compliance.

Noncompliance Sanctions and Rewards

"One man's freedom in health is another man's shackle in terms of taxes and insurance premiums," notes Dr. John Knowles (1977) in an essay on individual responsibility for health. Marcia Kramer (1979) suggests that patients with self-inflicted diseases should prepay the costs of their treatment in the form of an excise tax on cigarettes to pay for the extra medical care costs generated by smoking. A related application of this idea was the tobacco initiative circulated in California for a health education campaign against smoking to be financed by a cigarette tax. It was opposed strongly by the tobacco lobby and failed at the polls but could resurface.

Another way to promote individual responsibility for health is to offer positive incentives for patients who do comply with medical advice. The Mendocino County School District does this by its system of employee health insurance. The district establishes a $500 account for each employee; if the employee's health care claims are less, the person receives the difference. If health costs exceed $500, the district still pays them, but there is no financial reward for the employee. The annual cost of medical claims to the school district has been reduced 60 percent since the system was initiated.

Time Bomb for the Future

Noncompliance is everyone's problem and no one's responsibility. As a contributing factor to rising health care costs, it has received little attention as a clinical or managerial issue. When providers and purchasers of care develop more awareness of its consequences and costs, noncompliance will be one of the major health care issues of the 1990s.

In the coming era of alternative delivery systems, the New Hospital and its medical staff will share the financial risk with the HMO or insurer for keeping their enrolled population healthy—and out of the hospital. Then noncompliance will get the attention it deserves from providers, employers, insurers, and from patients themselves.

STRATEGIES FOR THE NEW HOSPITAL

Alternative health care delivery systems. Capitation and prepaid systems in which the provider is at risk for the cost of patient care have built-in incentives to keep patients well. Their profit margins may be eroded by uncooperative patients. As more of these integrated health plans are organized—as HMOs, PPOs, exclusive provider organizations (EPOs), or subsidiary contractors—patient compliance will become an increasingly important issue. Noncompliance is a time bomb for prepaid health care. Unlike auto insurers who can drop a subscriber who fails to comply with traffic laws and safety practices, health insurers must continue to serve their noncooperative beneficiaries.

Provider-patient relationships. To enhance patient compliance, health care providers should learn more about compliance. When medical recommendations involve life style changes, patients must act as partners in health. Only the patients can make the behavioral changes necessary to improve their health while under a treatment regimen. The relationship between providers and patients needs redefining in a way that emphasizes their shared goal—cure or control of the disease—and complementary contributions toward achieving it. The professional will provide expertise, advice, and treatment, and the patient will (ideally) modify behavior. Now the toughest question must be addressed: If the patient does not comply, does the provider have a right to drop the patient?

Health policy. Noncompliance raises some difficult policy questions that must ultimately be addressed. Who should pay for self-inflicted diseases? Where should the line be drawn in defining them? Is smoking a self-destructive behavior or an addictive disease? What about alcohol and substance abuse or obesity? Does the hypertensive patient who continues to use excessive salt contribute to the cost of illness? Should conscientious people who take care of themselves have to pay for their fellow citizens' poor health habits? Are there ways to provide rewards for healthy life styles and behavioral changes? What are appropriate compliance incentives for health insurers, employers, and government to offer? The New Hospital can help gain recognition for these issues and get them on the issue agenda in Washington, in the health benefits policies of corporate America, and in the minds of their customers.

Monitoring compliance with high-tech and high-touch methods. In *Megatrends* John Naisbitt (1982) notes that technological advances must be balanced by a personal touch or the technology is rejected. With an automated patient record system and word processing, the New Hospital has the technological capacity to monitor patient compliance quite effectively and design a program for periodic intervention to promote it. Electronic nagging, no matter how efficient, is likely to be counterproductive. However, computer models can indicate which patients are likely to be noncompliant and which kinds of interventions will be most effective for them.

Partnership with employers. Compliance is an area for a productive partnership between the New Hospital and health care providers and purchasers. Providers can identify high-cost noncompliant employees. Employers can utilize incentives to encourage compliance and reinforce physicians' advice. For hospitals this is a new service for employee assistance programs that could be marketed to employers. For HMOs and PPOs a compliance program is a strategy to keep costs—and prices—down. Employers who cooperate with the HMO and PPO in successful compliance programs could be given a discount rate or rebate incentive.

REFERENCES AND SUGGESTED READINGS

*Bruer, J.T. "Methodological Rigor and Citation Frequency in Patient Compliance Literature." *American Journal of Public Health* 72, no. 10, (October 1982):1119–1123.

*Cairns, J. "Cancer: The Case for Preventive Strategies." In *Healthy People: The Surgeon General's Report on Health Promotion and Disease Prevention*. Washington, D.C.: U.S. Department of Health, Education and Welfare, 1979, pp. 157–171.

California State Department of Health Services. *Report of the Prepaid Health Research, Evaluation, and Demonstration (PHRED) Project*. Sacramento, CA, 1980.

*Chamblee, R.F., and Evans, M.C. "New Dimensions in Cause of Death Statistics." *American Journal of Public Health* 72, no. 11 (November 1982): 1265–1270.

Davis, Milton S. "Variations in Patients' Compliance with Doctors' Advice: An Empirical Analysis of Patterns of Communication." *American Journal of Public Health* 58 (1968):274–288.

*Earp, J.L., Ory, M.G., and Strogatz, D.S. "The Effects of Family Involvement and Practitioner Home Visits on the Control of Hypertension." *American Journal of Public Health* 72, no. 10 (October 1982):1146–1154.

*Engstrom, P.F. "Overview: Cancer Education and Patient Compliance." *Advances in Cancer Control: Research and Development*. New York: Alan R. Liss, 1983.

*Ganda, O.P. "Morbidity and Mortality from Diabetes Mellitus: A Look at Preventable Aspects." *American Journal of Public Health* 73, no. 10 (October 1983):1156–1157.

Haynes, R.B., et al. "Improvement of Medication Compliance in Uncontrolled Hypertension." *Lancet*, 1, 1265–68.

*Haynes, R.B., Taylor, D.W., and Sackett, D.L., eds. *Compliance in Health Care*. Baltimore: Johns Hopkins University Press, 1979.

Knowles, J.H. "The Responsibility of the Individual." Daedalus 106, no. 1 (Winter 1977):57–80.

Kramer, M.J. "Self-Inflicted Disease: Who Should Pay for Care?" *Journal of Health Politics, Policy and Law* 4, no. 2 (Summer 1979):138–140.

Naisbitt, John. *Megatrends*. New York: Warner Books, 1982.

*Stachnik, T., and Stoffelmayr, B. "Worksite Smoking Cessation Programs: A Potential for National Impact." *American Journal of Public Health* 73, no. 12 (December 1983):1395–1396.

Stockwell, Serena. "Improved Compliance Called Key to Improved Health." *Oncology Times*, February 1982.

Weinstein, M.C., and Stason, W.B., *Hypertension: A Policy Perspective*. Cambridge, MA: Harvard University Press, 1976.

---

*Suggested reading.

Chapter 11

Baby Doe: The New Ethical Issues

11

On April 9, 1982, an infant known to the world as Baby Doe was born in a hospital in Bloomington, Indiana. He had an incomplete esophagus and Down's syndrome, which causes moderate to severe mental retardation. Due to advances in neonatal medicine, physicians would have been able to assure Baby Doe's survival by attaching his esophagus to his stomach. Because nothing could be done to prevent retardation, the parents chose to withhold surgery and intravenous feeding. That decision was challenged by the hospital and upheld in Indiana courts on two separate occasions. On April 15, 1983, after being denied food, water, and surgical aid, Baby Doe died.

REDEFINITION OF CIVIL RIGHTS

On May 18, 1985, the secretary of Health and Human Services (HHS), through the director of the Office of Civil Rights, informed the nation's 6,800 hospitals that on the basis of section 504 of the Rehabilitation Act of 1973 hospitals could risk losing their federal funding if they discriminated against handicapped persons. More specifically, hospitals were put on notice that it "is unlawful for a recipient of Federal financial assistance to withhold from a handicapped infant nutritional sustenance or medical or surgical treatment required to correct a life threatening condition if: (1) the withholding is based on the fact that the infant is handicapped; and (2) the handicap does not render treatment or nutritional sustenance contra-indicated."

In March 1983, HHS published its first Baby Doe Rule. As a condition of federal funding, the rule required hospitals to place poster-size notices in prominent positions in delivery rooms, nurseries, and maternity and pediatric wards, stating, "Discriminatory failure to feed or care for handicapped infants in this facility is prohibited by Federal law.'' These notices included a 24-hour, toll-free hotline number that anyone could use to report a suspected case of denying food or treatment to such infants. HHS also established a special assignment Baby Doe squad to follow up on specific complaints at a given hospital.

Baby Doe and Local Hospitals

Writing in the *New England Journal of Medicine*, Dr. James Strain (1983), president of the American Academy of Pediatrics, describes what happened at two hospitals when the hotline was used.

Strong Memorial Hospital, Rochester, New York

On March 29, 1983, an unidentified caller from another town, having read a newspaper account of Siamese twins with two heads and one trunk being treated at the hospital and apparently suspecting that they might be denied food or medical care, used the hotline. Strong Memorial was advised by telephone that a civil rights investigation was to be conducted. Within a day three investigators—two from New York and one from Washington—arrived at the hospital. They brought with them no written requests for medical information, no statement of investigative authority, no verification that a hotline call had been received. The hospital complied with the team's request for medical records, only to have team members disagree about which office was entitled to the information.

The investigators also arranged for a neonatologist from Norfolk, Virginia, to consult. After flying in, the consultant learned that the investigators failed to obtain the parents' consent to examine the children. He left the next morning but not before expressing full support for the care provided and the overall management of the case. No commitment was given by the investigative team as to when a final report would be issued. In addition to the trauma caused by the birth of the infants, the parents were forced to respond to the questions from the investigative team and local news media. On April 1, on the basis of newspaper accounts that implied the hospital was intentionally harming children, one family removed a seriously ill child before his treatment had been completed.

Vanderbilt University Hospital, Nashville, Tennessee

The investigation at Vanderbilt was prompted by a caller charging that 10 named children at the hospital were not being fed or given proper medical treatment. The Department of Health and Human Services office in Atlanta advised the hospital by telephone on March 23, 1985, that it wished to be provided, within one hour, with the current medical status, diagnosis, and prognosis of each of the children. The hospital stated that it would provide the information but could not do so in an hour.

That evening the team arrived at Vanderbilt: two investigators from Atlanta, one from Washington, and a neonatologist from St. Louis. A meeting from 9:30 to 11:45 PM was held with the investigative team, the attending physicians for each of the 10 children, the chief of pediatrics, the chief pediatric resident, and the associate director of nursing. After the meeting the physicians made rounds to visit each child.

The next day the investigative team examined medical records and interviewed selected nurses and hospital administrators. The investigators promised no final report for 30 to 90 days. Like the Rochester case, the neonatologist reported that the medical care being given to the children was exemplary in all respects.

As a result of the investigation one person remained in the pediatric intensive care unit longer than necessary. The need to retrieve charts from the outside investigators delayed the transporting of children from the pediatric intensive care unit to the operating room. Laboratory reports had to be reordered. Six nurses were diverted from patient assignments, which complicated shift changes and delayed patient reports forwarded to nurses on the next shift. The chief of pediatrics worked on the investigation for 8 hours; the associate nursing director for 18 hours; the chief pediatric resident for 10 hours; and six nurses for 3 hours.

Provider Counterattack

In the health care industry there was a vigorous protest over the intrusion of the federal government into the patient-provider relationship. A number of professional and trade associations, including the American Academy of Pediatrics and the American Hospital Association, brought suit against the federal HHS department to enjoin the interim rule before it was to become effective.

On April 14, 1983, U.S. District Court Judge Gerhard Gesell ruled that the regulation was invalid because HHS failed to follow proper procedures in promulgating it. In his decision Judge Gesell cited the Administrative Procedure Act, which was "designed to curb bureaucratic actions taken without consultation and notice to persons effected" (Annas 1983). The right to notice and comment was established to make sure that the rule-making agency at least considered all factors that the affected individuals believed were relevant so that rational decision making could be fostered. Judge Gesell cited HHS for failing to follow the 30-day notice and comment requirements of the Administrative Procedure Act, and ruled the Baby Doe regulation invalid.

HHS rewrote and reissued the Baby Doe regulations on July 5, 1983, and provided for a 60-day period for written comments. Significantly the hot-line telephone number was retained. Also an entirely new section required that each state's child protective services agency establish procedures designed to "prevent medical neglect of handicapped infants" within 60 days of the effective date of the regulation, including provisions for mandated health care provider reporting, review of such reports, provision of services, and notification to HHS of reports.

NEW BIOETHICAL DILEMMAS

Each year thousands of babies are born with life-threatening conditions, from congenital malformations and other genetic abnormalities to serious prematurity and low birth weight. With developments in neonatal intensive care, the number of these newborns whose lives might possibly be saved increases. Choices are posed for parents and physicians about what treatments should be used with which babies and for how long, in recognition that treatment will not have a successful outcome in all cases.

The controversy surrounding Baby Doe perhaps best typifies the issues involved. As Dr. Harry Jennison, director of the American Academy of Pediatrics, put it, "families of severely handicapped children are faced with great dilemmas . . . about the decision to sustain life. Their decision has become much more difficult now that medical advances allow us to keep such infants alive for inordinate periods of time" (Berseth 1983).

The issues surrounding Baby Doe are not a passing fad. They are the product of medical technology that is able, with increasing frequency, to prolong life to a point that some feel is too long. These feelings conflict with other's belief that any life should be preserved as long as possible regardless of the cost in pain, family crisis, and dollars. Feelings run high on both sides.

Ethics and Economics

Complicating the ethical dilemma caused by advanced medical technology is the potential legal dilemma of allocating scarce medical resources not only among the population of severely handicapped babies but among the population generally. Despite current debate no national data describe the amount of neonatal intensive care currently being delivered in the United States. Nor are there reliable figures describing total health care expenditures and per capita costs of Baby Doe type cases. In 1983 the President's Commission for the Study of Ethical Problems in Medicine and Biomedical and Behavioral Research put the cost of neonatal intensive care for 1978 at $1.5 billion. Given that each Baby Doe case includes multiple and different diagnoses, most hospitals are loath to offer any estimated charges. One major tertiary care institution in California put the typical daily charge of a Baby Doe infant at $10,000 to $15,000 and the typical total hospital charge at $30,000 to $45,000.

Added to this uncertainty is the cost of special care, quite possibly of lifelong institutionalization. Neither the surgeon general's office, Office of Civil Rights in the Justice Department, Maternal and Child Health in the Department of Health and Human Services, Health Care Financing Administration, nor the Office of Technology Assessment has formal projections for those costs.

From a broader perspective, the Baby Doe issue raises substantial economic and policy issues. In an era of limited resources, diverting resources to hospital care to prolong life of infants who will die regardless of medical intervention is not cost beneficial. George Annas, professor of law at Boston University School of Medicine, argues that "in other areas the Administration has attempted to avoid unnecessary regulations, and insists on subjecting even health-related regulations to cost-benefit and cost-effectiveness analysis. No attempt has been made to do any of this homework" for the Baby Doe regulation, however. Dr. Norman Fost (1982) suggests "there is a curious contradiction in the government's insistence that the handicapped infants be treated similarly to others while the funds necessary to accomplish that are being drastically reduced."

Threat to Physician-Patient Relationship

A number of physicians have been critical of the Baby Doe regulation because, according to Dr. Carol Berseth (1983) of the Mayo Clinic, "it inserts an unwelcomed participant into the doctor-patient relationship" and represents an intrusion by the federal government into matters that have traditionally been settled privately between physicians and patients. Dr. Harry Jennison is even more blunt. Referring to the July regulations, he states that such methods are "a serious threat to the privacy and confidentiality of families in agonizing circumstances" (Berseth 1983).

On a different note, physicians have been critical of the Baby Doe regulations because they provide little, if any, useful clinical criteria on which health care providers can make the determination as to whether treatment of severely handicapped infants is medically contraindicated. The problem, according to Dr. Norman Fost (1982), professor of pediatrics at the University of Wisconsin, "is that there is no customary medical care in the difficult and problematic cases."

This same point is made in an official statement by the Committee on the Legal and Ethical Aspects of Health Care for Children: "The complexities of each case make it impossible to define precisely a single decision that would be medically and ethically correct in all cases." The committee's statement goes on to suggest that the Baby Doe regulations "fail to resolve the fundamental question of whether it is *ever* appropriate to withhold or withdraw life-prolonging treatment when an infant's prognosis is death within days, months, or even several years, or when the child's existence will involve great pain and suffering" (Strain 1983).

Hospitals in Catch-22 Position

Hospitals see themselves in a Catch-22 situation, caught between pro-life advocates and legislators concerned about the potential of infanticide, and hospitals and physicians who are trying to ward off government interference with clinical decision making. The American Hospital Association has argued that the regulation "creates an adversarial relationship" between hospitals and parents (Wallace 1983). The AHA position is that the Baby Doe regulation constitutes an unwarranted form of coercion inducing hospitals to turn over medical records that violates the time-honored norm of confidentiality between doctor and patient. Lawyers representing the hospital industry cite Judge Gerhard Gesell's ruling that links the hotline and possibility of a "sudden descent of Baby Doe Squads" to an "intrinsic *in terrorem* effect" because of the anticipated consequences of outside bureaucrats coming in and demanding answers to sensitive and difficult questions.

The surgeon general, Dr. C. Everett Koop, counters provider criticism with the argument that the administration's intervention "on behalf of children is no different from what happens in child-abuse cases in which state and local authorities step in to protect battered youngsters. Agencies that investigate child abuse," he adds, "can't really determine the extent of the problem unless they see written reports . . . thus, our insistence on the right to see medical records of handicapped infants is in line with standard practice." Dr. Koop believes that the great majority of physicians can be trusted to do what is fitting and proper. Citing surveys that show that many physicians feel it is quite all right not to perform corrective surgery on an infant with Down's syndrome, Dr. Koop states, "we aren't sure that some physicians can be relied on not to break the law, which forbids discrimination against handicapped children" (U.S. News & World Report 1984).

COMPROMISE: HOSPITAL ETHICS COMMITTEES

Despite the diametrically opposed positions of the Reagan administration and health care providers, a compromise was developed around the role of ethical review committees as a means of monitoring cases when parents and physicians have decided to withdraw or withhold life-prolonging therapy on handicapped infants or when there is disagreement between parents or among parents and physicians regarding the proper course of therapy. The compromise marked a retreat from the administration's earlier position favoring quick federal review of the treatment of severely handicapped infants whose parents decide to forego surgery or other forms of treatment. The new Baby Doe rule still requires hospitals to post a notice with a list of phone numbers so people can report suspected cases of nontreatment.

Most importantly the emphasis appears to have shifted responsibility from federal enforcement to hospital committees. Such committees include physicians, clergy, social workers, nurses, administrators, laymen, and lawyers. According to a 1985 national survey conducted by the American Hospital Association, about

60 percent of the nation's hospitals had ethics committees, a 100 percent increase from 1983 (Wallace 1986).

According to former Health and Human Services Secretary Margaret Heckler, the new ethical review committees "strike a delicate balance in protecting severely handicapped infants while recognizing the natural, inherent role of parents and doctors" (Annas 1983). The surgeon general is somewhat less supportive though: "I'm all for bioethical committees," he contends, "but the mere fact that a committee exists does not provide any backup in case there is some abrogation of a patient's civil rights" (U.S. News & World Report 1984). A similar point is made by Paul Marchand, of the Association for Retarded Children, who warns that in cases where nontreatment is prescribed, "bioethics committees could not act quickly enough" (Wallace 1983).

The final Baby Doe rule governing the care of handicapped infants went into effect February 13, 1984. Notices were sent to all U.S. hospitals for posting in nursing and medical staff areas. The notices list telephone numbers for reporting suspected cases of discrimination against handicapped infants and recommend that callers first refer denial of care cases to hospital infant care review committees. Under the regulations the formation of these committees is recommended but not mandatory.

Unresolved Concerns

Within the medical profession there remains a deep and fundamental mistrust of the entire Baby Doe regulatory approach. Dr. James Sammons, executive vice president of the American Medical Association, put the AMA view succinctly: "although some cosmetic changes have been made to the interim final rule, the major concerns of the American Medical Assocation and other organizations have not been addressed" (Strain 1983). Strains in the compromise have become even more pronounced since the Reagan administration's refusal to say flatly that it will not support legislation now being considered in Congress to extend the definition of child abuse to include cases such as Baby Doe. Dr. Harry Jennison of the American Academy of Pediatrics, whose group was one of the first to file suit against the administration on the initial Baby Doe regulation, stated: "We expected the Administration to take a public stance that the legislation was not necessary. Instead, they just stayed silent. In my opinion, the legislation will supersede the regulation and continue the philosophical approach of punitive enforcement" (U.S. News & World Report 1984).

The physicians' concerns are broadly shared. In an editorial on February 28, 1984, the *Wall Street Journal* supported a U.S. Appeals Court decision the week before in which a 2-to-1 vote upheld a lower court decision denying the Justice Department access to Baby Jane Doe medical records. "What was most heartening about the court's decision," the editorial stated, was the recognition—shared by many judges who've had to deal with this issue—that the federal government is trying to force the legal system to provide a clear-cut solution to the problem for which no solution exists. The right solution to the serious questions raised by the "Baby Doe" issue is to allow the growth of a movement that is creating hospital committee-review systems at the local level.

"The clear implication of the 'Baby Doe' regulation," the editorial concluded,

> is that the nation's doctors, parents, clergy and local officials cannot be trusted to devise systems to deal with the endangered lives of newborn infants. If this is true, the U.S. has gone quite beyond the saving grace of anybody's laws. But it is not true. U.S. society is not . . . immoral or insensate . . . and it should be given the opportunity at the local level to prove that. . .

Round 1 of an Unresolved Issue

All social issues have life cycles and Baby Doe is no exception. The length of the life cycle depends in part on the strength of the constituencies involved. Two of the most powerful and established constituencies in the United States are diametrically opposed on the Baby Doe rule: the hospital industry and the medical profession on one side, the pro-life coalition on the other. The courts are consistently upholding the principle of confidentiality as it applies to government access to the patient's record.

For hospitals and physicians the threat of outside review by either the Office of Civil Rights in the Justice Department or designated state agencies will continue. The likelihood of hospitals having to turn over medical records has decreased. With increasing use of ethics review committees, hospitals may hope for less outside interference. Physicians remain skeptical and concerned about politicization of the doctor-patient relationship. Emotions stirred by the Baby Doe issue will almost certainly be channeled to other controversies as the American health care system moves further along the frontier of the biogenetic revolution. Baby Doe is only the beginning.

STRATEGIES FOR THE NEW HOSPITAL

Be prepared. Hospitals should anticipate the potential risk of a Baby Doe situation. Hospitals serving high-risk populations and those with intensive care newborn nurseries are particularly vulnerable to Baby Doe situations. Those facilities that believe they have a significant potential risk should develop a contingency plan. The plan should be developed by administration, medical staff, nursing, legal, public relations, and others who would be involved in a Baby Doe situation. The contingency plan might specify roles and responsibilities in preparation for the potential barrage of attention from media, Office of Civil Rights, pro-life groups, and others interested in this highly volatile issue. Legal battles have focused on medical records. Consequently appropriate attention to record-keeping will be essential. From the experiences of hospitals with Baby Doe situations, a circus atmosphere can be created by the media and interest groups.

Hospital ethics committees. The President's Commission for the Study of Ethical Problems in Medicine and Biomedical and Behavioral Research, the American Academy of Pediatrics, and the Reagan administration all support the establishment of review committees in hospitals to aid physicians and families in ethical decision making. These committees should be considered a must in hospitals that have neonatal intensive care units and would probably be of considerable use in all tertiary care institutions where decisions regarding life and death are confronted daily. Responsibilities of such committees would include:

- articulating and updating guidelines to suspend life-support procedures,
- monitoring all decisions to avoid life-saving treatments and suspend life-support activities, and
- establishing cost-benefit criteria to guide the use of major capital equipment, medical technologies, and costly medical and surgical treatment programs.

Trustees and ethical issues. Baby Doe raises a number of ethical issues that few hospitals have directly faced. It is not too early to start thinking and talking about these issues at the board level. Educational programs are a place to start. Whether or not the board chooses to establish an ethics committee, it may be important to surface their views and values before a crisis.

Public funding cutbacks. The likelihood of Baby Doe situations may be increased by current cutbacks in public funding programs for high-risk populations. With Medicaid Title 19 cutbacks in many states, there is already anecdotal evidence to suggest that more high-risk mothers are receiving inadequate prenatal care. This should be a significant source of concern to hospitals and health care organizations serving such high-risk populations. Hospitals can make a positive contribution to the setting of public priorities for health programs that would reduce the likelihood of Baby Doe situations.

REFERENCES AND SUGGESTED READINGS

*Annas, George. "A Wonderful Case and an Irrational Tragedy: The Phillip Becker Case Continues." *Hastings Center Report,* February 1982.

Annas, George. "Disconnecting the 'Baby Doe' Hotline." *Hastings Center Report,* June 1983.

Annas, George. "'Baby Doe' Redux: Doctors as Child Abusers." *Hastings Center Report,* October 1983.

"Babies and Big Brother." *Wall Street Journal,* February 28, 1984.

Berseth, Carol Lynn. "A Neonatologist Looks at the 'Baby Doe' Rule: Ethical Decisions by Edict." *Pediatrics* 72, no. 3 (September 1983).

*Budetti, Peter, et al. *Case Study #10: The Costs and Effectiveness of Neonatal Intensive Care.* Washington, D.C.: Office of Technology Assessment, 1981.

*Committee on the Legal and Ethical Aspects of Health Care for Children. "Comments and Recommendations on the Infant Doe Proposed Regulations." *Law, Health and Medicine,* October 1983.

Fost, Norman. "Putting Hospitals on Notice." *Hastings Center Report,* August 1982.

*McClellan, Dennis. "An Advocate for Ethics in Modern Medicine." *Los Angeles Times,* October 13, 1985.

*President's Commission for the Study of Ethical Problems in Medicine and Biomedical and Behavioral Research. *Deciding to Forego Life-Sustaining Treatment,* 1983.

Punch, Linda, et al. "'Baby Doe' Thrusts Administrators into Middle of Life-Death Decision." *Modern Health Care,* July 1982.

"Should Uncle Sam Protect Handicapped Babies?" Interviews with Dr. C. Everett Koop and Dr. Harry Jennison. *U.S. News & World Report,* January 16, 1984.

Strain, James. "The American Academy of Pediatrics Comments on the 'Baby Doe II' Regulations." *New England Journal of Medicine* 309, no. 7 (August 18, 1983).

Wallace, Cynthia. "Outcry over 'Baby Doe' May Revive Little-Used Hospital Ethics Committee." *Modern Health Care,* June 1983.

Wallace, Cynthia. "L.A. Physicians, Lawyers Prepare Guidelines on Withdrawing Treatment." *Modern Healthcare* 16, no. 7:62–64.

*Suggested reading.

Part III

Management Strategies for Tomorrow's Hospitals

Chapter 12

The New Age CEO*

*Adapted from "The 'New Age' CEO" by Russell C. Coile, Jr., and Dennis D. Pointer in *Healthcare Forum*, pp. 38–41, with permission of Association of Western Hospitals, © May/June 1985.

12

Tomorrow's health care executive will be a new breed, with new roles, goals, and management styles. The change may be as profound as the movement to professionalize health care management started by Malcolm MacEachern fifty years ago. These New Age managers will differ from their predecessors in important ways: in basic values and orientation, in the methods by which they motivate and manage people, in how they create and spend capital, in the organizational structures they build, in the ways they communicate with coworkers and customers, in their use of technology, and in how they relate their work and their lives. A new age of health care management suited to tomorrow's environment is coming.

Critical success factors for the last generation of health care managers were maintaining high-occupancy levels in hospital beds, a loyal, well-equipped medical staff, and the continuing certification of the quality of the hospital's care by the Joint Commission on Accreditation of Hospitals (JCAH). The best of yesterday's health care executives built elegant hospitals and maximized their revenues under cost-based reimbursement. There were challenges aplenty, but major environmental changes—usually by the government, as the dominant payer—could be anticipated years away and accommodated. Tomorrow's health environment will bring change on an almost daily basis. Maintaining organizational balance and making forward progress will take every facility of the New Age chief executive officer (CEO).

THE SHIFTING GROUND OF HEALTH CARE MANAGEMENT

Illness has been the base business of the health care industry since 1900. Now the health marketplace is shifting dramatically. Hospital use in the mid-1980s is

143

declining 5 to 10 percent in every region of the nation. This is not the last gasp of the 1981–83 recession. It is a permanent shift in consumer attitudes and demand. The golden age of hospitals is over, and the new age of health has begun.

The illness industry must reconceptualize its business as health. The old paradigm of curative medicine is being superseded by a new orientation toward health. As the values of individual consumers and major purchasers of health services change, the New Hospital of tomorrow must learn how to profit from keeping its customers healthy.

As the new paradigm accelerates in impact, hospital use will decline, perhaps to half of the current rate of 1,000 to 1,200 hospital days per thousand. This drop in hospital use will come not just from a decreasing length of stay but in actual reduction in admissions, as the hospital becomes the last resort of only the most acutely ill. Other healthier consumers will obtain treatment and support services from ambulatory care centers and other low-cost settings.

New Age CEO

Will hospital administrators be obsolete? Not if they can make the paradigm shift with their organizations, matching the swing in consumer attitudes and habits with new types of services and new styles of management. At the intersection of this mercurial pattern of tasks, technology, and market conditions is the health care manager. Tomorrow's new age CEO must be able to operate amid ambiguity, charting directions in a context that will frequently change. A constant challenge will be balancing financial, organizational, and human needs and coaligning these with the manager's personal and professional goals.

The health care organization of the future will need philosopher-managers, according to Leland Kaiser (1981), who will manage by ideas, not objectives. Philosopher-managers will guide health care organizations into paths that maximize both corporate and community goals. The biggest challenge for the new age CEO will be to create win win outcomes in which individuals, the organization, and the public interest are all winners.

Tasks of the New Age CEO

The manager of tomorrow's health care organization will have a number of new roles that will demand a different repertoire of skills and abilities than those taught today in schools of business and health administration:

- Information broker. In the new information era information will be abundant, even overwhelming. The task of the knowledge executive will be to provide key information to those closest to the situation who must act. The computer will be an enormous asset, and every manger will need to utilize its computing and communications power. Satellites and telecommunications will make management a global affair. The new age CEO will be the hub of an information network in which the ability to persuade using electronic media will be as important as traditional skills of face-to-face communication.

- Organization designer. In a dynamic environment, leaders must be organizational designers. Organizational structures will change constantly. As conditions shift, the manager must realign the organization with a minimum of delay. When new markets are identified, the competitive advantage will go to the first firm to capitalize on the opportunity. Fine-tuning structures for productivity will be essential in a marketplace of constant competition.

- Facilitator. With work site democracy increasing, the new age CEO must provide the conditions under which employees will do their best—not by telling them what to do but by providing a corporate culture that encourages risk taking and innovation at all levels of the organization. These are the "change masters," suggests Rosabeth Moss Kanter (1983), who make things happen through others. A major challenge of the manager will be to coalign the tasks of the organizations with the goals of its staff.

- Pathfinder. To position the organization in a competitive health care environment will require the skills of a master strategist. When the level of competition is high, the penalty for strategic error may be bankruptcy. Strategic analysis of industry and market, once the domain of staff planners, must be an executive function at the highest level.

- Intrapreneur. The challenge of health care management will be the creation of new products and services in a dynamic market. In the past, new business ideas have come primarily from individuals and small firms working on the fringe of the marketplace. The new age CEO must galvanize employees to become entrepreneurial within the context of the large health care organization (intra + entrepreneurial = intrapreneurial). The new rules of intrapreneurship begin with throwing the old rule book away. The future health care executive must provide flexibility in personnel policies, procedures, and ways of doing business. Intrapreneurs need control over capital, taking a personal share of risk, and gaining a significant reward if successful.

THE TYPE I ORGANIZATION

The corporation is one of the most pervasive institutions of the modern age. The classical hierarchical pyramid of top-down management is giving way to a new structure, the Type I innovative organization (see Figure 12–1). The new innovative organization looks more like a bubble machine than the well-ordered pyramid, which is just the point.

Figure 12–1 Classic versus Innovative Organizations

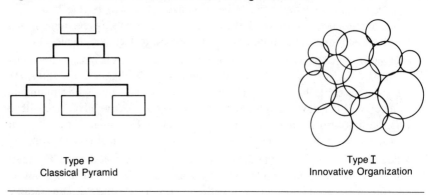

Type P
Classical Pyramid

Type I
Innovative Organization

The innovative organization is a constantly shifting network of overlapping task groups and functions. Each product line organizes its own network of producers and support staff for maximum advantage. No matter that it is not neat or lends itself to easy definition on an organization chart. This is a results-oriented structure, which is less concerned with turf than with outcomes.

The new age CEO is somewhere in the middle of the Type I organization, trying to keep it moving and in generally the right direction. The future manager is the pivotal central hub, at the intersection of many networks within the organization. But the notion of control is obsolete. Each work group sets its own goals and provides its own discipline. New members and new functions are added as needed and are shed just as quickly when no longer necessary.

Value-Based Management

Central to the success of industry leaders like IBM and Hewlett-Packard is a corporate culture with a widely shared set of core values. Brozovich has experimented with value-based management in a hospital setting, and it works (Brozovich and Shortell 1984). Its philosophical base is Theory Z, an amalgam of management concepts inspired by the managerial philosophy of successful Japanese firms like Matsushito and Nippon Electric. Its roots are in Eastern religion. Theory Z emphasizes the importance of creating a common culture that links the needs of the workers to those of the organization. It begins with definition of a shared set of values by all members of the organization. The management challenge for the new age CEO is to guide the organization in such a way that all decisions, designs, systems, processes, traditions, and reward structures emphasize and are consistent with the overall system of values.

Value-based management has a long-range perspective. Capital investments and human investments will have a long-range payoff. In contrast with short-term, bottom-line management, value-based management aims to develop a strong, healthy firm that is successfully meeting the needs of both its market and its work force.

Well-designed business strategy is critical to the success of the value-based organization. The new age CEO takes the long view of the firm in its industry and in society and positions it for dominance. Strategies must be consistent with values. The value-based organization is not pushed about by every minor shift in the marketplace. Such a market-driven strategy is seldom successful on a consistent and sustained basis.

CUSTOMER SATISFACTION

A business enterprise meets its moment of truth every time it comes in contact with a customer. If these moments satisfy some customer need, the business will be a success. Most of these moments of truth occur far from the executive suite. Customer relations expert Karl Albrecht (Albrecht and Zemke 1985) defines *service management* as a philosophy that imbues every aspect of the customer relationship. A number of hospitals and health organizations are instituting guest relations programs, inspired by the best examples of service in the private sector, from companies like Disney, Marriott, and Scandinavian Airlines (SAS).

Health care is in transition from a product-driven to a customer-driven industry. It is no longer enough to have the finest medical staff and most advanced technology. The success of the New Hospital will be determined by whether it services the needs of its three tiers of customers, illustrated in Table 12–1. Peter Drucker (1985) puts it plainest: "It is the customer who determines what a business is." The customer defines what has value and what they will pay. In a

Table 12–1 Customers of the Future

Customer Class	Customer Type	Customer Needs
Major purchasers	HMOs, PPOs, employers, insurance plans	Large volume Low price Predictable quality
Physicians	Broker/producer	Access to facilities Support Customer base
Mass market	Individuals Well Worried well Sick	Health care Information Reassurance Medical care

market-driven environment the success of the New Hospital will be direct response to how well it satisfies customers.

Attention to the details of service—making the most of those moments of truth—is the hallmark of the high-performance organization. It begins with common courtesy and in some hospitals is taken to new heights of pampering and luxury. The character of the hospital's service is reflected in the pride with which it is delivered. This is the distinctive stamp of the New Hospital: cutting through impersonality to attend to the unique needs and wants of every customer. Can it work in a 500-bed institution? Without a doubt it can. If Disney can manage to sustain the fantasy for 25 million Americans each year who spend a day in the Disney Worlds, a hospital can impress its customers with the quality of caring.

The average customer has little background with which to judge the quality of care provided by the hospital but can judge the quality of the service. Hospitals will differentiate themselves on the level of service and range of amenities, just as hotels and telephone companies do today, from no-frills to premium levels of service. That level of service must align with the hospital's strategic management and corporate culture, a test that managers of the New Hospital must meet every day in the thousands of moments of truth.

FUTURES MANAGEMENT

The new age CEO believes the future is a resource to be managed. Anticipating future conditions and charting organizational strategies toward a desired future is the essential task of leadership. In a turbulent marketplace where not all hospitals and health organizations may survive, it will take a mix of vision and pragmatism to be an industry leader.

There are many possible futures. The task of the new age CEO is to select the future that has the best fit with the strengths of the organization and the expected marketplace conditions. The intentional organization designs its preferred future and initiates strategies and organizational structures to reach it.

At bottom the new age CEO is not afraid of the future. Change and stress are the stimuli of growth and achievement. The macho manager is, like the cowboy, a vanishing myth. The new age CEO recognizes that management and leadership are a process in which many share. For all the new age CEO's of tomorrow's health care organization, the future is a door and vision is the key.

STRATEGIES FOR THE NEW HOSPITAL

Profitability—not occupancy or market share. Be clear about the goal of the ''new age'' hospital manager in tomorrow's competitive marketplace: it is to maximize the profitability of their organization. Two motivations apply. First, regardless of type of ownership, every health corporation must be profitable if it is to survive. Second, profits are symbols of the achievement of a wide range of financial and community service objectives. Profits represent the value of the hospital's services to its customers. Without continuing profitability the organization will be hardpressed to change, grow, or obtain capital from financial markets. Traditional symbols of success—high occupancy levels and dominant market share—may or may not be associated with success in the future. If services such as trauma, obstetrics, or neonatal intensive care are not profitable, then higher volume only increases losses.

Nichemanship—not generalship. The new age CEO must be an adroit niche-finder. The secret to success in tomorrow's crowded health industry is finding profitable niches and establishing leadership within those niches. These may be vertical markets, such as the elderly or an enrolled group, or product niches, such as long-term care. Whatever the market sector, the organization should focus its strengths in becoming the brand name recognized by customers in those niches. Unlike the past, when hospital name recognition was sufficient to retain physician and customer loyalty, that strategy of broad market position can only be held by a few large multihealth corporations. Every other hospital and health organization must find its own niche.

Continuous innovation. The hallmark of tomorrow's most successful health companies will be continuous innovation. Ideas, as much as capital, are the key to maintaining market-niche leadership. Sustaining that desired leadership position means constant change and continuous improvement. Casio, the world's most successful watchmaker, enhances or extends its products every three months. That is the lead-time Casio has before competitors copy their innovation, and in the meantime, of course, Casio has already innovated again. Tomorrow's business climate will be unrelenting: product life cycles will be short and competitors will vigorously pursue every profitable opportunity. The new age CEO must foster a corporate climate in which managers and employees are constantly improving the character of established businesses and exploring new product lines in anticipation of changing customer needs.

Entrepreneurial risk. The hospital industry has been a risk-adverse industry and with good reason. Malpractice is a continuing threat. Health care must be a zero-free-defects process. This has had a chilling effect on organizational risk-taking. As diverse a set of industrial observers as Peter Drucker, George Guilder, and the Atari democrats, Magaziner and Reich, place their faith in the future of America in the hands of the entrepreneur. This is the age of enterprise. Like the airlines, banking, and communications, hospitals are being swept up in a wide wave of entrepreneurship that will leave no industry untouched. Some hospitals will be blessed to be led by a natural entrepreneur. For those hospitals who are now risk-bound, hiring experienced risk takers is a shortcut to an entrepreneurial future. Already a number of health organizations are hiring executives from high-competition industries who will bring a risk-taking perspective to the management of the New Hospital. As long as the entrepreneurial outsiders are balanced by managers who know and care deeply about the base business of health care, these hospitals will be winners.

Bias for action. Cost reimbursement in the pre-prospective payment era (1965–82) created a safety net to protect every hospital's financial management. It was difficult to make serious financial mistakes since reasonable costs were reimbursed without question. That is history. Today hospitals must operate within much finer financial margins. The penalty for strategic error can be executive termination. A critical success factor for the new age CEO in tomorrow's challenging environment is a bias to act—rather than react—to change. The bias for managerial action must be informed by anticipation of the changing environment ahead and a vision of the New Hospital's preferred future. In times of change there are three types of leaders: those who make it happen, those who watch it happen, and those who never know what is happening until change has passed them by.

REFERENCES AND SUGGESTED READINGS

*Ackoff, Russell C. *Creating the Corporate Future*. New York: John Wiley & Sons, 1981.

Albrecht, Karl, and Zemke, Ron. *Service America: Doing Business in the New Economy*. Homewood, Ill.: Dow Jones-Irwin, 1985.

Brozovich, John P. and Shortell, Stephen M. "How To Create More Humane and Productive Health Care Environments." *Health Care Management Review*, Fall 1984, 43–53.

*Cleveland, Harlan F. *The Future Executive*. New York: Harper & Row, 1972.

*Cleveland, Harlan F. The Knowledge Executive. New York: Harper & Row, 1985.

*Clifford, Donald K., and Cavanagh, Richard E. *The Winning Performance: How America's High-Growth Midsize Companies Succeed*. New York: Bantam Books, 1985.

*Coile, Russell C., Jr., and Pointer, Dennis D. "The 'New Age' CEO." *Hospital Forum* 28, no. 3 (May/June 1985):39–41.

*Deal, Terrence E., and Kennedy, Allen A. *Corporate Cultures: The Rites and Rituals of Corporate Life*. Reading, Mass.: Addison-Wesley, 1982.

Drucker, Peter F. *Innovation and Entrepreneurship: Practice and Principles*. New York: Harper & Row, 1985.

*Ferguson, Marilyn. *The Aquarian Conspiracy: Personal and Social Transformation in the 1980's*. Los Angeles: J.P. Tarcher, 1980.

*Guilder, George. *The Spirit of Enterprise*. New York: Doubleday, 1985.

*"Innovation: The Agenda for American Business." Report by Arthur Young, The Institute for Innovation and The Foresight Group, New York, 1985.

*Johnson, Richard L. "Old Memories and New Dreams: Economics for Nonprofit Hospitals." *Health Matrix* 3, no. 1 (Spring 1985):15–21.

Kaiser, Leland R. "Futurism in Health Care." *Hospital Forum*, parts I–III, November/December 1980, March/April 1981, May/June 1981.

Kanter, Rosabeth Moss. *The Change Masters*. New York: Simon & Schuster, 1983.

*Kimberly, John R., and Quinn, Robert E. *New Futures: The Challenge of Managing Corporate Transitions*. Homewood, Ill.: Dow Jones-Irwin, 1984.

*Maccoby, Michael. *The Leader: A New Face for American Management*. New York: Simon and Schuster, 1981.

*Magaziner, Ira C., and Reich, Robert B. *Minding America's Business: Decline and Rise of the American Economy*. New York: Harcourt Brace Jovanovich, 1982.

*O'Toole, James. *Vanguard Management: Redesigning the Corporate Future*. New York: Doubleday, 1985.

*Pascale, Richard T., and Athos, Anthony G. *The Art of Japanese Management*. New York: Simon and Schuster, 1981.

*Peters, Tom. "Common Courtesy: The Ultimate Barrier to Entry." Parts I–II, *Hospital Forum*, January/February 1984, March/April 1984.

*Pinchot, Gifford III. *Intrapreneuring*. New York: Harper & Row, 1985.

*Pointer, Dennis D. "Preparing for the 'New Age.'" *Hospital Forum* 27, no. 6 (November/December 1984).

---

*Suggested reading.

Chapter 13

Multihealth Corporations

13

The future will belong to multihealth corporations (MHCs). This new type of health care organization is more than a hospital and more than a holding company. It is a totally integrated horizontal and vertical system. Looking to the future, the health care industry will be dominated by 25 to 50 large MHCs.

The good news for hospitals is that the health industry is at the threshold of a significant period of industry growth and consolidation. Many of tomorrow's multihealth corporations do not exist today. In the process, however, this new wave of corporate development will wash away a number of today's free-standing hospitals and totally alter the way in which health care services are organized and delivered by the year 2000.

CRITICAL SUCCESS FACTORS

In any industry there are a small number of critical success factors on which rest the rise and fall of individual companies. In the health care industry the multihealth corporation has a set of critical success factors that will shape its destiny, and that of the health industry.

- Size. MHCs will be large. At the regional level small MHCs will own or operate a minimum of 10 to 20 hospitals, with combined corporate revenues of $250 to $500 million per year. National MHCs will include a base of at least 100 hospitals and $1 billion revenues. Corporate potency will be essential to mount competitive advances and withstand the coming price wars.
- Alternative delivery system. The MHC is not hospital-centered. At the heart of each MHC will be a health plan with a minimum of 100,000 subscribers, to provide the financing and consumer base to support the MHC.

155

- Corporate practice. The MHC must control the type and quality of medical care provided. Contracts with professional medical corporations will be the dominant pattern, but some MHCs will utilize the salaried physician approach.
- Information systems. Information systems will provide the linkages for the highly decentralized MHC. Telecommunications and satellite communications will link the widely dispersed organizational units to each other and to their consumers.
- Central finance. Financial control is centralized in the multihealth corporation. Strategic management begins and ends with finance, controlling access to capital and setting goals for financial performance.
- Core values. The factor that will distinguish the great multihealth corporations will be a distinctive set of organizational values, providing the corporate culture that binds a large, decentralized company together.

CONSTRUCTION OF THE MHC

This is the decade in which hospitals must make two important decisions. The first is whether they will transform themselves into a health care corporation, providing a range of services, and leaving their hospital self-concept behind. The second question, and the most critical, is which MHC to join.

There is only a limited future for free-standing hospitals. Some—perhaps 25 percent of America's hospitals—for example, will find a specialized market niche, e.g., children's hospitals. Even sole-provider hospitals in rural areas will not be secure. They can expect new competition from out-of-state hospital chains and even from their own medical staff.

Only through mutual association will today's hospitals become tomorrow's multihealth corporations. There are two ways to organize MHCs: (1) build and (2) buy. The low-cost approach to building a multihealth corporation will be voluntary affiliation, but it is slower. When mergers are voluntary, capital is not wasted on hospital acquisitions but can be protected for system development and marketing. Hospitals who choose to affiliate will have a greater commitment than those who are purchased. They are more likely to share common values and be willing to accept the financial and information systems ties that will bind them together.

Acquisition, the strategy utilized by investor-owned systems, has been highly successful. Equity capital and long-term debt have provided the funding for rapid growth and development by for-profit systems such as: HCA (Hospital Corporation of America), AMI (American Medical International), and NME (National Medical Enterprises). In 1985 the for-profit companies owned or managed 15 percent of the nation's hospitals. By 1990 it could be twice that: 30 percent.

Profile of an MHC

Using the alliance model, American Healthcare Systems (AHS) was formed in 1984 by 15 corporate members of United Health Care Systems of Kansas City and 11 multiinstitutional system members of Associated Health Systems, Phoenix. Additional voluntary affiliations have added 10 systems. AHS is a for-profit entity, created to nationally market health care service such as health maintenance organizations, preferred provider organizations, and alternative health care services jointly developed on behalf of AHS members. Through the AHS business subsidiary, this MHC develops and markets purchasing, materiels management, and shared service programs. AHS buys more than $1 billion of goods and services annually. With nearly 500 member hospitals and another 975 affiliated institutions, the combined revenues in 1985 totaled $14 billion.

AHS is the largest nonprofit conglomerate in the health industry, followed by Texas-based Voluntary Hospitals of America, with more than 1,000 hospitals. Formation of Associated Healthcare Systems through voluntary association gives the member local and regional multihealth corporations a voice in Washington. The AHS institute provides policy research and representation of AHS views with the largest health care buyer in the nation: the U.S. government. AHS is the beginning of a new era of competition among very large companies in the health industry.

Organization of the MHC

The MHC is a totally different organization from any model previously utilized in health care. It is not a traditional pyramid, nor is it simply a holding company. The multihealth corporation is a network (Figure 13–1). The multihealth corporation is a diversified company. At its center is a small corporate apparatus, including the president, chief executive officer, and the staff functions of finance, information systems, and strategic business planning.

Figure 13–1 The Multihealth Corporation Network

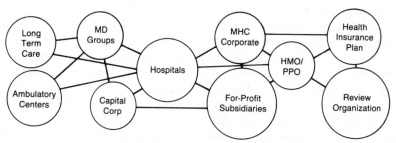

The MHC is not organized along division lines, for example, hospitals, nursing homes, home care. Its subunits are geographic market clusters of vertically integrated services, including one or more hospitals, long-term care facilities, home care, ambulatory and convenience care centers, and affiliated subsidiaries. These regional and subregional cluster systems have the license and the venture capital to compete to the maximum in their local markets.

Only the functions of finance, information systems, and strategic planning are centralized. The MHC provides policy, leadership, and vision for the system. Through the joint pledging of assets, the MHC controls a large pool of investment capital and acts as banker for the system.

Alternative Delivery System

At the heart of the MHC is the health plan that provides the consumer base for the health care activities of the MHC's services and facilities. The health plan may be organized as a health maintenance organization (HMO) or other type of integrated health financing/insurance/delivery plan. The health plan will not necessarily be limited to use of MHC facilities to meet its subscribers' needs. This will force the MHC to be price competitive and give the health plan an incentive for maximum marketing and financial performance.

As related business activities, the health plan may operate an administrative services organization (ASO) to provide claims review for employers and administrative support for physician groups. The health plan should not be a captive of the MHC but given a wide entrepreneurial focus.

People and Productivity

There is a danger in becoming a very large company: losing your people in the process. As the multihealth corporation grows, adding new hospitals and health care systems, the new people must share the goals and vision of the company. The experience of the private sector in the accommodation of acquisitions is that a company can become big without losing the corporate family feeling, but it requires a dedicated effort.

A primary task of the new multihealth corporation will be to establish a companywide corporate culture. Publicizing corporate goals widely is the first step. Establishing a distinctive image for the MHC across all operating units is important. Choosing a corporate color and logo is symbolic in a conscious campaign to create that corporate identification.

The critical element in the success of the multihealth corporation from the inside is its people. Human resource development systems must be sufficiently flexible to recognize and reward talent at all levels of the organization. Publicizing the heroes and champions across the MHC's far-flung operating and administrative units will provide role models across the MHC.

Management education is an important shaping force. At the Lutheran Hospital Society of Southern California, a management education program called INFORM—Innovation for Managers—brings the latest state of the art to its health care executives and top staff. A concern for people needs to be reinforced through a systemwide productivity monitoring system. A new system developed by management engineers at LHS marketed as the C.A.R.E. System measures productivity on a monthly basis, in multiple formats for appropriate levels of management.

THE FUTURE AND MULTIHEALTH CORPORATIONS

While the future is far from certain, a number of key trends point toward the emergence of the multihealth corporation as the model for tomorrow's large health care organizations. The key driving forces, and their implications for MHCs, follow:

- Competition. The door to competition in health care has been opened, and there is no closing it. Hospitals will compete on price. By some estimates, 1,000 hospitals will close in the 1980s due to competitive pressures. Multihealth corporations will prosper. The MHCs will have the capacity to be large vendors to major corporations and insurance carriers buying health care in large volume and at discount prices. Having the needed service capacity, location, and financial strength to compete on a volume and price basis will accelerate the growth of multihealth corporations and leave the free-standing hospital in a precarious position.

- Conglomerates. The multihealth corporation is a conglomerate. Today one of three hospitals is affiliated with a multiinstitutional system. By 1990 it will be one of two hospitals. Most multihospital systems are small—10 hospitals or fewer. By 1990 at least 10 multihealth corporations will own or manage more than 100 hospitals. Health care expenditures will reach nearly $700 billion by 1990; in 1990, 20 percent of those revenues will go to multihealth corporations. The health care industry is about to be totally restructured.

- Corporate practice. Three forces—conglomerates, the information era, and the shifting dollar—will combine to fundamentally change medical practice. One of 2 physicians practices in a group setting today; in the year 2000 it may be 9 of 10. Physicians will work with hospitals, not for them, through professional medical corporations. Hospitals and physicians will share financial risks and rewards, as reimbursement shifts from fee-for-service to capitation and prospective payment for diagnostically related groups. Some multihealth corporations will acquire, own or manage medical groups, but in most cases professional corporations will negotiate independently with the MHC. Case management systems will incorporate the philosophy and style of practice of the MHC.

- Diversification. Most hospitals are still dependent on inpatient-related revenues: 95 to 99 percent of all revenues. The multihealth corporations will have a significant advantage in diversification and new business development. The MHC has the expertise, entrepreneurial experience, and access to capital for venturing. Diversification has an expensive learning curve. The multihealth corporation can provide centralized assistance to its hospitals and subsidiaries in developing new product lines. Marketing diversified services requires skills still limited in most hospitals. Multihealth corporations can take advantage of experiences across their system, bringing people and expertise from one part of the company to bear in another.

- Shifting dollars. Health care dollars are shifting: from inpatient to outpatient; from fee-for-service to capitation and at-risk contracting; from public to private; and from acute care to long-term care and health promotion. Multihealth corporations will be the first to establish effective new case management systems and have the discipline necessary to use them effectively. The MHCs will have real market advantages in being chosen preferred provider organizations, having the critical mass and management discipline to be low-cost producers.

BARRIERS TO MHC FORMATION

Not all multihealth corporations will succeed. Barriers that can be anticipated by those seeking to organize MHCs will include the following:

- Board leadership. Hospitals' boards of trustees will need a combination of foresight, an awareness of how the future will change, with perspective, the ability to see beyond their four walls, to give up local independence in exchange for united strength in a MHC.

- Capital. Like small business, some multihealth corporations will fail because they are undercapitalized, but are likely to be acquired by bigger MHCs if they stumble.

- Medical staff. Physicians must be fully committed partners in these new ventures.

- Outside competition. The health industry should anticipate new market competition from non–health care providers, as Sears has provided in real estate and financial services.

THE NEW FACE OF THE HEALTH INDUSTRY

Major changes are taking place in the health care industry. New financial and competitive pressures are just beginning to be felt. Some hospitals will find a protected market niche. But for most hospitals the future lies with multihealth corporations.

The multihealth corporation will be the dominant organizational model, but it is a flexible concept. Some MHCs will be tightly run from the center; others will operate decentralized franchises. There will be an MHC to fit most styles and organizational cultures. What can be predicted about all MHCs for the future is they will be large, potent, and dominant in their markets.

STRATEGIES FOR THE NEW HOSPITAL

Benefits of early affiliation. Many hospitals are sitting on the fence. Affiliating with a multihealth corporation, or starting a new one, will be the most critical decision hospital boards and CEOs will make in the 1980s. For those who join early, there will be risks but also the potential for higher rewards. While not all MHCs will succeed, the first MHCs will be in the best position to gain dominant market shares in their regions.

Entrepreneurial building blocks. One of the fastest ways to build an MHC will be to buy small (2–10 hospitals) and mid-sized multihospital systems. This is a strategy utilized by investor-owned MHCs and is the most likely market entry strategy for new competitors. Expect it to be used also by nonprofit MHCs. Those who stand to profit most are the entrepreneurs who put together the small and mid-sized systems that will be the building blocks for tomorrow's large companies.

Join now. Two words of advice to hospitals thinking about multihealth corporations are *join now*, to gain maximum advantage from early membership.

Sell now. Many MHCs will buy—not build—their systems. Hospitals that sell early are much more likely to bring premium prices. The best hospitals are fomenting bidders' wars among competing MHC suitors, and getting top prices. If selling is an option, look at it closely now.

SUGGESTED READINGS

Barkholz, David. "Midwest Not-for-Profit Systems Diversify, Enter Insurance Field." *Modern Healthcare,* October 11, 1985, pp. 42–46.

Bisbee, Gerald E., Jr. "Hospital Management Industry: Delivering the Goods in Difficult Times." Part 1. Kidder Peabody & Co., November 5, 1984.

Brown, Montague, and McCool, Barbara. *Multihospital Systems: Strategies For Organization and Management.* Rockville, Md.: Aspen Systems Corp., 1980.

Deveney, Kathleen, and Tarpey, John P. "Humana: Making The Most of Its Place in the Spotlight." *Business Week,* May 6, 1985, pp. 68–69.

"Health Care System in the 1990's." Study conducted by the Health Insurance Association of America by Arthur D. Little, Inc., January 1985.

Hull, Jennifer Bingham. "Medical Turmoil: Four Hospital Chains, Facing Lower Profits, Adopt New Strategies." *Wall Street Journal,* October 10, 1985.

Johnson, Donald E.L. "Investor-Owned Chains Continue Expansion, 1985 Survey Shows." *Modern Healthcare,* June 7, 1985, pp. 75–90.

Johnson, Donald E.L. "Will Outsiders Buy Hospital Chains?" *Modern Healthcare,* November 8, 1985, p. 5.

Johnson, Everett, and Johnson, Richard. *Hospitals In Transition,* Rockville, Md.: Aspen Systems Corp., 1982.

Johnson, Richard L. "Health Care 2000 A.D.: The Impact of Conglomerates." *Hospital Progress,* April 1981, pp. 48–51.

Mannisto, Marilyn. "Five Distinct Traits Foreseen for Healthy Hospital Systems." *Hospitals,* April 16, 1984, pp. 26–27.

Mannisto, Marilyn. "Multis 1984 Growth: Small in Numbers, Large in Impact." *Hospitals,* December 16, 1984, pp. 40–42.

Mason, Todd. "Lifesaving Partnerships For Nonprofit Hospitals." *Business Week,* August 26, 1985, p. 84.

Sandrick, Karen. "Investor-Owned Growth Shifts from Numbers to Niche." Part 1. *Hospitals,* June 1, 1984, pp. M16–28.

Sandrick, Karen. "Not-for-Profit Growth Has National Look." Part 2. *Hospitals,* September 1, 1984, pp. M16–22.

Chapter 14
Capital Strategies

14

The capital crunch is not a new breakfast cereal. It symbolizes the fear by hospitals that the supply of long-term capital is drying up. Harold Ting and John Valente (1982) of ICF, Inc., believe there will be too many hospitals chasing too little capital in the 1980s. The problem is that many of the 2,500 hospitals built with federal Hill-Burton funding in the 1950s and 1960s are aging and need replacement. They estimate the potential demand for capital at $150 to $200 billion in the 1980s or $15 to $25 billion a year of hospital long-term borrowing.

Fueling the pressure for capital are rising construction costs. Some hospital projects have risen to $150 to $200 million, and $30 to $50 million is commonplace. That amount of capital is probably not going to be available to hospitals. A shortfall of $50 to $100 billion is predicted for U.S. hospitals in the 1980s from the capital market.

Potency will be a critical success factor for tomorrow's health care organizations. Health care, like all enterprises, begins and ends with capital. Without capital there is no investment in new services, new technology, new facilities, or marketing to customers. Every health care activity requires capital.

CAPITAL MARKETS

Who buys and sells capital? The buyers come from all sectors of the economy. In 1983, $615 billion of capital was borrowed: 25 percent by households, 25 percent by business, and 50 percent by government at all levels. Using tax-exempt municipal bonds, nonprofit hospitals in 1985 took $29.7 billion out of the capital market. The sellers in the municipal bond market have changed dramatically in recent years (Table 14–1).

165

Table 14-1 Sources of Hospital Capital: Tax-Exempt Bonds

Year	Bonds ($ in billions)	Insured Issues	Uninsured Issues
1984	$10	27%	73%
1985	$29.7	40%	60%

Source: *Modern Healthcare*, vol. 16, no. 7, pp. 114–116, Crain Communications Inc., © 1986.

As the market changed and the large institutional investors abandoned bonds, the gap was filled by new mutual funds and by individuals. Interest rates moved up, to attract individual buyers, are still rising, and will continue to stay high, given current economic uncertainties, believes Bruce Mansdorf (1983) of Merrill Lynch. Capital markets will ask higher prices for hospital capital until the impact of DRG payment, selective contracting, and the fate of the Medicare trust fund becomes clear to investors.

The health industry's uses of capital are shifting. Hospitals have traditionally used capital to build new facilities only as the old wore out. That is still true for nonprofit hospitals and not-for-profit (NFP) multihospital systems. Investor-owned health care corporations have used capital for acquisitions as well as construction, and the deals are getting bigger. The merger of American Hospital Supply with Baxter Travenol of America in 1985 was a $6.5 billion deal in the health industry and the fourth largest megadeal of the year, mirroring the merged activities in the oil industry and elsewhere in the private sector.

NFP multihospital systems are acquiring new subsidiaries in their diversification activities. Without access to the equity market, however, the deals are small because the NFP multis must fund these acquisitions primarily from internal operations. Larger NFP multis with more internal resources have begun to use acquisitions more aggressively. Baptist Hospital of Phoenix purchased Manatee Memorial, a county hospital, in 1983 for $65 million. An increasing use of capital is to refinance existing debt. Nearly half of the capital borrowing in 1983 was to restructure existing debt, as opposed to new construction and reinvestment.

End of the Capital Pass-Through

The days of easy access to capital may soon end. The federal government plans to end the capital pass-through for hospitals. Until now, the costs of borrowing have been simply passed along to consumers, third party payers, and government. The federal government's former cost-based reimbursement system covered all capital costs as long as the capital projects had obtained certificates of need from state planning authorities.

Passage of the Tax Equity and Fiscal Reform Act of 1982 (TEFRA) ushered in a new form of government control over hospital finances, which hospitals are actively resisting. Hospital associations are lobbying vigorously to slow down implementation, phasing out the pass-through over 10 years. The proposal by government to create a capital pool raises hospital fears of a national cap, or limit, on available capital.

CAPITAL STRATEGIES

All market strategies are capital strategies. There is a limited supply of capital. The primary strategic responsibility of management is to protect its capital and expand its share of available capital. Hospitals and health care organizations provide services to the public, but they are not public services. The ability of a health care company to subsidize those consumers who cannot pay part or all of the cost of their care must come from prudent capital management. In a highly competitive marketplace like health care, those companies that most successfully manage capital strategies will prosper. Others who do not, and they may be numerous, will flag or fail. Ten capital strategies for the New Hospital and tomorrow's health care companies follow.

Leverage

Investor-owned hospitals have been leading advocates of the leverage strategy. They have successfully demonstrated it is possible to borrow safely at levels exceeding 80 percent of long-term debt to assets. Not-for-profit hospitals have been more conservative; their long-term debt seldom exceeds levels of 60 to 70 percent. Despite market rumors of a capital crunch, for-profit hospital and health care companies with a proven record of financial performance have had little difficulty gaining access to taxable long-term capital. State health care financing authorities have been major underwriters of capital to the not-for-profits. If the capital crunch worsens, state funds may be the only substantial source of large-dollar financing available in the capital market for small nonprofit hospitals.

Tax-exempt capital borrowing in 1985 neared $30 billion, an increase of 200 percent over $10 billion in 1984. With the capital pass-through for Medicare reimbursement guaranteed only through 1986, the capital window is lowering. Hospitals and health care companies should plan alternative capital strategies now, in anticipation that their capital costs may not be fully covered by government programs in the future.

Acquisition

New capital assets may be developed or acquired. Most nonprofit hospitals have developed their capital asset base on their own over a long period. For-profit health care companies have aggressively used acquisition as a strategy for capital growth. Using a combination of private venture capital, equity funding, and long-term debt, the for-profits have grown dramatically since 1975. Today, investor-owned companies constitute 20 percent of all multihospital systems. The for-profit chains grew 15 percent in 1983; by 1990 the for-profits may own 30 percent of all American hospitals. From a capital perspective the larger the asset base, the larger the debt that may be supported to finance further acquisitions. In this way the Hospital Corporation of America was able to acquire its number 2 rival, Hospital Affiliates, for more than $300 million.

Equity Funding

The greatest market advantage for-profit health care companies have enjoyed is their access to equity capital. Of the five largest multihospital systems in the United States, all are for-profit (Hospital Corporation of America, American Medical International, National Medical Enterprises, Humana, and Universal Health System). Now not-for-profit health systems are tapping the equity pool, by converting nonprofit activities to for-profit and taking them to the equity market. When U.S. Health Care Systems converted to for-profit, it raised $23 million from two stock offerings. As a publicly held health maintenance organization, a $3 million investment in 1981 became worth $80 million in three years.

Nearly 20 percent of all new stock offerings in 1983 were health-related, indicating a high level of investor interest in new health issues. Not all are repaying investor confidence. Home Health Care of America rose quickly when issued in 1983 but then fell more than 50 percent after initial earnings were low. Only 1 in 30 publicly held home health companies was profitable in 1984. The equity strategy is not without risk.

Cash Management

As health care companies have grown larger, they have increasingly utilized strategies from the private sector to obtain short-term return on cash reserves. Today cash management is an established specialty of financial management. Sophisticated cash managers can increase the rate of return on their short-term investments by one to three percentage points over current interest rates. The most common vehicles for cash management held by health care companies are still certificates of deposit and short-term treasury bills. A limited number of companies like American Hospital Supply have begun to utilize financial futures as a hedge against currency fluctuations abroad and short-term swings in interest rates at home. Knowledgeable cash managers can do better than break even in the financial futures market, while providing additional security to their companies against fluctuations in the capital market.

Diversification

Today's hospitals are still primarily dependent on inpatient revenues. In many hospitals more than 95 to 99 percent of all revenues are from inpatient and related services. With increasing pressures on hospital reimbursement, particularly squeezing inpatient expenditures, many hospitals have begun to diversify. In a survey by the Health Industry Manufacturers Association (1985), more than 20 health-related and unrelated diversification opportunities for alternate (non-hospital) site providers can be identified. When subjected to financial and feasibility criteria, there are a number of promising business opportunities for hospitals and health care companies:

- HMO/PPO
- diagnostic medical imaging
- home health care
- ambulatory care centers
- wellness programs

The key financial criteria for diversification are typically 12 to 15 percent return on investment (ROI) and 16 to 20 percent net return on revenues. The underlying test for all business diversification activities is whether it outperforms leaving the money at the highest rate of interest available. Hospitals and multihealth corporations are diversifying with considerable energy and innovation. Health Central of Minneapolis has established an international trading company to represent U.S. equipment and suppliers to overseas health care buyers. Hospitals are finding it easier to create new activities than to make money from them. Break-even on new ventures seldom occurs sooner than two to three years, and high-level profitability may take longer. Goal setting for diversification should recognize these longer lead times. Achieving a goal of 25 percent of revenues from nonpatient care sources will take most hospitals and health care companies a minimum of five years.

Venture Capital

Hospitals have made only limited use of the venture capital market. Venture capital has been an increasingly important source of funding for new business development since 1980. More than $9 billion of venture capital for new businesses was invested in 1983, mostly from private investors. California's share of that capital pool for entrepreneurs was an estimated $2 billion. In health care $114 million of venture capital was invested in starting new businesses in 1983.

Venture capital has played an important part in the development of the new biogenetic industry.

Genetech, Cetus, and several hundred other new companies have been established since 1980 with venture capital. More than 100 of these companies have gone public, converting the initial venture investment into stock, or paying off the original loans. While 90 percent of the $11.5 billion venture capital market consists of limited partnerships, there are established venture capital companies like Merrill Lynch and Allied Capital. These publicly held companies raise their capital through sale of stock to investors. There are also venture capital brokers who assist in matching investors with entrepreneurs.

Risks are high in this market, but so can be rewards. Five of 10 new ventures fail within two years. Only 1 of 10 is likely to be a long-term success, and only 1 of 100 will turn out to be a Data General or Digital Equipment Company (DEC). These high-performance companies made their venture capitalists rich.

Joint Ventures

The joint venture is an increasingly popular approach to business development. It brings together companies with complementary interests that pool resources, capital, and expertise. Joint ventures are particularly useful when a company wishes to transfer new or established technology from one market into another industry or geographic area. In today's business environment there are no rules about who will do business with whom. The Hospital Corporation of America, for example, is involved in a joint venture with nonprofit multi Intermountain Health System in a hospital project in Colorado.

Working with an established company can dramatically shorten the learning curve for a company entering a new market. Start-up capital costs can be lower in joint ventures. The venture partners invest their time and effort—sweat equity—to assist with front-end and initial operating costs. Traditional boundaries in business relations are blurring. Memorial Hospital of South Bend, Indiana, is joint venturing a free-standing surgicenter with its physicians. Joint ventures between insurers and providers preview the interaction of healthcare financing and delivery. Aetna is involved in a joint venture, the "partners" plan, with Voluntary Hospitals of America while Equitable is venturing with the Hospital Corporation of America.

Joint ventures provide a low-cost solution to the problem of capitalizing and managing large, complex projects. Real estate developers, architects, and venture capitalists are involved with hospitals in a wide range of projects. At one California hospital the existing medical office building was purchased by a developer, along with the site for a second medical office building (MOB) and adjacent parking structure. Through this sale the hospital was able to remove the existing long-term debt from its balance sheet, get an AAA rating, and sell bonds in two days to cover a $70 million replacement facility.

Short-Term Capital

Commercial paper and other instruments are beginning to fill a much-needed gap for the health industry between short-term borrowing to cover fluctuations in cash flow and long-term financing for capital improvements. As hospital inpatient revenues shrink under new payment schemes like Medicare's diagnostic related groups, it is getting tougher to generate adequate working capital out of operating revenues. For-profit health companies have access to the equity market, but nonprofits do not. A key question for hospitals trying to diversify and develop new product lines is, Where's the working capital? The answer may be short-term financing (1 to 10 years) utilizing a variety of financial instruments, such as the following:

- secured and unsecured short-term notes
- variable rates financing (some interest rates are adjusted daily)
- lines of credit
- loan guarantees

Leasing

To avoid tying its capital into fixed assets, and to tap existing assets for new capital, hospitals are making wider use of leases for plant and equipment. In its simplest form the hospital sells its plant to another company, leases back the facilities on a long-term basis, and uses the capital proceeds of the sale for other purposes. This is nothing new in the private sector. Bank of America sold its San Francisco building for $600 million, and a number of other companies have made similar deals for their corporate headquarters. In more complex lease-back arrangements, a third party investor provides the initial capital and builds the new facility that the hospital leases. Several for-profit chains have used this strategy extensively with local governments that lacked the capital to replace their county and municipal hospitals. Harvard turned down a reported $80 million build and lease-back offer from the Hospital Corporation of America. The University of Southern California has accepted a similar plan from National Medical Enterprises to build a 250-bed hospital for USC's private-pay patients in downtown Los Angeles.

Research and Development

America's economic woes in the 1980s may be due to the failure to reinvest through R&D in the 1970s. The authors of *Minding America's Business*, Magaziner and Reich (1982), have been dubbed the Atari democrats for their championing of a high-technology future. R&D spending is central to retaining leadership in biotechnology, communications, medicine, and computer technology. Research and development outlays by U.S. companies rose 9.8 percent in 1983, continuing a five-year trend in outspending inflation to develop new technologies. Energy and high-tech companies have led the growth trend: General Motors heads the list with $2.6 billion in 1983, followed by AT&T and IBM. Information-processing companies invest most: 7 percent of sales, followed by pharmaceuticals with 6.1 percent. Even such nontechnical firms as Pizza Time Theater spent more than $6 million.

Total R&D spending, both public and private, exceeded $100 billion in 1984. This level of investment is essential to create alternative technologies. A public-private partnership between government and industry is needed if the United States is to meet the Japanese challenge, advocates Theory Z author William Ouchi in *The M-Form Society* (1984). President Reagan agreed. The federal R&D budget for fiscal year 1985 proposed to increase R&D spending 14 percent to $35 billion, concentrating on defense, supercomputers, biotechnology, engineering and manufacturing, and the first manned space station.

STRATEGIES FOR THE NEW HOSPITAL

Access to capital. Access to capital markets will be a critical success factor for growth and development in the health industry. The winners in the capital competition will be health care conglomerates with the balance sheet and combined revenues to win the confidence of the capital market. Free-standing hospitals, public hospitals, and small chains will be losers.

Rising money costs. Interest costs will continue to rise for hospitals in the long-term capital market regardless of how the economy shifts. Lenders and institutional investors believe hospital profits will be hard pressed by competition and DRGs. Hospitals must exercise cost discipline to achieve top bond ratings and gain the substantial savings in interest costs that a better rating brings.

Use of commercial paper. Hospital use of commercial paper, loan extenders, and loan guarantees will become commonplace. The key need for capital by hospitals in the 1980s will be to finance diversification and business development. This working capital will come from major banks and other capital sources that private businesses routinely tap. Hospitals may utilize capital brokers to assist in the search for working and venture capital.

Bankers on boards. The banker may join the board and even the management team as hospitals are forced to live within the constraints set by their lenders. Key management decisions will have a new set of constraints, imposed by the lenders and bond underwriters as conditions of financing. In private business, when a commercial loan becomes shaky, the bank may insist on adding new board members to guard the company's performance. This is a real possibility for health care companies that become extensively leveraged or financially troubled.

No rules. No rules apply in who will do business with whom in the health industry of the future. Joint ventures will cross all traditional lines. The 1980s will see much experimentation in business development. Hospitals are not traditionally entrepreneurial, lacking both skill and daring. Like gamblers going to Las Vegas, hospitals should decide how much they can invest in new business ventures. Experts can assist in risk assessment, and use of arms-length subsidiaries can wall off legal and financial liability. As the base business of hospitals erodes, health care companies can prosper through innovative capital strategies.

REFERENCES AND SUGGESTED READINGS

"Alternate Site Providers: Managing During a Period of Transition." Report by Health Industry Manufacturers Association, Washington, D.C., 1985.

*Ansley, C.E. "Lease Financing and Risk in the Hospital Industry." *Topics in Health Care Financing* 9, no. 4 (Summer 1983):69–77.

*Bekey, Michelle. "Venture Capital." *California Business,* February 1984, pp. 31–35.

*Bradford, C. "The Hospital Capital Crisis: Issues for Trustees." *Harvard Business Review* 60, no. 5 (September-October 1982):56–68.

*Brown, Montague, and McCoor, Barbara. "Bidding for Hospitals." *Hospitals* 57, no. 1 (March 1, 1983):53–60.

*Bruton, Peter, and Waterman, John. "Capital Financing Demands New, Innovative Practices." *Healthcare Financial Management,* April 1985, pp. 38–46.

*Cohodes, Donald. "Which Will Survive: The $150 Billion Capital Question." *Inquiry* 20, no. 1 (Spring 1983):5–11.

*Cohodes, Donald. "Is New Capital Policy Needed?" *Modern Healthcare,* (June 1984):178–179.

Graham, Judith. "Insurers Will Raise Premiums, Be More Selective about Issues." *Modern Healthcare* 16, no. 7 (March 28, 1986):114–116.

*Hee, Dickson, and Henkel, Arthur J. "Tax Exempt Bonds: Operational Statistics and Bond Ratings." *Healthcare Financial Management* 37, no. 10 (October 1983):52–59.

*Hee, Dickson, and Henkel, Arthur J. "Tax-Exempt Hospital Revenue Bonds: What Are the Options in 1984?" *Healthcare Financial Management* 33, no. 4 (April 1984):40–47.

*Heckler, Thomas M. "Some Capital Notions." *Hospitals* 58, no. 1 (January 1984):89–92.

*Long, H.W. "Preserving Capital: Asset Choice and Program Selection in a Competitive Environment." *Healthcare Financial Management* 36, no. 7 (July 1982):40–42; 36, no. 8 (August 1982): 42–50.

Mansdorf, Bruce. "Hospital Capital-Raising after TFRA: More Changes for the Industry." *Review of the Federation of American Hospitals* 16, no. 1 (January-February 1983):41–44.

Magaziner, Ira C., and Reich, Robert B. *Minding America's Business: The Decline and Rise of the American Economy.* New York: Harcourt Brace Jovanovich, Inc., 1982.

*Mistarz, Jo Ellen. "Capital Outlook." *Hospitals,* March 16, 1984, pp. 60–64.

Nauert, Roger. "Cash Management: An Effective Way to Plan and Budget Available Resources." *Healthcare Financial Management* 38, no. 2 (February 1984):64–71.

Ouchi, William. *The M-Form Society*. Reading, Mass.: Addison-Wesley, 1984.

*Seermon, Lynn, et al. "Alternative Services Offer Hospital Systems Local Market Control." *Modern Healthcare* 14, no. 6 (May 1984):79–87.

Ting, Harold M., and Valante, John D. "The Future Capital Needs of Community Hospitals." *Health Affairs* 3, no. 1 (Summer 1982):14–27.

*West, David A. "Debt Financing in the 1980s: Is the Risk for Non-Profit Hospitals Too Great?" *Healthcare Financial Management* 37, no. 4 (April 1983):56–63.

---

*Suggested reading.

Chapter 15
Nichemanship

15

IBM did not invent the computer. Sperry Rand did, but who remembers? Since 1960, IBM has dominated the computer market as the standard against which others competed. Big Blue, as IBM is called by competitors, has been a blue-chip investment for one good reason. It has been the leader in the computer industry, with no competitor achieving half of IBM's market share—in large mainframe computers, that is.

When hobbyists began building home computers in basement workshops, IBM ignored them. When Tandy introduced the first mass-market personal computer and sold it for under $1,000 through its Radio Shack outlets, IBM ignored them. And when Steven Jobs started selling Apple computers from his garage, IBM ignored him. Then in 1981 IBM was ready with its entrant in the microcomputer field—the PC personal computer, aimed at the business market, not the home. In two years IBM captured a 35 percent market share.

That's nichemanship! A *niche,* according to Webster, is a suitable place or position. Without a niche any product faces the danger of being considered a commodity and being priced (or ignored) as such.

In a spectrum of products or services, a niche is a suitable position such that buyers choose it in preference to competitors. The ideal niche has only one occupant—your product or firm. The ground rules are simple: find a need and fill it, better or cheaper than competitors.

THREE GENERIC STRATEGIES

Michael Porter of the Harvard Business School is the guru of nicheseekers. Porter's *Competitive Strategy,* published in 1980, is already a classic in its field. In

177

coping with competitive forces, there are three generic strategic approaches to successfully outperforming other firms in an industry.

Strategy 1: Overall Cost Leadership

Having a low-cost position yields the firm above-average average returns in its industry despite the presence of strong competitive forces. Its cost position defends the firm against rivalry from competitors because its lower costs mean that it can still earn returns even after its competitors have competed away their profits through rivalry.

Achieving a low-cost position requires aggressive construction of efficient scale facilities, vigorous pursuit of cost reductions, tight cost and overhead control, and cost minimization in areas such as services, sales force, and advertising. A great deal of managerial attention to cost control is necessary to achieve these aims, but it has paid off for companies like Briggs & Stratton (50 percent market share), DuPont, and Black & Decker, which dominate their industries.

As the health industry becomes more competitive, expect that a number of health care companies will take the low-price position. In other industries 20 to 25 percent of the market is dominated by low-cost producers. Republic and Summit are health industry examples, following the strategic path set by low-cost pioneer Hospital Affiliates of Nashville, acquired by Hospital Corporation of America in 1982.

Strategy 2: Differentiation

The essence of nichemanship is differentiation—creating something that is perceived by customers as unique. Approaches to differentiating can take many forms:

- design or brand image (Mercedes in automobiles)
- technology (Sony in audio-video products, Coleman in camping equipment)
- features (Jenn-Aire in electric ranges)
- customer service (IBM in mainframe computers)
- dealer network (Caterpillar in construction equipment)

Strategy 3: Focus

The focus strategy rests on the premise that the firm is able to serve a narrow strategic market of customers more effectively or efficiently than competitors who are competing more broadly. As a result, the firm achieves differentiation from better meeting the needs of the particular target, lower costs in serving this target, or both.

Federal Express focused on the need of some customers for fast, overnight delivery. In doing so, it created a niche in package delivery, which has evolved into a new mini industry. Volkswagen created the compact auto niche and Southland's 7-11 created the convenience food store. Innovation is the wellspring of nichemanship.

POSITIONING: THE BATTLE FOR THE MIND

The battleground of competition is not the marketplace—it takes place in the minds of the customers. Positioning starts with a product, a piece of merchandise, a service, a company, an institution, or even a person. Positioning is not what happens to a product. Positioning is what the firm does to the mind of the prospect.

Positioning has changed the way the game of nichemanship is being played today: .

- third largest-selling coffee in America (Sanka)
- Number 2 in Rent-a-Cars (Avis)
- the other computer company (Honeywell)
- the uncola (Seven-Up)

Along Madison Avenue these are called positioning slogans, and the advertising agencies who write them look for niches in the hearts and minds of American consumers. Is positioning creativity? Is it magic? There are many nichemanship strategies to success in the battle for the mind.

Looking Out for Number 1

The preferred position is easy to find: number 1. In every industry, every market and buyer's shopping list, the leader has the best position to outperform competitors. IBM's return on investment has consistently exceeded its mainframe competitors—averaging 19.4 percent compared to Burroughs (13.7 percent), Honeywell (9.3 percent), and Control Data (4.7 percent).

Who was the first person to walk on the moon? Neil Armstrong, of course. Who was second? Few Americans can recall. The point is simple: The first product or the first company to occupy the number 1 position in the mind is going to be hard to dislodge.

The Product Ladder

Ask someone to name all the brands remembered in a given product category. Rarely will anyone name more than seven. For low-interest products the average consumer can usually name no more than one or two brands. Try it yourself: rental cars? shampoos? nursing home chains? Four thousand magazines today compete for readership, 300 models of cars, 10,000 items on the supermarket shelf.

To cope with this product explosion, people have learned to rank products and brands in the mind. Visualize a series of ladders in the storage room we can call the brain. Each ladder is a product category, and on each step is a brand name. Some ladders have many steps (seven is many). Others have few, if any. A competitor that wants to increase its market share must either dislodge the brand above or somehow relate its brand to the other company's position.

Positioning a Follower

What works for a leader doesn't necessarily work for a follower. Leaders can often cover a competitive move and maintain their leadership over followers. When Datril tried a price attack on Tylenol (first in aspirin sales), Johnson & Johnson immediately covered the move. It cut Tylenol's price even before Bristol-Myers started its Datril price advertising. As a result, Johnson & Johnson repelled the Datril attack and inflicted heavy losses on the Bristol-Myers marketing entry. Tylenol is an exception. Most leaders should cover a competitor's competitive move toward discount pricing by introducing another brand.

In the Southern California HMO market, Blue Cross announced its price increase for 1985: 0 percent. How should competitors respond? Kaiser, the giant of the HMO industry (largest in the United States), responded by announcing plans to seek a merger with Health Insurance Plan of Greater New York, the nation's second largest HMO. The combined plans would have a total of 5.5 million members. Although that merger fell through, Kaiser has aggressively launched a national market expansion.

Look for the Niche

To compete successfully against a leader, a follower must find—or create—a niche in the mind of the customer not occupied by someone else. The ideal niche has only one occupant: your company or product.

A group of young physicians in the highly competitive San Francisco market (highest physician/population ratio in the United States) opened a 24-hour ambulatory care practice and called it an Emergicenter. In the field of ambulatory-emergency medicine, they created a new niche and a new industry, which grew 65 percent in 1983–84.

Stouffers created a new niche in convenience foods with Lean Cuisine, 300-calorie entrees for the diet-conscious. A new competitor, Budget Gourmet then cut a new niche out of Lean Cuisine's market, the low-cost, low-calorie convenience food. Today, a number of the national food chains have their own house-label convenience entrees, taking the low-price position in competition with Budget Gourmet.

Repositioning the Competition

There comes a time in every industry when it appears all niches have been exploited. Because there are so few niches to be filled in the minds of customers, a company must create one by repositioning the competitors that hold the current leadership.

In other words, to move a new idea or product into the mind, you must first move an old one out. Take Tylenol. "For the millions who should not take aspirin," said Tylenol's ads. "If your stomach is easily upset . . ." six words of copy before any mention of the product. Today Tylenol is America's best-selling analgesic, ahead of Anacin, ahead of Bayer, ahead of Bufferin. Miller's Lite Beer repositioned the entire brewing industry. Advertising agencies are repositioning themselves as marketing consultants, to get a share of this $3.5 billion market. Who knows the market better than we? say the ad agencies.

In the same way accounting firms have repositioned themselves as management and strategic planning consultants in the minds of their clients. What aspect of management is more crucial today than finance? they say.

Power of a Name

The name is the hook that hangs the brand on the product ladder in the mind of the customer. In the era of nichemanship the single most important strategic decision is what to name the product.

Some companies have done well with descriptive names that begin the positioning process: Lite Beer, Head & Shoulders shampoo, Close-up toothpaste. Hospitals that broadened their scope of services often dropped *hospital* in favor of *medical center*. Now some are renaming themselves *health centers* to reflect their diversified health care product lines. A name should not be so close to the product that it becomes generic, a general name for all products of its class. Already this problem has occurred in the health industry: surgicenter, emergicenter, and urgent care centers. Those companies picked names so descriptive of the product that they lost their exclusivity.

Humana was the first national health care company to rename its hospitals with the corporate brand. Then Humana launched its well-publicized heart transplant program to gain name-brand recognition. It has followed with a national marketing strategy for its HMO. Med Care Plus grew from 40,000 enrollees in 1984 to 360,000 subscribers in 1985.

No-Name Trap

Why is General Motors widely known as GM, but American Motors is barely recognized as AMC? Both are practicing phonetic shorthand. But GM is the giant of its industry, with the biggest revenues and net profits of any U.S. corporation in 1984. American Motors is the smallest U.S. auto maker, barely holding a 2 percent market share.

There is a simple lesson here: the monogram of recognition must be earned. GM is a winner. AMC is still struggling. Switching to initials can cut into consumer recognition. In a consumer survey the average consumer awareness of initial companies was 49 percent, compared with 68 percent awareness for a matched set of name companies (Ries and Trout 1981). The results show the answer to the time-honored question, What's in a name?—a lot.

Vertical Integration: Linking the Niches

Buying health services today is like shopping on Beverly Hills' Rodeo Drive. Every provider operates from a boutique independent location, and there are few bargains. Vertical integration is just the opposite—owning or controlling every aspect of the production, distribution, and sales processes within a single firm.

The Kaiser Health Plan is a well-developed example of vertical integration. Pursuing a strategy of vertical integration results in repositioning the company in its industry. The merger of American Hospital Supply with Baxter Travenol brings the complementary product lines of both into a total system with few product gaps.

Forward Integration: Closer to the Customer

Texas Instruments' forward integration into consumer products such as watches and calculators allowed it to develop a brand name, whereas its computer chips were essentially commodities. Forward integration can help the company to differentiate its product more successfully because the firm can control more elements of the production process or the way the product is sold.

IBM's new network of product centers will allow IBM to compete with retailers of office equipment and microcomputers. Can you imagine the impact on distributors if IBM decided to sell its products only through its own outlets? Humana's Med-Plus ambulatory care centers perform a similar function for its hospitals, providing a feeder network of customers.

Backward Integration: Controlling the Source

Meat packers a century ago and steak houses illustrate the strategy of backward integration, producing to meet needs internally by buying their own ranches, raising their own livestock and feed, and fattening the animals on company-owned feet lots. Controlling the sources of supply allows a firm to differentiate its product better, or say credibly that it can. For a hospital, owning a HMO or PPO provides a supply of customers for their base business: inpatient hospital care.

Where product quality is a significant factor, as it is in health care, vertical integration provides more opportunity to control the consistency and level of quality across a range of services. It distinguishes that service from competitors whose services are not integrated or of uniform quality.

Marketing: You Deserve a Break Today

McDonald's spends over $300 million each year in advertising, more than twice as much as its nearest competitor, Burger King. "You deserve a break today" is one of the world's best-known slogans. The health industry will spend about $3 billion in 1986 advertising health care products including pharmaceuticals, to get its messages heard.

Few hospitals today spend more than 1 percent of budget on marketing and advertising. (At Procter & Gamble, it's 50 percent.) Much of this investment may be wasted if hospitals do not understand that nichemanship is not a shoot-out with competitors—the battle is in the mind of the customer. If you don't know what business you're in, advertising experts say, the market is an expensive place to learn.

Drill More Wells

In the oil industry a critical success factor is to drill more wells than competitors. In the nichemanship game it's drilling more holes in the minds of the consumers. McDonald's is piloting a new product in five locations in Southern California, which may create a new market niche: the Lite Mac.

STRATEGIES FOR THE NEW HOSPITAL

The merchandising of health care. Health care is entering a new era of retail market competition. Physicians will still make 70 to 80 percent of the big-ticket decisions—surgery and hospitalization—but individual consumers are playing a larger role in making these choices. Hospitals and health care companies will move to position themselves on the preference ladder through marketing and advertising campaigns. Health organizations that have not developed a marketing and advertising strategy are already falling behind. Remember the preferred position: first. Every product and product line needs its own marketing strategy and its own niche.

Brand name. Creation of brand names in the health industry is beginning to pick up speed. Who will be the Century 21 (largest real estate franchise company in the United States) of health care? Multihealth corporations have a potential edge here, if they move early to create brand name recognition in their local or regional markets. The investor-owned systems are already moving. Now is the time to take the initiative.

Professionals. Niche finding is not for amateurs. Health organizations can reduce groping for positions in the marketplace by bringing in outside expertise in marketing and advertising. Every hospital over 250 beds should have a full time vice president for marketing. Hiring someone with training and experience outside the health industry may yield quicker return on investment than job enlargement of existing public relations or planning staff. Upgrading in-house staff can work if they are buttressed by consultants. Marketing as a corporate function will be cost-effective for multis.

Vertical integration. Now is the time to build or buy the additional components to become a vertically integrated health care provider. It is not necessary to cover the entire waterfront. Some companies will create a niche in ambulatory care, long-term care, or psychiatric care and provide a vertically arrayed service spectrum within that niche. Build vertically integrated niches, then link them when capitation makes full-service packaging of health services feasible.

"Advertising Age." As an industry that will make increasing use of advertising, health care management needs to be an informed purchaser. Start reading *Advertising Age* or *Ad Week*. There is much to be learned from the private sector experience in advertising and marketing. These lessons will be learned much cheaper by reading about them versus first-hand in the school of hard knocks.

REFERENCES AND SUGGESTED READINGS

*Caltan, Vicky, et al. "Health Care Costs: The Fever Breaks." *Business Week*, October 21, 1985, pp. 86–94.

*Davis, Robert T., and Smith, F. Gordon. *Marketing in Emerging Companies*. Reading, Mass: Addison-Wesley, 1985.

*Deveney, Kathleen, and Tarpey, John P. "Humana: Making the Most of Its Place in the Spotlight." *Business Week*, May 6, 1985, pp. 68–69.

*Hull, Jennifer B. "Medical Turmoil: Four Hospital Chains Facing Lower Profits Adopt New Strategies." *Wall Street Journal*, October 10, 1985.

*Inguanzo, Joe M., and Harju, Mark. "Creating a Market Niche." *Hospitals*, January 1, 1985, pp. 62–67.

*Johnson, Donald E.L. "Multi-Unit Providers: Survey Plots 475 Chains Growth." *Modern Healthcare*, May 15, 1984.

*Kotler, Philip. *Marketing Management: Analysis, Planning and Control*. 4th ed. Englewood Cliffs, N.J.: Prentice-Hall, 1980.

*Kotler, Philip. *Marketing for Non-Profit Organizations*. 2nd ed. Englewood Cliffs, N.J.: Prentice-Hall, 1982.

*Lazarus, George. "New Frozen Food Hot Shots?" *Adweek*, September 3, 1984.

*Levitt, Theodore. *The Marketing Imagination*. New York: Free Press, 1983.

*MacStravic, Robin Scott. "Boutiques and 'Shopping Malls' Threaten Hospitals' Traditional Roles." *Modern Healthcare*, September 13, 1985, pp. 144–148.

*Morgan, Richard. "Next Step for Agency Growth: Compete with Consulting Gurus." *Adweek*, August 20, 1984.

*Porter, Michael E. *Competitive Advantage*. New York: Free Press, 1985.

*Porter, Michael E. *Competitive Strategy*. New York: Free Press, 1980.

*Punch, Linda. "Major Alliances Focusing Efforts on Creation of New Businesses." *Modern Healthcare*, August 15, 1984.

*Punch, Linda. "Emergicenters Cut Themselves Free From Their Emergency Room Roots." *Modern Healthcare*, October 1984.

Ries, Al, and Trout, Jack. *Positioning*. New York: Warner Books, 1981.

Seerman, Lynn, Sachs, Michael, and Thompson, Kent. "Alternative Services Offer Hospital Systems Local Market Control." *Modern Healthcare*, May 1, 1984.

*Walch, William E., and Tseng, Simone. "Marketing: Handle with Care." *Trustee*, August 1984.

---

*Suggested reading.

Chapter 16

Preferred Provider Organizations

16

For preferred provider organizations (PPO) the future health system offers a multitude of possibilities. The PPO is a new concept. Perhaps the best thing about these new health care organizations is that so little is known about them. There is no model PPO. The PPO will be a vehicle for experimentation. Many forms of sponsorship, payment, and provider arrangements are possible. The survivors will be those PPO organizations that meet the challenge of the marketplace.

FROM A CONCEPT TO A MOVEMENT

The PPO sprang on the health industry overnight, enjoying a booming growth since its initial formulation by InterStudy, the Minneapolis health policy organization, in February 1981. InterStudy noted the rise of a new form of health plan, beginning in Colorado and California, which it dubbed preferred provider organizations. In little more than a year, the PPO was the cover story of health industry publications and mentioned prominently in articles on health care competition in the *New York Times, Business Week,* and *Kiplinger's Changing Times.*

There is no central source of information on PPO formation, but it is evident from a variety of sources that PPOs are one of the hottest topics in health care. An estimated 1,000 PPOs were in operation or under development in 1985 (Potzmann 1985). As the concept evolved from a simple discounting operation, PPOs are now a complementary business strategy for hospitals, physician groups, insurance plans, and even HMOs. New integrated health plans offer employers a full-service line including an HMO, PPO, and a traditional indemnity plan. Such plans are now being brought to market under brand names "Flexcare" (CIGNA health plan and Connecticut General Life Insurance) and "U.S. Healthlink" (Lincoln National Corp. and U.S. Health Care Systems).

189

Since the California legislature authorized private sector contracting for hospital and physician services in 1983, California has been a hotbed for PPOs. By some estimates as many as 150 PPOs are under various stages of discussion and development by a variety of California organizations. After the state of California completed the initial round of contracting with selected hospitals, Blue Cross moved to develop its own network of 240 preferred providers, which provide services to subscribers at alternative (discounted) rates. Aetna's PPO plan, called Choice, began marketing activities in 1983, and many commercial insurance carriers have followed suit. Aetna is involved in a PPO-type arrangement in a joint venture with Voluntary Hospitals of America, with a national marketing effort.

Major Employers

There are a small number of employers' PPOs, and the trend is growing. Companies that have been active in employer health coalitions, like Rohr Industries and Hewlett-Packard, have been actively working on developing their own PPOs. One of the 19 employer health coalitions in California has developed an employer-sponsored PPO, the Community Care Network in San Diego. Employer coalitions have been a mechanism for educating the business community about the potential of the PPO concept. As yet business has been listening but keeping its checkbook in its pocket. Despite initial ballyhoo there have been fewer signed PPO contracts with major employers than advocates had predicted. Employers are utilizing insurers and insurance brokers to create PPO networks and remain skittish of provider-sponsored organizations.

Discounts Not New

The concept of a preferred provider organization may be new, but discounts by hospitals and physicians are well-established market practices. Indeed the Medicare and Medicaid allowances under the former cost reimbursement programs were simply discounts by another name. Insurance carriers and intermediaries have negotiated discounted rates with selected providers on behalf of major buyers.

What is new in the PPO concept is the scale of the purchasing—California Medi-Cal's $2 billion, for example—and the limited number of preferred providers who received Medi-Cal contracts. Blue Cross of California's health net PPO contracts with only one-third of 600 hospitals in California.

Double-Edged Sword

Preferred provider organizations are a doubled-edged sword for hospitals and physicians. Those providers who are preferred and successfully negotiate contracts with one or more purchasers are at risk to provide services at the negotiated price. If their costs are lower, the providers keep the difference, but there is no protection if costs occur above the preset price.

Not to be selected as a preferred provider is also risky. If too many of a hospital's payers shift to other facilities, the impact on census and revenues may be drastic. One small Los Angeles hospital reportedly had its average daily census fall below 10 patients after losing a major PPO contract. Hospitals fear a domino effect. If they fail to gain a PPO contract, other payers may bypass them for hospitals with PPO agreements that have demonstrated a willingness to negotiate prices and services.

PPO Sponsorship

Hospitals are clearly interested in the PPO concept, but they are not the only potential sponsors. InterStudy's survey of 81 developing PPOs indicated that 25 percent of the new organizations were hospital-based. Nearly as many were being formed by physicians, and another 20 percent were joint hospital-physician ventures. Third party payers were active in organizing 14 PPOs. Only two of the PPOs were being formed by employers. As the PPO movement heats up, it is distinctly possible that it will attract entrepreneurs as did the prepaid health plan program in California in the early 1970s.

THREE FUTURE SCENARIOS

Of the many possible futures for health, three scenarios for the health system in the year 2000 may illustrate the potential of this new organizational arrangement: the preferred provider organization.

High Technology: Upscale PPO

The first scenario, High Technology, extends the progress in treating and preventing disease through advances in biomedical technology. There will be superdrugs targeted to receptor sites on cells to cure cancer and other diseases without surgery. Not only will organ transplants be commonplace, but micro minicomputers will be implanted to direct their activities. Artificial joints will replace damaged natural parts. Genetic engineering may make it possible for children born after 1990 to live to be 150 years old. Medical technology will be widely available, and the American health system will grow through multinational corporations delivering health care technology across the world. The information revolution will link consumers and providers through low-cost two-way communications.

Under this scenario for the health system of the future, we can imagine a scenario for PPOs entitled upscale PPO. This PPO is designed to appeal to the upscale consumer: affluent, well-educated, and discriminating. The PPO would provide special guest relations amenity services, such as personalized followup after services to check posttreatment satisfaction. The PPO package would include special health promotion and fitness services through a network of health and fitness spas. Two-way communications would provide education, and advice and consultation from the PPO provider network to consumers in their homes or offices. In this package the full array of high-technology medicine would be applied, with minimum concern for cost considerations except for procedures considered cosmetic. Employers would purchase the upscale PPO package as a desirable form of executive compensation. The upscale PPO would be available internationally for an elite clientele who can afford and seek the best that technology and the health system have to offer.

Conglomerates: PPO Network

In the second scenario, conglomerates, a fundamental restructuring of the health industry occurs. In a process of acquisition and corporate growth that parallels development of multinational firms in the private sector in the 1960s, the health industry comes to be dominated by a handful of large companies. By the year 2000 more than 90 percent of all hospitals are members of multiinstitutional systems. Several of the largest for-profit systems have become part of large conglomerates, being acquired by companies like General Foods.

The PPO scenario driven by the vision of future conglomerates is the PPO network. The new conglomerates are both horizontally and vertically integrated systems of local and regional PPOs. PPOs are the building blocks of the health conglomerate. Each PPO is unique, providing a complete package of services to enrollees and corporations in its market. Prepayment on a capitation basis is the dominant mode of financing. Some employers and insurance companies still prefer to pay on a fee-for-service basis, a mode that is rapidly disappearing. PPOs compete, sometimes intracompany, with different levels of service packages from basic no-frills to deluxe.

Wellness: Live-Well PPO

The third scenario, wellness, assumes a basic transformation in consumer attitudes and health behavior. The life style known as voluntary simplicity becomes a majority consensus. Consumers take more responsibility for their own health. The health promotion providers, who had been on the fringe of the health marketplace, become mainstream providers. Inpatient days fall below 300 per thousand population, and physician visits drop to less than 3 per year. Virtually no one dies in the hospital. Most of the elderly die at home or in hospices.

The live-well PPO embodies the new paradigm of health that drives the wellness scenario of the future. This PPO network is strongly decentralized. Its base is the alternative healers and therapists who provide holistic and human-centered services to the PPO consumers. Organized as an alternative to hospital-based PPOs, the live-well program is a financial success because it makes relatively little use of the higher cost resources like inpatient care. Employers like the program. Employee morale is up and costs are down. Live-well is a flourishing PPO alternative.

THREATS TO PPOs

The future for PPOs is a kaleidoscope of threats and opportunities. The best management strategies for one PPO may lead to failure for another. Each developing PPO must be sensitive to its future environment, aware of both the hazards and the opportunities of the future health care market in its strategic planning and management. There are a number of real dangers for the future of preferred provider organizations:

- Quick fix. The PPO may be only a temporary solution to today's health costs problems. The lack of a long-term vision for the PPO leaves it vulnerable to premature termination if it experiences market shifts and developmental problems that are highly likely in the early years. The PPO must be more than a band-aid solution.
- Limited incentives. The PPO does not stimulate any fundamental change in the attitudes or behavior of either consumers or providers. Consumers are under no incentive—other than financial—to use the PPO and are given no incentive to alter or reduce their use of health services. Providers share only limited financial risk in the arrangement, and their incentives are to encourage more use of services—contrary to the interests of the payers, which want to cut both costs and utilization.
- PPO failure. The failure of some PPOs is likely due to a variety of business hazards. Hospitals do not have many of the needed skills in marketing and entrepreneurial management. Some PPOs will be poorly designed, others will experience financial losses. Given there are no statutory requirements for reserves, some payers and providers could be unpaid creditors of bankrupt PPOs. The default experience of multiple employer trusts (METs) in California and Washington demonstrates the financial fragility of some of these new health care arrangements.

- Health maintenance. There is no incentive for health maintenance in the PPO scheme. Consumers gain no benefits from controlling their health services use, and providers only benefit from expanded service demand. If a long-term goal of payers is to improve the health status of their consumers so they require fewer and less intensive services, the PPO will need modification to provide incentives for such behavior.

- A fad? Are preferred provider organizations only a transitory phenomenon? Certainly some skepticism is in order. So far the PPO concern is long on promise and short on performance. The first successful PPOs have had only limited market penetration and generate less than 5 to 10 percent of the inpatient service demand for their sponsor hospitals. Payers have been reluctant to commit to the PPO concept in significant numbers. Expectations for PPO performance should be kept in perspective.

- Postponing the real issues. There is valid criticism of the PPO concept; that it fails to confront some of the most fundamental issues between consumer, provider, and payer of health services. Some of these issues will occur early in the PPO's development, in confrontations around issues of cost versus quality between the PPO organization that must control its costs and its providers, who seek to provide the highest and best level of care available. Consumers and payers are caught directly in the middle of the cost-quality dilemma. More than one developing PPO will flounder on these issues.

- Quality. With the dominant emphasis on limiting costs so the PPO can make a reasonable rate of return at below-market prices, quality may suffer. Utilization review may be used by the PPO primarily as a mechanism to keep service use down rather than protecting a floor of acceptable quality. HMOs have dealt successfully with the quality protection issue but had more incentive to do so since the HMOs have a long-range and contractual relationship with their consumers. PPOs will have to be sensitive to the quality issue.

- Lack of regulatory oversight. At this early stage PPOs are not covered by any federal regulation and by state regulation in only a few states. There are certainly dangers in this lack of regulatory oversight. California's experience with prepaid health plans for Title 19 Medi-Cal beneficiaries in the early 1970s demonstrates that unscrupulous operators will take advantage of unregulated businesses. On the other hand premature regulation—before experience with the problems and the potential of the PPO concept—could have a real dampening effect on this promising organizational form.

OPPORTUNITIES FOR THE FUTURE

In the future of PPO development there will be opportunities to achieve goals of all three parties at interest: providers, consumers, and payers:

- Savings. The primary interest of PPO purchasers is the potential for reducing health expenditures. The more their consumers choose the PPO, the greater the savings over more costly fee-for-service care.

- Control. There are two ways PPOs will reduce costs: (1) discount payments to providers, and (2) the potential they offer for greater control over utilization. Discounts are only effective during the initial phase of competition. If prices settle at a new, lower level, the PPO must then compete on its ability to control both the type and level of service by the consumer. The PPO advantage over traditional insurance plans, as well as over HMOs, is its flexibility. The PPO can design health service plans tailored to the budgets and preferences of its major purchasers and even build the purchaser into the utilization review process.

- Network. The PPO concept can be packaged and marketed through a network of preferred provider organizations on a statewide, regional, and national basis. Not-for-profit and proprietary health care systems have an excellent potential to negotiate large-scale contracts with national employers or with consortia of local or statewide employers. Franchising offers a ready alternative for marketing the PPO on a state, regional, or national basis.

- Flexibility. There are practically no rules for the PPO arrangement. Its sponsorship, pricing, administration, provider relations, utilization review, consumer incentives, and other features are not fixed by tradition or regulation.

- Customize benefits. Each PPO may be unique to its environment and the interests of the three major parties. There is so little experience with PPOs, developers have little background on which to judge what will work. This may provide the license for PPO designers to break tradition, eliminating parameters such as full coverage for inpatient care or including nontraditional services such as biofeedback. An employer that has experienced a higher level of back problems, for example, can design a program with its PPO that provides prevention, education and health promotion, and fitness programs directed toward special needs.

- Competition. The advent of the preferred provider organization will stimulate competition in the health marketplace in three directions: (1) with traditional sources of health services or insurance, (2) with other PPOs, and (3) with health maintenance organizations. In an already competitive market, the Twin Cities metropolis in Minnesota, the seven established HMOs are being undercut on price by new PPOs. The PPOs believe that they can take business away from the less flexible HMOs, and the HMOs can be expected to counter. Competition is only beginning.

- Partnership. The PPO provides an opportunity to break with tradition in the organization, payment, and delivery of health services. As the first innovation in health care financing in a decade, it gives purchasers, providers, and payers a clean slate on which to design the health care organization of the future.

- HMOs. A major beneficiary of the PPO movement is the HMO industry. As PPOs discover the need to exercise greater control over utilization and costs, they are likely to reorganize as IPA-model (Independent Practitioner Association) HMOs. As physicians and hospitals become more accustomed to working within PPO price structures and constraints, they will become more amenable to the HMO concept. As consumers and major purchasers discover the limitations of the PPO model, they are likely to move to the HMO organization by choice, for the guaranteed quality and price an HMO can provide.

VEHICLES FOR CHANGE

While the future is not perfectly clear, emerging trends provide early evidence that PPOs will have a powerful effect on tomorrow's health care system. The preferred provider organization is a vehicle for change. It is a transitional mechanism toward new forms of health organizations, new styles of medical practice, new patterns of health expenditures, and perhaps even a new definition of the business of health delivery.

How many hospitals will participate in PPOs? Estimates vary, but it could become nearly universal by 1990 if major insurance companies join the PPO bandwagon. The percentage of patients covered by a PPO will rise much more slowly.

There has not been such anticipation in the health industry since the passage of Medicare and Medicaid in the 1960s. PPOs are having a galvanizing effect on the industry. Competitive forces are being unleashed, and creative energies flowing. A new generation of health care organizations is coming: the preferred provider organizations.

STRATEGIES FOR THE NEW HOSPITAL

Build, buy, or join now. The window of opportunity is lowering. Build, buy, or affiliate with a PPO now. Tomorrow's health system will be dominated by integrated health plans that contract with a select number of providers: hospitals and physicians. Few hospitals can afford to be nonpreferred providers. PPOs are ground-floor strategies for involvement.

Multiple affiliations. One California hospital has affiliated with more than 60 PPOs and HMOs. It is too early for these arrangements to make a substantial difference in the patient load and revenues of today's hospitals, but by 1990 hospitals can expect that 50 to 75 percent of their nongovernmental patients will be derived from prenegotiated contracts.

Physician involvement. Early and extensive involvement of the medical staff is essential for PPO arrangements to be successful. In the long term, physician and hospital care is converging into an integrated form of patient care management. Without physician support, no PPO can succeed. Building in physician collaboration in all aspects: patient care, management, and finance is essential. These strong partnerships will outcompete PPOs whose only bonds are economic interest.

Experiment. The best thing about PPOs is that there is no one way to do them. PPO developers should use constraint-free thinking in designing new PPOs. They are designing the health organization of the future built to suit their concept of the future. Revision the PPO as an experimental form of the New Hospital.

Becoming HMOs. The real future of PPOs is to become HMOs. Capitation will be the dominant form of payment, and PPOs will evolve toward the HMO concept. It is inevitable. If the PPO is to survive, it must have HMO-type controls in place over costs and utilization. In the process the evolution of PPOs will change the HMO model, opening up this organizational form to new forms of ownership, provider relations, capitalization, and customer relations. The face of the health industry will be reshaped between 1985 and 1995.

REFERENCES AND SUGGESTED READINGS

*Berger, Judith D. "Selective Contracting: California's Hot Potato?" *Hospital Forum*, November/December 1982, pp. 7–14.

*Boland, Peter. *The New Healthcare Market: A Guide to PPOs for Purchasers, Providers and Payors*. Homewood, Ill.: Dow Jones Irwin, 1985.

*Brukardt, Gary. "Mountain Medical PPO: A Case History of Marketing a New Concept in the Denver Area." *FAH Review*, July/August 1982, pp. 29–32.

*Cassidy, Robert. "Will the PPO Movement Freeze You Out?" *Medical Economics*, April 18, 1983, pp. 262–274.

*Ellwein, Linda Krane, and David D. Gregg. "InterStudy Researchers Trace Progress of PPOs, Provide Insight into Future Growth." *FAH Review*, July/August 1982, pp. 20–25.

*"Health Care Industry, Business Show Increasing Interest in PPO Concept." *FAH Review*, July/August 1982, pp. 12–17.

*Koder, Karen. "Competition: Getting a Fix on PPOs." *Hospitals*, November 16, 1982, pp. 59–66.

*Kuntz, Esther Fritz. "Hospitals Forming PPOs to Fend Off HMO Rivals." *Modern Healthcare* 13, no. 2 (February 1982):22–24.

*O'Connor, Maureen L. "Preferred Provider Organizations: A Market Approach to Health Care Competition." *Hospital Forum*, November/December 1982, pp. 16–21.

Potzmann, Mary Ann. "Environmental Assessment: Moving Forward: An Integration of Interests." Minneapolis, MN: Health Central Corporation, 1985.

*"Preferred Providers: Discount Health Care." Washington Report on Medicine & Health. *Perspectives*, July 12, 1982.

*Shaw, John M., and Giacomazzi, Allyn L. "Self-Funding Insurance Helps Cut Costs." *Hospitals,* August 16, 1980, pp. 71–79.

*"Three Networks Reflect Growing Interest in the Development of California PPOs." *FAH Review,* July/August 1982, pp. 36–39.

*Tibbitts, Samuel J., and Manzano, Al. *PPOs: An Executive Guide.* Chicago: Pluribus Press, 1984.

---

*Suggested reading.

Chapter 17
Intrapreneurship

17

Three-fourths of the new jobs since 1975 have been created by small, new companies. In microelectronics, biogenetics, business services, fast food, and other high-growth industries, new products and services are being created by entrepreneurs working outside the mainstream, in companies like Compaq Computer, which did not exist in 1975. Fortune 500 companies are beginning to respond, using the concept of intrapreneurship—creating new, little businesses within established, big businesses.

IN-HOUSE ENTREPRENEURSHIP

The concept of intrapreneurship was coined by Gifford Pinchot (1985) to encourage entrepreneurship within the corporate structure. Once Pinchot worked on a rural commune in New York. Today his companies, the New Directions Group and Pinchot & Co., are among a growing number of management consulting firms advising management on ways to encourage innovation, develop new products, and reward entrepreneurship. The concept was refined and tested by the ForeSight Group in Sweden, and is being popularized by blue-chip management consultants Arthur Young and Company, as a strategy for revitalizing and decentralizing large organizations.

Too often major firms lose their brightest talent, who take ideas for new products and form new companies. Ex-IBM employees founded several of IBM's competitors. In a precedent-setting move, IBM successfully sued two former employees from bringing to market an idea they had developed while at the company. The lesson was clear: ideas developed on company time belong to the company. Now IBM is utilizing the concepts of intrapreneurship to create new product lines, and it's working. The best-selling IBM PC personal computer was developed by an in-house group that was given the license to create a new computer in 18 months. The result was not only a new product but a whole new industry, dominated by IBM. Since 1981, IBM has founded 14 new Independent Business Units (IBUs) and Strategic Business Units (SBUs), abandoning its long-held strategies of market dominance in a few product lines through slow product introduction and no discounts.

Greenhouse for New Ideas

Thinking entrepreneurial is the first step, but many ideas never make it to the marketplace for lack of implementation. At Uniroyal, for example, a new weather-resistant plastic was introduced in 1982—and went nowhere. Then Uniroyal hired a corps of entrepreneurs and technicians to work in its greenhouse for new product ideas. Under intrapreneurial management Uniroyal created a mini-company to produce and market the new plastic, with its own manager and intraboard of directors drawn from company operations.

Now the product has been repositioned, prices raised, and it is breaking even. Eventually it will be returned to the chemical division that spawned the original concept. That is the carrot that gives operating units an interest in new ventures. Uniroyal intrapreneurs have a half-dozen similar projects in the works, giving the company a much-needed mechanism for self-renewal.

From a Cost Center to a Revenue Center

Here is a challenge for entrepreneurs: transforming Ma Bell into an intrapreneurial market-driven company. The breakup of the biggest company in the world forced AT&T to break with many traditions. Its view of the world as a protected monopoly has been shattered. Instead it is nine companies competing with each other to provide telecommunications to the nation. New competitors, like MCI and Sprint, have already eroded the highly profitable long-distance business. Now IBM and Rolm have developed a joint venture to compete head to head against the telephone system, beginning with the instrument itself: replacing the telephone itself with a new data and communications device.

Under such competitive pressures the new telephone companies like Pacific Telesis are looking at cost centers such as Information as revenue centers. Converting cost centers to contribution centers means a new entrepreneurial orientation. For example, the Residence Telephone Order Center will be motivated to sell more high-margin versus low-margin services when it will be credited with the revenues created. In 1985 Pac-Tel initiated one of the largest management incentive programs in American industry, putting 25,000 midlevel and senior managers at risk for earnings-based compensation.

In-House Companies

New ideas for products and services are deliberately stimulated in the intrapreneurial company. One process utilized in a Swedish corporation solicits proposals from employees who compete for funding of their new ventures from a special intrapreneurship risk-capital fund.

Economist Norman Macrae (1982) encourages companies to permit competition among departments of large companies to win the business of revenue centers. One typing pool put on an intrapreneurial footing doubled its productivity per typist from 12 pages to 24 per day. The market test for these in-house businesses is the right of operating divisions to contract outside the company for services, if they can find them cheaper or better.

NEW RULES OF INTRAPRENEURSHIP

One California hospital converted five departments to independent business units: housekeeping, dietary, laundry, engineering, and information systems. Most of the outside customers are health-related, including medical office buildings and nursing homes. The need to be competitive in the outside world has reduced their internal operating costs.

The intrapreneur should share a well-defined risk, to underline personal commitment, and if successful, receive a well-defined reward. According to Gustaf Delin (1982), the Swedish experiments in piloting intrapreneurship underscore the need for flexibility from standard organizational policies—new rules—to facilitate experimentation and risk taking while protecting the corporation's interests in the venture.

The intrapreneur's right to work with capital in the conduct of the new business should be unquestioned. Personnel policies, purchasing procedures, and work rules should be eased or suspended for a specified period. Intrapreneurs need their own board of directors, who may be drawn from within or outside the company. Delin recommends that the intrapreneur be given strong personal influence in the choice of intraboard members.

Intrapreneurial groups may be isolated, to avoid corporate intrusions. These skunkworks, a concept developed by Lockheed and popularized by Tom Peters, need protection from company red tape, which tends to stifle innovation. IBM's PC computer was developed in a remote rural facility in Boca Raton, Florida. Members of the PC development group were all volunteers, another new rule of intrapreneurship. Peters now leads Executive Skunkcamps to teach innovation and entrepreneurship to major corporate leaders.

On Becoming Intrapreneurial

For intrapreneurship to flourish, the corporate culture must support and reward risk-taking. Peter Drucker (1985) cautions that two of every three new corporate ventures fails within five years. There must be a tolerance for failure. Persistence is essential. At Pilkington's Glass, researchers made—and broke—more than 100,000 tons of a revolutionary form of glass before they produced it in a form durable enough to sell. The potential market, auto glass, was so attractive that the intrapreneurs persisted until they made the breakthrough.

Deal and Kennedy, authors of *Corporate Cultures* (1982), believe that large companies must decentralize to be competitive in tomorrow's environment. Small is beautiful is the rule of organizational designers seeking to make a company more adaptive. How many is too many for initiation of an intrapreneurial group? One designer recommends 10 to 12; Deal and Kennedy suggest 50 to 100. Loose ad hoc organizational structures minimize barriers to doing what needs to be done by those who can do it best.

Tomorrow's organizational building block may be the network, recommends John Naisbitt (Naisbitt and Elkins 1983). This informal organization works on a task basis, across organizational lines, drawing on those with skills appropriate to the job. New communications technologies like computer conferencing can link dispersed workers at low cost, allowing each to communicate when convenient.

Personal Incentives

Money is an important incentive for intrapreneurship, but only one. A strategy recommended by Gifford Pinchot (1985) at his New School for Intrapreneurs in Tarrytown, New York, is that the intrapreneurial employee share the risk, such as 10 percent of the initial project cost or an investment of up to 20 percent of salary for two years. The company would then contract to buy completed research or development for cash bonuses and to provide capital to pursue the new venture. If successful, the intrapreneur would gain another cash bonus and more risk capital for new projects.

Trading job security for opportunity may need a safety net. At Air Products the company protects intrapreneurs with the corporate umbrella of benefits, in case of failure. Intrapreneurs downplay getting rich as a motivating factor; it is the opportunity to pursue a new idea that drives the intrapreneur. In Tracy Kidder's account of the development of a new computer by a Massachusetts computer firm skunkworks in *The Making of a New Machine* (1981), the project leader described his most powerful incentive—the chance to play pinball again, pitting himself and his team against the odds to solve new problems and create new machines.

INVENTURE CAPITAL

Finding funds for new ventures is the classic bane of entrepreneurs. In an intrapreneurial company, corporate capital can be allocated for new development, creating a pool of inventure capital. There are a number of sources of funds for new ideas.

From the Innovations in Health Care Management project funded by the W.K. Kellogg Foundation, the Center for Health Management Research in Los Angeles has identified a number of sources for inventure capital formation. Loans from a capital pool put the intrapreneurs at risk to be successful. An intrapreneurial group may sell assets, or services, to raise funds or to broker for needed services from elsewhere in the company.

Finding a benefactor within the company's top management who will commit the needed monies is a successful strategy. Some organizations set aside a percentage of the budget for research and development activities. A variation is to earmark a percentage of all new revenues over past performance levels. Employees may donate a sixth day (and a seventh) to a new enterprise. Direct employee investment of a percentage of salary, or foregoing fringe benefits, can contribute to start-up funds.

Signature capital takes advantage of corporate policies allowing managers to spend up to certain levels without higher authorization. This can allow a promising project to proceed incrementally until it can demonstrate its worth. The strategy of stone soup follows the parable of starting a pot of soup with a stone. All members of the intrapreneurial group bring whatever individual skills or funds they have to invest in the effort.

Investing for Success

Which intrapreneurial projects will succeed? There are no unique intrapreneurial criteria for screening the potential of new ventures for market success. The fact that intrapreneurship is being promoted within the company does not reduce the need for business planning and rigorous analysis before a decision to invest corporate resources. In the private sector only 1 in 10 new companies is a high-profit success. Venture capital companies may screen 50 business plans for every investment made.

Like the venture capitalists, the New Hospital promoting intrapreneurship should focus on the management team and the competitive edge and growth potential of the new service or product in its market. The new product line must have an inherent cost advantage or address a new market that will grow quickly and substantially. Intrapreneurial investments should be no less carefully made.

STRATEGIES FOR THE NEW HOSPITAL

Hospital diversification. As traditional sources of revenue (inpatient care) are restricted by Medicare and other payers, hospitals are increasingly interested in diversification. This is hardly news to today's hospitals, but most are still overwhelmingly dependent—95 percent and more—on inpatient care. Hospitals must turn an important corner. They need to reconceptualize themselves as health care corporations, not just hospitals. In the 1980s health care corporations will diversify such that patient revenues account for only 50 to 75 percent of gross revenues. Intrapreneurship is one strategic path to diversification. More importantly, it signals to employees they can do it here without leaving the company to pursue their dreams.

More than marketing. The Uniroyal experience is instructive for hospitals. Even an excellent new product failed to move forward because of a critical lack of skills in taking a new product to market. Many hospitals today are hiring directors of marketing. That is a step forward but does not go far enough. Intrapreneurship includes marketing but as only one of several key capabilities essential to successful diversification. Others include finance, planning, product development, project management, and an important intangible, the drive to succeed. New product line development will need a team approach of skilled professionals, supported by outside consultants as needed.

Business planning. In becoming intrapreneurial, health care organizations must become highly skilled in planning new business development. Preparing business plans for new programs and product lines provides essential information for evaluation of profitability potential. Sound business planning will reduce risks and provide a base on which the hospital can make a prudent decision on the investment of its inventure capital. Few health care corporations have this skill and may want assistance from experienced entrepreneurs. Intrapreneurship will be an organizational learning experience.

Public capital. The rising interest of venture capitalists in new companies is extending to health. Promising areas for health care organizations to develop equity-supported companies include health maintenance organizations, long-term care, urgent care, ambulatory surgical centers, rehabilitation, substance abuse, and home care. The equity market may be the source of substantial investment funds for the health industry in the future, accessible to both not-for-profit and investor-owned health care corporations that can demonstrate the management capability and profit potential to attract investor capital through limited partnerships and initial public offerings (IPO) to outside investors.

Risk taking. With all new ventures there is risk. The health industry has been risk-adverse. As the health marketplace becomes more competitive, some diversification efforts will certainly fail. Health care organizations have limited experience with the rough and tumble of a price-sensitive competitive market.

Management and boards of trustees will need to learn how to evaluate risk in business development, when to be bold, and when to cut losses. This is a time to strengthen the management team with new people from outside the health industry and broaden the board with new members who come from highly competitive industries.

REFERENCES AND SUGGESTED READINGS

*Brandt, Steven C. *Entrepreneuring*. Menlo Park, Calif.: Addison-Wesley, 1982.

*Colip, Terry, and Clinton, John. "Healthcare Entices Venture Capital Firms." *Modern Healthcare*, October 1983.

Deal, Terrence E., and Kennedy, Allan A. *Corporate Cultures: The Rites and Rituals of Corporate Life*. Reading, Mass.: Addison-Wesley, 1982.

Delin, Gustaf. "Intrapreneurship: An Opportunity for Business Development in Large Corporations." Corporation for Enterprise Development, 1982.

Drucker, Peter F. *Innovation and Entrepreneurship: Practice and Principles*. New York: Harper & Row, 1985.

*"Here Comes the Intrapreneur." *Business Week*, July 18, 1983.

Kidder, Tracy. *The Soul of a New Machine*. New York: Little-Brown, 1981.

Macrae, Norman. "Intrapreneurial Now." *Economist*, April 17, 1982.

*Mancuso, Joseph R. *How to Prepare and Present a Business Plan*. Englewood Cliffs, N.J.: Prentice-Hall (A Spectrum Book), 1983.

Naisbitt, John, and Elkins, John. "The Hospital and Megatrends." Parts 1 and 2. *Hospital Forum*, May/June, July/August, 1983.

*Petre, Peter D. "Meet the Lean Mean New IBM." *Fortune*, June 13, 1983.

*"Personal Computers: And the Winner Is IBM." *Business Week*, October 3, 1983.

Pinchot, Gifford. *Intrapreneuring*. New York: Harper & Row, 1985.

*Shays, E. Michael. "Bringing the Entrepreneurs Out at Pacific." *Management Journal*, June 1983.

*"Uniroyal's 'Greenhouse' for New Ideas." *Business Week*, October 10, 1983.

---

*Suggested reading.

Chapter 18
Innovation

18

Few of today's health care organizations are organized for innovation. Their systems and processes are oriented toward incremental improvement, minimizing risk and muddling through.

Status quo maintenance worked as long as the health care environment remained stable. Industry growth allowed even the most inefficient providers to survive but no longer. Now the health industry is in transition. Hospitals face a rising threat of widespread hospital failures, under pressure from payers and competitors. The health care marketplace is undergoing revolutionary change suggests Dennis Pointer (1985), not just the rules by which the game is played but the game itself. Health service organizations must become far more creative and innovative if they are to thrive, let alone survive, in the new health care marketplace.

THE NEED FOR INNOVATION

Hospitals need only to look at other industries—airlines, banking, and communications—for inspiration in handling deregulation and increased competition. The experience of the ABC industries is instructive: competition will unleash a wave of innovation that will totally restructure the hospital industry.

In general, hospitals have lagged two to five years behind business and industry in adopting the latest management ideas. With regulatory impediments diminishing and competition increasing, hospitals today have the motivation to innovate. What hospitals have lacked is a systematic management process for transfer and adapting innovations from the private business sector into the health field.

Why Hospitals Don't Innovate

In the health care industry this lack of innovativeness is an important problem because many of the assumptions under which hospitals have operated since the 1960s are no longer valid. Given the massive changes the health industry is facing, hospitals have two choices: (1) adapt through innovation and (2) drift into obsolescence.

Yet the management of health care organizations lags behind. Although a substantial body of knowledge has emerged in the management literature since the 1970s on such topics as organizational change and managing innovation, few of the results have found their way into the conventional wisdom of hospital management. A number of reasons might be cited.

- Cost reimbursement has buffered hospitals from the rough and tumble of the marketplace to which other industries are routinely exposed.
- Risk aversion was rewarded and risk taking was considered unnecessary and potentially hazardous to the health (and tenure) of hospital executives.
- Hospital management was isolated through specialized professional education and professionalization of the field.
- Limited venture capital was available for entrepreneurial business development in the health industry, except for the investor-owned corporations' access to equity funds and taxable securities.
- Regulation, not competition, has been the dominant pattern within the medical marketplace; in the absence of competition, hospitals have had little economic incentive to innovate.

In today's rapidly changing health care environment, though, these factors are no longer applicable. The hospital industry has reached the mature phase in the product cycle; innovation can break through the life cycle barrier (Figure 18–1).

Networking

There is a promising new management approach to increase the level of innovation by America's hospitals: planned management innovation (PMI). At the core of this approach is networking—reaching out to the best-managed companies in the private sector for new management ideas, then transferring and adopting them into the hospital environment.

A three-year R&D project begun in 1981 demonstrates that hospitals can successfully innovate at management's selected targets and under management's control. A new process called planned management innovation was devised as part

Figure 18–1 Product Life Cycle and Innovation

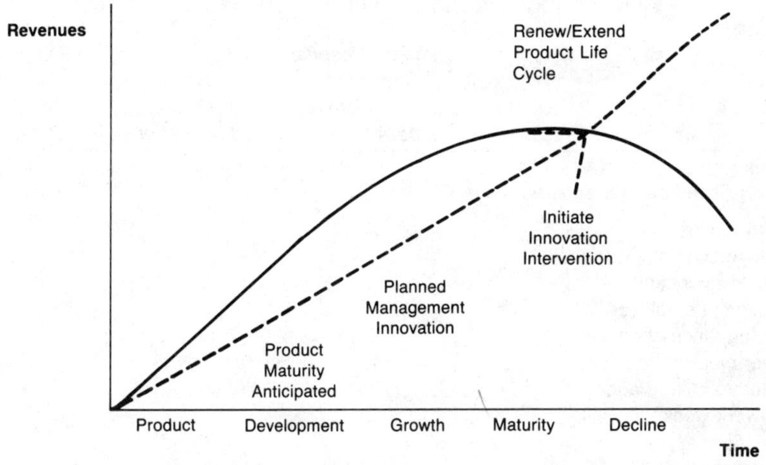

of the demonstration project that institutionalizes the process of networking and innovation.

Seven hospitals participated in a research and demonstration project, Innovations in Health Care Management, funded by the W.K. Kellogg Foundation, and conducted by the Center for Health Management Research of the Lutheran Hospital Society of Southern California. Two areas were targeted for innovation by the demonstration hospitals: (1) marketing and (2) human resources management. The seven participating hospitals identified key problem areas, then used networking to identify potential solutions already in use by leading private-sector corporations. More than 100 Fortune 500 companies cooperated in the program.

The results are highlighted in the box score of hospital innovation (Table 18–1). Not all were equally successful. Some innovations took more time to implement than planned. The greatest gains came in improved managerial efficiency. Participants agree that networking reduced the search for innovation measurably, speeding implementation 6 to 16 months over home-grown solutions. Most telling from an evaluation perspective, more than two-thirds of the innovations have become institutionalized after the demonstration period.

BREAKING THROUGH WITH INNOVATION

Hospitals can break through the product life cycle's inexorable decline phase through innovation. Customer relations is a prime example. At California Medical Center in Los Angeles a guest relations program called P.R.I.D.E. is helping to offset the hospital's inner-city location by providing a premium level of service.

Table 18–1 Innovations in Health Care Management Funded by
W.K. Kellogg Foundation (1981–1984)

	Lutheran Hospital Society of So. California (Los Angeles)	Health Central (Minneapolis)	Samaritan Health Services (Phoenix)
Human Resource Management			
Quality circles	X		
Employee communications			X
Productivity incentives	X		
Nonexempt employee performance appraisal			X
Career mobility	X		
Corporate culture audit			X
4/40 work week	X		
Marketing			
Customer relations	X	X	X
Market-based planning	X		
Product development model		X	
Emergency room marketing	X		

The program was inspired by the customer relations programs of Pacific Southwest Airlines and Disneyland.

In downtown Phoenix Good Samaritan Hospital of the Samaritan Health Services system instituted a V.I.P. customer relations program to personalize the service of the 785-bed teaching hospital. After networking with companies such as Marriott and the Goldwater's retail chain, Samaritan Health Services made a corporate decision to develop a customer-relations—not a guest relations—program in the mode of the private-sector business community. In Minneapolis the Health Central System's Building Bridges program proved so popular with other hospitals that the program is being nationally marketed to the health industry.

All three hospitals are located in overbuilt, highly competitive markets. They believe that innovation in customer service will give them a competitive advantage in being the hospital of choice with three tiers of customers: (1) major buyers such as employers and insurance companies; (2) physicians, as they chose where to admit and refer patients; and (3) individual customers, who are playing an increasingly large role in selecting their health care provider.

Hospitals today face competitive pressures to contain costs, acquire new medical technologies, respond to rising consumer expectations, cope with the graying of America and chronic morbidity patterns, and rebuild plant and equipment in the face of growing capital shortages. All factors are driving hospitals' top-level managers to be innovative in management efficiency and business development. Hospitals cannot wait for spontaneous innovation to adapt to a rapidly changing environment. Peters has advocated a skunkworks approach to organizational innovation, isolating the innovators from management interference. That is not the only way to innovate. Hospitals can strategically plan and manage change, using a process developed in the demonstration project called planned management innovation.

The secret of this needed management process is networking. The central goal of the Kellogg-funded demonstration project was to identify innovative management practices in the private business sector and transfer and adapt them in hospitals. By so doing, the hospitals would shortcut the traditional innovation process.

Redefining Innovation

First, the hospitals had to learn a new concept for innovation. The classic definition of innovation is "the act of introducing something new or novel," but the popular concept of innovation is invention. Invention focuses on the creative process. Not every company has a Thomas Edison. Where will new ideas come from in tomorrow's hospital?

Redefining innovation provides a solution that is facilitated by networking: *innovation* is a practice or product that is new to the adopting organization. Management practices from business and industry can be identified, transferred, and adapted by health care organizations through the networking process.

Health Networking

Innovation and networking have not received the attention in the health care management literature they deserve. The networking concept is a method by which health care managers may expedite the process of identifying and implementing innovative management practices from the private business community for use in health organizations.

There is a rich literature on the diffusion of innovation, to which networking should be added. Networking is a powerful new mechanism for organizations and individuals to gain innovative concepts and practices.

In Search of Innovation

The excellent companies make conscious use of the networking process to promote more effective organization, as chronicled by Peters and Waterman (1980). In these organizations networking provides a "rich, informal communication," "a virtual technology of keeping in touch," and a fluid, project-oriented approach to organization." *Chunking*, another management innovation Peters and Waterman founded, simply means pulling people together from various places, positions, and levels within the organization to facilitate information exchange in product development.

Chunking closely resembles the interdisciplinary approach utilized by health care managers in the search for innovations under the Kellogg-funded R&D project. Participants were typical department heads or line supervisors from various areas within the hospital, using ad hoc "quick-hit task forces," in Peters and Waterman's (1980) lexicon. They appeared on no organizational chart but were pulled together to help manage selected problems.

The idea of task forces is hardly new. Alvin Toffler (1970) calls them adhocracies. In the search for innovation the hospital task forces were ad hoc networks. The excellent companies in business and industry, and the hospitals participating in the Innovations project, know that networks exist. Rather than perceiving them as threats, the networks were deliberately used by management to facilitate innovation.

Information Society

This is the age of information, a time of unprecedented growth in the development and exchange of information. Health is an information industry. Much of what is provided to health care consumers is information. As a knowledge-based industry, health is well-suited to utilizing networks and the new information technologies.

Networks are to the organization of information societies what bureaucracies were to the organization of industrial societies. Where the latter fragmented tasks and functions to maximize control and instill discipline, networks cut across tasks and functions to promote a fluid work environment in order to achieve genuine cross-discipline.

Quality circles are a form of networks. When the Santa Monica Hospital Medical Center sought a model for quality circles, they sought advice from high-tech giants Hughes and 3M. Santa Monica's initial success expanded the program from one to six departments and now is virtually hospitalwide.

Networks

Networks are people talking to each other, sharing ideas, information, and resources. Networks are interpersonal relationships within organizations in which people consciously develop linkages for the exchange of information to foster self-help and promote some kind of change. Networks exist for more than communication. They represent a new evolutionary stage in the structure and organization of society. Information transmitted through networks represents a transaction between individuals that is perceived as beneficial to the participants in the exchange.

Networks can also be thought of as the underground of formal organizations, like Chester Bernard's informal organizations. They are known but never documented. They do not appear in organizational charts delimiting offices, departments, and chains of command. Networks are flexible. They are practical and they are portable. People take their networks with them. Networks are not developed by organizations but by individuals.

While their existence may be known and even used by those within organizations who have power, they represent the nonorganizational side of power. It is the perception of the network by others that gives its members power. Contact power is one key to the effectiveness of networks. Contacts provide information, and information is the real stock-in-trade of networks. The more one trades, the more contacts are strengthened, the more powerful and effective are individuals within the network, and the more likely a network's goal will be achieved.

In the Kellogg experience each business contact was a source of referral to peers, often in other companies. Networks were constructed through a series of interviews that extended relationships through personal linkages.

From the standpoint of networking, the interactive process between people in different subsystems breaks down the boundaries which separate them. The Kellogg innovations experience in networking illustrates this interactive process. California Medical Center in Los Angeles formalized its network of business-based strategic planners into an advisory committee to guide the hospital in its long-range market planning. Santa Monica Hospital instituted a monthly luncheon meeting series, Ticket to Health, to extend its network of contacts in the local business community.

Networking Culture in Organizations

Networking has real utility inside organizations too. Networking reflects a style of management that emphasizes communication that is lateral, diagonal, and bottom-up. Networking is rooted in informality and equality. On this point Naisbitt (1982) cites an executive from a major hi-tech corporation who places a great deal of emphasis on networking: "We simply can't afford to have the hierarchical barriers to an exchange of ideas and information that you have at so many corporations. Too many valuable ideas can get lost in a company's bureaucratic quagmire."

Openness to change is an essential element of the organization culture to promote successful innovation. As hospital CEO Richard Norling (1983) stated, "There has to be a willingness by the management team to put an idea on the table without criticism, to give new ideas a chance."

Fostering Business and Health Relations

Under the stimulus of the Kellogg grant the seven demonstration hospitals initiated networking activities with IBM, Security Pacific Bank, General Foods, Honeywell, and other companies with reputations for excellence in the human resources and marketing areas. Their experience and expertise were tapped directly by the project's hospitals in the search for management innovations. There was considerable resistance at first to networking with business and industry among all seven demonstration hospitals. They feared being perceived as naive. Some hospital executives feared criticism from business corporations over the issue of health care costs.

Once the networking process was underway, advantages to both the hospital and corporate communities quickly become apparent. The hospitals were given access to a pool of relevant management information at no cost, as well as useful assistance in translating that information to the hospital setting. Private industry saw first-hand that its local hospitals were genuinely trying to do something about rising costs and in a number of instances were given helpful tips relating to health benefits, health promotion, and employee assistance programs.

CONDITIONS FOR INFORMATION TRANSFER

Research from the Innovations project suggests four basic conditions must be present for the successful transfer of management practices. First, the management practice must have already demonstrated its utility in the donor organization. Second, the receiving organization must have a need to change and be willing to commit necessary resources. Third, the donor organization must be willing to share its management practice and willing to provide technical assistance where necessary. Finally, the receiving organization must have a structure in place to facilitate the transfer, adaptation, and implementation of the management practice. The eight step process of information transfer is outlined in Exhibit 18–1.

Stages of Transferring Innovation

Information transfer can be viewed as a sequence of four stages within the receiving organization, each of which includes specific tasks that must be accomplished if external ideas are to be transferred and successfully adapted.

Stage 1.   An organization needs to identify a problem. Experience from the Innovations project would suggest that familiar problems, or problems in which the organization already has sunk costs, are more likely to benefit from the transfer and adaptation process than newer problems with which the culture is less familiar. Hospital familiarity with

Exhibit 18–1 The Networking and Innovation Process

Step 1. Accepting the need for innovation

Step 2. Initiating the networking process with business and industry through formal and informal discussions and exchanges

Step 3. Sifting out most worthwhile management practices for potential adaptation and implementation

Step 4. Developing a plan of action including time frame, task allocation, and determination of rules and responsibilities

Step 5. Developing a network within the organization to provide technical and political support

Step 6. Communicating project developments with key stakeholders within the organization, up, down, and across the organization

Step 7. Promoting the acceptance and use of the innovation by the organization

Step 8. Testing the innovation, modifying, and adopting (or eliminating) the innovation

---

human resource management expedited the implementation of innovation in this area. In marketing, the hospitals' lack of familiarity slowed the transfer process of innovations requiring marketing expertise.

Stage 2. Management makes an assessment of the degree of readiness for innovation (and resistance to change) in its culture and the resources the organization has available and is willing to commit. In a hospital that adapted a quality circles program, for example, the task force spent six months investigating the Japanese Theory Z concept of participative decision-making at management's request. The task force completed its work before management's decision to implement. In that same hospital the CEO explicitly stated at a department head meeting that despite the necessity for reduced budgets, he would not cut innovative programs like quality circles. As a result, the program was implemented ahead of schedule and is considered a resounding success by both top and middle management.

Stage 3. The organization needs to align formally the goals of the project with its larger strategic goals and then commit those resources that were previously identified as available to the project. If the alignment is not close, or the willingness to commit designated resources is not strong, the project is almost certain to flounder.

In a hospital that implemented a productivity incentives program, management commitment was not formally expressed in either its strategic or one-year operational goals. The pilot program was not initiated until every financial aspect had been detailed. This demand for advance knowledge was a form of risk-aversion and had a deleterious effect on the enthusiasm and effectiveness of the project staff.

By contrast, a CEO skeptical of strategic planning made personal visits to major corporations. He came back a believer in the value of planning and market research. The result was a new long-range 20-year statement of mission and goals, with a matching set of 5-year plans and a marketing department to refine and implement them.

Stage 4. The organization needs to establish a networking mechanism to support transfer and adaptation. In some instances this mechanism consisted of separate planning and implementation teams in which the planning team (usually top management) defined the innovation area and delegated virtually all other networking responsibilities to the implementation team. In other instances networking responsibilities were combined in one group or a subcommittee of the planning team (top management) assumed these responsibilities.

Critical Success Factors for Innovation

Judging from the experience of all seven demonstration hospitals in planned and managed innovation, eight factors would predict success for the transfer and adaptation process:

1. a strong need for change
2. a definite readiness within the organization for change
3. a genuine commitment from top and middle management
4. clearly stated goals and objectives
5. realistic time frames
6. adequate technical and staff support
7. a positive working relationship with the donor organization
8. effective leadership from top management for the networking mechanism to promote the transfer and adaptation process

The Innovative Edge

Winning performance—how does a company gain it and sustain it? An indepth study by McKinsey & Company's Don Clifford and Dick Cavanagh (1985) of 750 midsize growth companies defined their success in a word: *innovation*. These companies are the innovative leaders of their market niches. More than a third got their start through introduction of a new product or service. Although many rank in the top 10 to 15 percent of their industries, few rest long on their reputations.

Innovation, R&D and product improvement are continuous. Peter Drucker (1985) believes their success is due to new technology. But the technology is not electronics or genetics. It is the technology of innovation and entrepreneurship.

STRATEGIES FOR THE NEW HOSPITAL

Innovate continuously. The price of leadership in a competitive environment will be continuous change and improvement in every aspect of product development and service delivery. Leaders get their competitive edge through innovation, and they never rest on the past. The innovative health care organization must bring new products to market constantly. Set high goals. The 3M company aims for 25 percent revenues from products less than five years old.

License creativity. The New Hospital must create a climate for innovative performance and foster it in every aspect of corporate life. Every organization has its myths and stories. Too often they are sagas of overcoming company policies and narrow-minded management. Let them be about successful innovation by creative employees whose new ideas were welcomed. The message will be reinforced when employees are given tangible—at least 15 percent of salary—rewards for innovation.

Expect failure. Not all new ideas will succeed. Plan for failure, and learn from it. Be a two-mistake company where employees are not fired or demoted after failure.

Break the rules. Top management sets the limits of acceptable corporate risk-taking behavior. Symbolically breaking or bending the rules telegraphs a message to employees that company rules are not a barrier to innovative performance.

Invest in innovation. Innovative performance is no accident. It needs to be nurtured and capitalized. Forget the corporate mission statement. The real priorities of any company are reflected in its budget. Set aside a line item in the budget for innovation, R&D, and new ventures. This form of reinvestment is essential for the New Hospital to maintain the vitality of its products and the responsiveness of its service.

REFERENCES AND SUGGESTED READINGS

*Bell, Daniel. *The Coming of the Post-Industrial Society*. New York: Basic Books, 1973.

*Bernard, Chester. *The Functions of the Executive*. Cambridge: Harvard University Press, 1938.

Clifford, Donald K., and Cavanagh, Richard E. *Winning Performance: How America's High-Growth Midsize Companies Succeed*. New York: Bantam, 1985.

Drucker, Peter F. *Innovation and Entrepreneurship: Practice and Principles*. New York: Harper & Row, 1985.

*Galbraith, Jay R. "Designing the Innovating Organization." *Organizational Dynamics*, Winter 1982, pp. 5–25.

*Kaiser, Lee. "Innovation." *Hospital Forum,* March-April 1982.

*Kanter, Rosabeth Moss. *The Change Masters.* New York: Simon and Schuster, 1983.

Naisbitt, John. *Megatrends.* New York: Warner Books, 1982.

*Naisbitt, John, and Elkins, John. "The Hospital and Megatrends." Parts 1–2. *Hospital Forum,* May-June, July-August 1983.

Norling, Richard A. Interview with author. January 1983.

*Perow, Charles. *Complex Organizations: A Critical Essay.* 2nd ed. New York: Scott, Foresman, 1979.

Peters, Thomas, and Waterman, Robert. *In Search of Excellence: Lessons From America's Best-Run Companies.* New York: Harper & Row, 1980.

Pointer, Dennis D. "Responding to the Challenges of the New Health Care Marketplace: Organizing for Creativity and Innovation." (1985).

*Porter, Michael. *Competitive Strategy.* New York: Free Press, 1980.

*Rodgers, E.M., and Shoemaker, F.F. *The Communication of Innovation.* New York: Free Press, 1971.

*Strum, Dennis W., and Coile, Russell C., Jr. "Transferring Lessons from High Performance Organizations." *Hospital Forum,* May/June 1984, pp. 62–64.

*Strum, Dennis, and Classen, Barbara. "Networking: A Process for Enhancing Interaction among Business and Industry, Health Care and Academic Institutions." Los Angeles: Center for Health Management Research, 1982.

Toffler, Alvin. *Future Shock.* New York: Random House, 1970.

*Zaltman, G., Duncan, R.B., and Holbek, J. *Innovation and Organizations.* New York: John Wiley & Sons, 1973.

---

*Suggested reading.

Chapter 19

High-Output Management

19

In this high-speed "Federal Express—I need it yesterday!" world, there is a new challenge for managers: high-output management. Increasing productivity, especially managerial productivity, is *the* management challenge of the New Hospital. Hospital care is still a labor-intensive—not capital-intensive—industry. The New Hospital needs to learn how to be more productive, cutting labor costs 25 to 35 percent to be competitive in the 1990s. As America's hospitals become the health care factories of the future, the private sector experience can be instructive here.

Take Intel, one of Silicon Valley's success stories. In its brief 15-year life span, Intel has pioneered the computer chip and the microprocessor. There are two keys to Intel's success: the first is technological innovation, but the factor that has maintained Intel as one of America's premiere computer companies is management. Andrew Grove, Intel's president, is a true believer in his message. Not only has he written a book about the techniques that made Intel profitable, but he has appeared tirelessly, and without compensation, to present them to business audiences across the nation. Like Alfred Sloan, guru of the last generation of American managers, Grove is a practitioner. More to the point, he is an engineer whose manufacturing experience provides the principles on which high-output management (1983) is based.

THE BREAKFAST FACTORY

Andrew Grove's lessons on productivity start with breakfast, literally. Using the analogy of preparing a simple breakfast in a restaurant, Grove lays out the basic sequence of the manufacturing process. Using system analysis, Grove identifies boiling the eggs as the limiting step in the process. The key idea is to construct a

225

production flow by starting with the longest (most difficult, most sensitive, or most expensive) step and work backward. In this simple analogy are the three fundamental types of production operations: (1) process manufacturing, (2) assembly, and (3) testing.

Extending the lesson further, Grove looks for the most cost-effective way of producing his egg. Hiring specialists, keeping overhead to a minimum, investing in capital equipment are all ways of optimizing the process. With careful analysis, the one best way will be identified.

All production flows have a basic characteristic: the material becomes more valuable as it moves through the process. A boiled egg is more valuable than a raw one, a fully assembled breakfast egg is more valuable than its parts, and finally the breakfast placed in front of a customer is more valuable still. Here is another lesson: Grove recommends detecting and fixing problems in the production process at the lowest-value stage possible. This minimizes the cost as well as the risk of a quality defect when the product gets to the customer.

Assuring quality is a critical success factor in the computer and the health industries. At Intel, quality is checked in three places: (1) incoming inspection of raw materials, (2) in-process inspection of production, and (3) final inspection before delivery to customers. Remember Grove's admonition: detect problems at the lowest-value stage of the process. How often should quality be measured? Grove has a common sense suggestion. Use variable inspections. Because quality levels vary over time, it is only common sense to vary how often to inspect. If problems begin to develop, test more frequently until quality returns to the previous high levels. It is cheaper than continuous or periodic inspection, and probably more effective. The same principle applies to managing subordinates.

MANAGERIAL LEVERAGE

To improve productivity, managers of the New Hospital must improve their leverage. An activity with high leverage will generate a high level of output. Automation is certainly one way to improve the leverage of all types of work. So is work simplification. Management engineering can achieve as much as 20 to 30 percent reduction in effort (and cost).

These techniques have been widely applied in manufacturing. Now management engineers are turning them to improving the productivity of the soft professions: the administrative, professional, and managerial work place. The major problem to be overcome is defining what the output of such work is or should be. In the work of the soft professions it is difficult to distinguish between output and activity. Boosting managerial output is the key to improving productivity, while increasing activity can result in just the opposite. The key to raising productivity of these knowledge workers, Peter Drucker (1982) suggests, is to distinguish between "contribution" (output), not effort (activity).

What is a manager's output? Is it judgments and decisions? directions? mistakes detected? products planned? or commitments negotiated? From a management analysis viewpoint these are not outputs. They are activities, descriptions of what managers do rather than what managers create.

The answer is deceptively simple. A manager's output equals the output of the organization plus the output of neighboring organizations under one's influence. A manager can do individual work, and do it well, but that does not constitute output. The distinction between line and staff is not meaningful here. By this broader definition the output of a manager is the result achieved by a group either under supervision or under influence. While the manager's own work is clearly important, that in itself does not create output. Only the organization does—in tangible goods, services, or other measurable units.

While the job of managerial work is difficult to categorize, more important is its focus. Is the manager investing the greatest proportion of time where leverage is most significant? Information gathering is not an end in itself. Its purpose is to focus the manager's critical attention on those areas with the highest leverage. Companies like Intel increase managerial leverage by focusing on the particular place in the company where output is below expectations. The proc   s more efficient and certainly more direct. At neighboring competitor Hewlet.. ackard, they call this walking around management, or WAM.

While managers move about, doing their daily work, they are role models for others in the organization. No single managerial activity can be said to constitute leadership as directly as leading by example. Values and behavioral norms are not transmitted easily by talk or memo but are conveyed effectively by doing, and doing them physically. There is no one preferred style of leadership, and the principle applies at the bottom of the organization as well as the top. How a manager handles time may be the single most important aspect of being a role model and leader, in the view of Michael Maccoby, author of *The Leader* (1981).

Successful managers are those who concentrate on high-leverage activities. There are three basic opportunities for a manager to achieve high leverage:

1. when many people are affected by one manager
2. when a person's activity or behavior over a long period is influenced by a manager's brief, well-focused set of words or actions
3. when a large group's work is affected by an individual supplying a unique, key piece of knowledge or information.

Leverage is enhanced by timely action. Or it can be set back, for example, when a manager is a key participant but is unprepared to make a decision when needed. Managerial meddling is another way in which managers can negatively affect output. The art of high-output management lies in the capacity to select from the many activities of seemingly comparable significance the one or two that provide the most leverage and concentrate on them.

MEETINGS: THE MEDIUM OF MANAGERIAL WORK

Meetings have a bad name. Some call them the curse of a manager's existence. Managers often spend up to 50 percent of their time in formal meetings. Spending more than 25 percent of one's time in meetings is the sign of a manager's malorganization, believes Peter Drucker (1982).

But there is another way to regard meetings. Grove believes in them. Rather than fighting their existence, use the time spent in meetings as efficiently as possible. In the New Hospital meetings are not a distraction from managerial work—they are high-priority management tasks that play a critical role in productivity.

The two basic managerial roles produce two basic kinds of meetings: (1) process-oriented meetings for information exchange and (2) mission-oriented meetings which frequently produce decisions. To make the most of process-oriented meetings, Grove recommends infusing them with regularity. Those attending should know how the meeting will be run, what kinds of substantive matters will be discussed, and what is to be accomplished. It should be designed to allow a manager to batch transactions, using the same production set-up time and effort to take care of many similar managerial tasks. At Intel there are three kinds of process-oriented meetings: (1) one-on-one, (2) staff meetings, and (3) operations review.

One-on-One

At Intel a one-on-one is a meeting between supervisor and subordinate. It is the principal way their business relationship is maintained. Its primary purpose is mutual teaching and exchange of information. By talking about specific problems and situations, the supervisor teaches the subordinate skills and know-how and suggests ways to approach things. At the same time the subordinates provide the superior with detailed information about what they are doing.

How frequently are one-on-one meetings needed? It depends on the job or task-relevant maturity of each subordinate. The frequency of contact is not dependent on how long the employee has been with the company but on the level of experience in handling similar tasks. When events change at a rapid rate, as in marketing, such meetings are needed with a high order of frequency.

A key point about a one-on-one: it should be regarded as the subordinate's meeting, with its agenda and tone set by the subordinate. There is good reason for this. Someone needs to prepare for the meeting. The supervisor with eight subordinates would have to prepare eight times; the subordinate only once. So the latter should be asked to prepare an outline, which is important because it forces the employee to think through in advance all issues and decisions that need to be raised. From the outline the supervisor knows at the outset what is to be covered and can help set the pace of the meeting according to the significance of the items. The outline also provides a framework for supporting information, which the subordinate prepares in advance.

Meetings should cover progress, problems, and perhaps most importantly potential problems. These may be surfaced by review of indicators or simply from the subordinate's intuition. Both parties can take notes on the outline, and save them for the next meeting. This provides a continuing stream of information, applying the production principle of batching to minimize unscheduled interruptions.

Staff Meetings

Staff meetings are the key to effective teamwork. What should be discussed at staff meetings? Anything that affects more than two of the people present. Meetings should be mostly controlled, with an agenda issued far enough in advance that subordinates have a chance to prepare for the meeting. But it should also include an open session for discussion of any topic. The role of the supervisor as chairman is key, to keep the discussion on track with subordinates bearing the brunt of working the issues.

Staff meetings are an ideal medium for decision making. Decisions are most likely to be implemented when there is a shared consensus about the problem and its solution.

Operation Reviews

The least common but highly significant form of business meeting is the operation review. This is the opportunity to keep the teaching and learning going on between employees several organizational levels apart: people who don't have one-on-one's or staff meetings with each other. Such meetings are a source of advice and direction from senior managers. They are also a source of motivation. Such meetings are almost universally formal. Grove recommends prepared presentations with audiovisuals. Operation reviews are an opportunity not only to focus on production progress and problems, they are critical in the promotion process for subordinates. Successful presentations pave the way for increased responsibility.

Mission-Oriented Meetings

Unlike process-oriented meetings, which are regularly scheduled to exchange knowledge and information, the mission-oriented meeting is usually held ad hoc.

It is designed to produce a specific output, frequently a decision. The key to success here is what the chairman does. These meetings are valuable and costly. One estimate of the dollar cost of a manager's time, including overhead, is about $100 per hour. A meeting involving 10 managers for two hours costs the company $2,000. The chairman's role is pivotal. The chairman sets the agenda, invites the participants, and maintains discipline. As you might expect, Grove is a stickler for punctuality. There is a formal agenda and afterwards written minutes. If all went well, such meetings would never be needed except on a regularly scheduled basis. Grove estimates 80 percent of business can be handled routinely.

Electronic Meetings

Managers of the New Hospital do not have to wait until the year 2000 for the meeting of the future. Electronic meetings via computer teleconferencing offer a technological alternative to face-to-face meetings. Electronic meetings have an agenda, someone in charge, invited participants, and discussion, dialogue and debate—all the aspects of a typical business meeting except one: the participants never meet.

In an electronic meeting most participants never leave their own desks, but they could just as easily join the meeting from a hotel room or a remote retreat. With access to a telephone, and a computer terminal or portable computer with modem, electronic meetings can be carried out worldwide without the time, travel, and expense of face-to-face meetings. New age companies like Network Technologies of Ann Arbor, Michigan, make it possible for multinational companies to hold global meetings—and little companies to hold meetings under a single roof—but at the time and convenience of each participating manager or employee.

Time and distance are obviously not a factor in electronic meetings. Participants may join the meeting at an appointed time and communicate simultaneously (synchronously) or at their own preferred time (asynchronously). Because most messages are keypunched, communication tends to be brief and direct. Since the computer is the meeting host, there is a detailed written record available to all. Levels of security can tier participation in certain decisions. Productivity is enhanced by the focused nature of this communication modality and the time gained by avoiding travel and delay that accompanies most meetings.

MANAGING BY THE NUMBERS

Running counter to Andrew Grove's vision of a high-tech, systems engineered business world is Harold Geneen's bare-knuckled approach to productivity management. Geneen is a throwback to the days of John D. Rockefeller. His management credo is hard work, long hours, and a relentless attention to the numbers. The numbers are symbols of business activity, a thermometer to measure the health of the enterprise. As president of ITT, the worldwide conglomerate, Geneen was responsible for overseeing 250 profit centers, whose annual budgets and supporting documents occupied 30 feet of shelf space in Geneen's office.

Geneen believes that modern managers squander entirely too much of their limited time on the social responsibility of the corporation and not nearly enough of managerial attention is directed to the business side. Striving to gain employee participation in decisions, from Geneen's viewpoint, is a distraction from the essential task of driving performance toward quantified business objectives: the numbers.

Each quarter Geneen gathered his 250-plus managers around an enormous conference table known as the pit and grilled them for three intense days on their numbers. Aided by a staff of accountants and sharp-eyed MBAs, and his own nearly photographic recall, Geneen would lead the inquisition for hours without interruption.

The results showed the benefit of this exercise in managerial leverage. When Geneen managed ITT, the firm achieved better than 10 percent growth and 15 percent profitability for almost 60 consecutive quarters and was the envy of Wall Street. When Geneen finally retired, his successor reportedly cut the huge conference table in half with a chain saw and adopted a more participative management style. Since Geneen, ITT has been unable to sustain growth and has survived only through divestiture of assets. If there is a lesson in productivity management here for managers of the New Hospital, it is to reinforce the need for management discipline and a well-focused concentration on the numbers of their enterprise.

VANGUARD MANAGEMENT

The success of Japanese companies in gaining world-power economic status has prompted a spate of analyses of the differences in Japanese management: Theory Z: the art of Japanese management, and even Zen and creative management. U.S. companies have much ground to regain. In the 1980s the Japanese consistently achieved 3 to 4 percent annual productivity gains, while U.S. productivity was a relatively flat 0.5 percent.

Rather than innovation by imitation, business school professor James O'Toole (1985) of the University of Southern California advocates a new style of uniquely American management dedicated to high purposes and a commitment to excellence. Vanguard management enhances productivity with employee practices such as the following:

- stockholder status for unions
- employee stock ownership

- a fair measure of job security
- lifelong training
- benefits tailored to individual needs
- participation in decision making
- freedom of expression
- incentive pay

In the hard-hit wood products industry, for example, Weyerhauser reopened a mill after extensive planning and collaboration with the union. Management staffing was cut 31 percent and employees reduced 37 percent. Productivity rose 30 percent. Before the closing, the mill's highest production was 23,500 board feet per hour. Weyerhauser figured break-even at 24,500 feet. With new equipment and incentive pay, workers broke the old record on the second day and now consistently cut 31,000 to 32,000 board feet per hour. That's vanguard management in action.

DOWNSIZING

From multinational giant IBM to one-location companies, the trend is toward lean and mean in staffing and operation. Before deregulation and breakup, AT&T had 23 levels of management and workers. Trying to achieve a flatter organizational profile, AT&T cut 6 layers in the first year and aims to reduce 3 to 4 more layers before 1990, reducing labor costs 30 percent.

Continental Airline's close call with bankruptcy led to a dramatic productivity turnaround. Under the protection of Chapter 11 receivership, management cut employee wages in half and reduced its work force from 11,000 to 4,000. Only a third of the pilots came back to work. Those who did accepted lower pay, longer work periods, and more work days per month. So did all other Continental workers. This gave the airline the ability to compete aggressively as a low-fare carrier on high-traffic routes. Within two years the airline was in the black.

One of the most ambitious attempts at downsizing is General Motors Saturn project. The Saturn is a new economy-sized car aimed to compete head-to-head with Japanese auto firms. The competition is formidable. Honda needs only 75 labor hours per car; GM requires 150 hours per auto. General Motors aims to establish not just a new car but an entire new automaker. Saturn will be a brand new company with no labor agreements or contracts around its neck to limit its productivity potential. The Saturn effort is being planned with the full cooperation of the United Auto Workers. In the new plant 6,500 workers are organized in small teams that control much of their own work. Flexible staffing is a key goal. Only six classifications of employees will work in the new plant, and all will be paid on a salary-incentive basis. Gone are the hourly wage scales, Byzantine work rules, and scores of job classifications. The changes should add up to a 30 percent productivity improvement over standard GM operations and may set a new standard for the entire auto industry.

THE CHALLENGE OF HIGH-OUTPUT MANAGEMENT

America's hospitals are vulnerable on the productivity issue. With more than half of every hospital dollar spent on payroll, the labor component is an obvious target for cost cutting and productivity improvement. In a number of respects the hospital industry lags 5 to 10 years behind other industries that have undergone deregulation and increasing competition. Hospitals can learn much from the private sector about high-output management.

Health care is a labor-intensive industry. Hospitals average 4.0 to 4.5 full-time equivalent (FTE) employees per occupied bed. In teaching hospitals the labor input can be 6.0 to 8.0 FTEs. Labor costs still comprise more than half of average hospital's budget. An estimated 75 percent of hospital employees are knowledge workers—prime targets for high-output management.

STRATEGIES FOR THE NEW HOSPITAL

Cut FTEs by 25 percent. Despite the several rounds of cost cutting most hospitals have conducted, more radical surgery is needed. The magnitude of the cuts most hospitals need is a minimum of 20 to 25 percent to make them cost competitive. The reason is simple. By 1990 more than half of all hospital inpatient business will be prenegotiated through competitive bidding. Only those hospitals that can operate at expense levels below their discounted prices will survive.

Look at health care as a commodity. Health care has always been a custom product. In the past each hospital or physician customer has been given a treatment regimen custom-tailored to unique needs (and insurance coverage). The shift to a payment scheme based on standard diagnoses by the federal government is the death knell for customized health services (and to profits based on a la carte billing). The more that health services can be standardized, the more that modern management technology can be applied to driving their costs down. The firms that accept this market reality first will be the first to enjoy the competitive advantages of lower costs and preferred provider contracts.

Apply management engineering. Think of each DRG cluster as a three-minute egg and apply Andrew Grove's management engineering to find the most efficient way to produce it: a standardized treatment plan for all major DRG categories. The task is not simple. It will need the expertise of management engineers, guided by the skill and experience of physicians, nurses, and employees as well as financial analysts and managers.

Become a low-cost producer. One business strategy is always recommended: become the lowest-cost producer in your market or niche. It is always an advantage to be the lowest-cost producer. The hospital can charge whatever the market will bear, and even discount, and still achieve higher profitability than competitors whose production costs are higher than yours.
Move to the vanguard. Invest heavily in managing for maximum output. This is an R&D effort that can really benefit from economics of scale. Multihospital corporations can gain cost-effective benefits from extending the lessons of this research across all member hospitals. Inevitably this will move hospitals (and physicians) to a corporate style of practice management. Some teaching or specialty hospitals with a protected market niche may resist standardization of the process of care. But that is where the health industry is going, and where you will find the New Hospital—in the vanguard.

REFERENCES AND SUGGESTED READINGS

Brozovich, John P., and Shortell, Stephen M. "How to Create More Humane and Productive Health Care Environments." *Health Care Management Review*, Fall 1984, pp. 43–53.

Clifford, Donald K., and Cavanagh, Richard E. *Winning Performance: How America's High-Growth Midsize Companies Succeed.* New York: Bantam, 1985.

*Coile, Russell C., Jr., Longe, Mary E., and Dizon, John O. "Computer Conferencing: A Technology Ahead of Its Users." *Hospital Forum* 27, no. 6 (November/December 1984):20–22.

*Dobrzynski, Judith H., Peterson, Thane, and Armstrong, Larry. "Fighting Back: Some Companies Are Finding Ways to Keep Japan from Always Winning." *Business Week*, August 26, 1985, pp. 62–68.

Drucker, Peter. *The Changing World of the Executive*. New York: Truman Talley/Times Books, 1982.

*Edid, Marilyn. "A New Labor Era May Dawn at G.M.'s Saturn." *Business Week*, July 22, 1985, pp. 65–66.

*Geneen, Harold. *Managing*. New York: Doubleday, 1984.

Grove, Andrew S. *High-Output Management*. New York: Random House, 1983

*Johansen, Robert, Vallee, Jacques, and Spangler, Kathleen. *Electronic Meetings*. Reading, Mass.: Addison-Wesley, 1979.

Maccoby, Michael. *The Leader*. New York: Simon and Schuster, 1981.

*Magaziner, Ira C., and Reich, Robert B. *Minding America's Business*. New York: Harcourt Brace Jovanovich, 1982.

O'Toole, James. *Vanguard Management*. New York: Doubleday, 1985.

*Peters, Tom, and Austin, Nancy. *A Passion for Excellence*. New York: Random House, 1985.

*"The Revival of Productivity." *Business Week*, February 13, 1984, pp. 92–100.

*Thurow, Lester C. "Top-Heavy Management Stifles Productivity." *Los Angeles Times*, September 15, 1985.

Tibbitts, Samuel J. "Vision." 1983 Annual Report, Lutheran Hospital Society of Southern California, Los Angeles.

*Suggested reading.

Chapter 20

High-Performance Organizations

20

Futurist Leland Kaiser believes tomorrow's most successful health care companies will be high-performance organizations (HPO). These industry leaders have a continuously expanding potential. What do they do right? They possess a combination of the key characteristics for success in the future. High-performance organizations are self-initiating and self-designing. HPOs thrive on competition and crisis. They are successful because they provide an opportunity for fulfillment: aligning personal and organizational goals. HPOs are future-oriented. They can't wait for tomorrow.

High-performance organizations are templates that the rest of the industry will imitate. HPOs are the true leaders. There is no one path to becoming an HPO. The characteristics of each HPO are unique combinations, suited to each company's environment and consistent with its vision of the future. For each health care corporation there is a unique tao (the way in Eastern philosophy) to becoming a high-performance organization.

CHARACTERISTICS OF HIGH-PERFORMANCE
ORGANIZATIONS

The health industry is in its adolescence. That is the good news, not the bad news. There are only a half dozen hospital corporations among the Fortune 500 companies, and yet health is the second largest employer industry in the United States. There is an enormous opportunity for growth and development. Those health organizations that can and will learn from the experience of others will prosper. There are characteristics of the most successful companies—the high performance organizations—that can be identified, transferred, and adapted to our industry.

237

Foresight. Foresight is the awareness—the critical awareness—of the environment. It is a process of continuously monitoring the environment for change, looking for both threats and opportunities. Security Pacific—the "Looking Forward" bank—is an example of a successful company that has invested in futures research and is committed to change. Security Pacific has leveraged itself from a regional bank to the sixth largest national bank, in part because it was among the first banks to take a major position in consumer finance. McDonald's also has a futures research and issues management program. McDonald's believes in staying close to the customer, and it is the most successful franchise organization in the world.

Potency. Potency is power, the might to do right. Resources are the key factor, and first among these is capital. Access to capital is widely recognized as one of the primary factors for the success of investor-owned health care corporations, and probably the driving force for development of not-for-profit systems like American Health Care Systems (AHS) and Voluntary Hospitals of America (VHA). Hospital Corporation of America became the largest private health care company in the world because it had the multimillion dollar capital with which to buy the second largest health company. Now the price tag for acquiring major hospital systems is billions. HPOs need potency to fuel rapid growth and diversification. Those with it will prosper; those without will wither.

Image. The high-performance organization has a clear image, both internally and in its marketplace. Employees and customers know what the company stands for: the quality of its products, the integrity of its people, and its business mission. This is particularly a problem for the large, diversified company that does not have a central, consistent self-image. A company with a standout image is IBM, consistently among the top 10 of Fortune magazine's 250 most admired companies. IBM stands for integrity and customer service, and its products command premium prices. Hewlett-Packard believes its reputation for quality is a strategic weapon. Procter & Gamble vaunts its marketing prowess for decades of high performance. Their image reflects their success.

Position. Positioning is power of another kind, the marketplace of strategic positioning for maximum advantage. It has to do with timing of initiatives, risk taking when windows of opportunity open, and sufficient strength to follow through to take advantage of the opportunity. IBM's 16-bit personal computer (PC) came on the market at precisely the right time, enabling IBM to set the industry standard and achieve a 30 percent market share in barely 18 months from product introduction. Many of the top performers in the McKinsey & Co. study of 750 midspeed growth companies gained their leadership status by finding and servicing niches within vertical markets (Cavanagh and Clifford 1985).

Flexibility. In an increasingly turbulent environment, where uncertainty is higher and product life cycles shorter, organizational flexibility is a must. Flexibility means the willingness to experiment with organizational design as often as the environment changes. Zero-base organizational design means developing organizational structures without preconditions—the ability to change in the face of psychological and organizational investments in the status quo. General Electric—selected in 1983 as the best-managed Fortune 500 company—decided its business is not electronics or appliances. GE's self-chosen mission is creating new businesses. National Medical Enterprises (NME), one of the nation's five largest multihospital companies, never limited itself to hospitals. Instead NME has diversified broadly into nursing homes, durable medical equipment, and insurance. Today more than 50 percent of NME's profits come from its nonhospital product lines.

Electricity. There is something special in the atmosphere of a high-performance organization. People are excited at the prospect of coming to work. There is a sense of electricity in the air—of change, growth, and opportunity. An example of companies with electricity is 3M. Innovation and new product line development are its forte. One of the hottest new products of the 1980s is 3M's yellow post-it note. It's everywhere. Engineers at 3M don't hide their new designs at the end of each business day. Prototypes are left out, for other engineers to play with them and cross-fertilize ideas. Employees can't wait to get to work at Trammell Crow. This real estate development company has dozens of millionaires among its employees. Ten percent of profits are channeled back into employee incentives and even secretaries have become rich. There is a heady atmosphere at Trammell Crow: the smell of enterprise and success.

Myths and Stories. All the great organizations have heroes and champions. Their heroic success stories are told and retold, an oral history that provides continuity over generations of employees. Myths and stories are about persistence demonstrated in the face of incredible odds. Frito-Lay has a record of 99 percent effectiveness in delivering fresh chips to 50,000 locations—each and every day, despite blizzards and obstacles of all kinds. Mary Kay of Mary Kay Cosmetics, in her pink Cadillac, is a legend in her own time. While the cosmetics conglomerate is a highly personalized organization, it is also one of the most highly successful direct-sales companies in America. Mary Kay rewards everyone at every level. Even the most casual visitor to a Mary Kay weekly rally will be drawn into the circle and initiated with pink ribbons, gold pins, and recognition. And they never talk of failure at Mary Kay, only success.

Technique. One dominant characteristic of high-performance organizations is their technique. They are good at what they do. They are consistently better than their competition. They are cost-efficient, and it is always desirable to be a low-cost producer. They are effective and they are productive. The Los Angeles Dodgers is baseball's most successful franchise since 1960. The Dodgers sell over 4 million tickets each season and presell nearly 40,000 season tickets in the 57,000-seat stadium owned by the ball club. This team is a winner, finishing first or second in the division 7 of 10 years from 1975 to 1985.

Vision. First and last, a high-performance organization has a vision of its preferred future. As the CEO of Samuel J. Tibbitts (1983), the Lutheran Hospital Society of Southern California believes, "Tomorrow's successful health organizations will be those who create their vision of the future, and build towards it." Vision is the gift of intuitive leaders to their organizations. It is a compound of art and science, based on foresight. Vision is the ability to perceive opportunities and take the risks to achieve them. This is the role of the master strategist that every company needs to achieve greatness. These core values drive the company, rather than simply allowing it to be pushed around by the marketplace and competitors. It is the quality of vision that differentiates the intentional organization from the accidental organization.

HIGH-PERFORMANCE PLANNING AND MANAGEMENT

Strategies for high-performance organizations are developed through a four-step process illustrated in Figure 20–1.

Foresight and Farsight

Becoming a high-performance organization begins with futures awareness: scanning the future environment to identify future trends and key factors in tomorrow's health care environment. That is balanced by an inner awareness, developed through an organizational self-assessment of strengths and weaknesses. The third critical factor is the organization's preferences, the concept of intentionality. Where does the organization envision its preferred position in tomorrow's environment? Once an organization has achieved this awareness through foresight, it can begin to practice farsight—managing by aligning the three processes of future scanning, self-awareness, and organizational visioning.

Figure 20–1 High-Performance Planning and Management

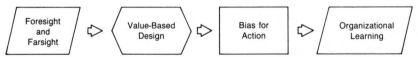

Value-Based Design

Phase 2 is the design process—the design of the business, marketing and sales strategies, management systems, and the organizational structure—based on corporate values. Values are one of the most important keys to high performance, maximizing the close linkage between personal and organizational values. Brozovich and Shortell (1984) argue that organizational design must be based on values. Their experiment in a Wisconsin community hospital demonstrates the utility of value-based design.

Values are the deep-seated, pervasive standards that influence every aspect of life: moral judgment, commitment, motivation, and pursuit of lifetime goals. Organizations, too, have values. Virtually all of America's high-performance organizations have a common trait: a core set of values. These value-driven organizations, like Hewlett-Packard, have a pervasive management concept and philosophy that infuses every aspect of their operations. High-performance organizations believe their uniqueness and capacity to be competitive in their market is fundamentally based on their human resources.

Value-based design begins with a review of alternative scenarios of the organization in alternative future environments. Each scenario provides an alternative design for achievement of organizational goals under different market conditions. Optimization analysis is the application of the tools of cost-benefit analysis to the preferred scenario: how the organization can optimize the path to the intended future at minimum cost with maximum effect, consistent with its core values. Optimization analysis looks at the treats and opportunities in the preferred scenario—the risk factors, cost factors, human and organizational factors—and which design will give maximum advantage from its strengths and minimize damage from its weaknesses. Optimization analysis is the opportunity to take advantage of decision support and the new decision analysis tools. Strategic management by objectives (MBO) is the development of action plans and objectives consistent with the optimal design for achievement of organizational goals, be they growth, rate of return, or market position.

Bias for Action

High-performance organizations have a bias for action. The successful organizations align planning with management, so that resource allocation—that critical first step—is the commitment of organizational resources to carry out the plan. If the optimization analysis has been done well, the resource allocation will be optimal. Where the tire meets the road is putting the product on service to the test of the market: does it sell? The third important phase of action—which health care organizations have been insensitive to in the past—is the promotion and marketing phase. Hospitals now understand the importance of marketing. Value-based marketing infuses the hospital's beliefs into its advertising, to differentiate the hospital vis-à-vis competitors by promoting its distinctive values such as customer service and premium quality.

Organizational Learning

Becoming a high-performance organization is a continuous process of organizational learning. The fourth phase of HPO strategic planning and management is evaluation, making a critical analysis of how new products and services have fared in the marketplace. The New Hospital faces considerable risk in product development. Designing an evaluation process that takes an early look at consumer response provides insurance that the organization will not take a bath with a new product or service. The assessment process generates hard information on market experience against forecasts of consumer acceptance, sales, market penetration, unit cost, and initial profitability (or loss) levels.

The realignment phase takes advantage of the new information that has been gained from the assessment to redesign the product, to optimize further the production and sales process, or to customize the product or service to make it more responsive to consumer preferences. The final phase of this process has two strategic choices: (1) product elimination or (2) product life cycle renewal, taking an existing product as the market evolves, adding to it, modifying it and spinning its successor using the profits from today's product to finance the next generation of products and services. Hospitals that fail to evolve will drift badly, while those willing to face risk and failure—and charge as often as needed—will thrive.

FUTURE HPOs

There are many paths to the future for the New Hospital that seeks to be a high-performance organization. Here are options for future HPOs:

- Boundary-jumper. The organization that can break the paradigm—the mindset—of all other organizations in its market and industry will be the leader of the next generation of businesses. The first nonprofit hospital organization that created a for-profit subsidiary was a boundary jumper. So was the first to buy a nursing home or home health agency, open a health food restaurant, or start an unrelated business. The first health organization that sees itself in the information industry instead of the health industry will be a boundary-jumper. Sears was a boundary-jumper when it decided it was in the consumer services business rather than retail sales and acquired Coldwell Banker to provide its real estate services. Imagine the scenario if the giant Sears conglomerate decided to invade health insurance or health care.

- Cosmopolite. The cosmopolites are the multinational organizations that will have the potency, desire, and savoir-faire to operate in the international marketplace. There are enormous risks in the global market, and there are also some large potential profits. The cosmopolites will be those health organizations that have the political and cultural sensitivity, combined with their capital and management expertise, to be successful outside their established environment. The U.S. health industry has a surplus of capacity and will seek new markets. Think of the potential in countries like India, Taiwan, Japan, even China.

- Star seeker. The star seekers are those who are not limited by today's vision. Star seekers will conceive totally new strategies and take risks in uncharted waters. Who will be first to practice corporate medicine, by controlling case management parameters through the artificial intelligence of the computer? Who will have the hospital without beds? Who will have the health care conglomerate that does not own a hospital? Who will operate the first satellite clinic in space? These are the star seekers, who will make the first leaps into the unknown, beyond the limits of today's strategic imagination.

ALIVE WITH POTENTIAL

The health industry is in enormous transition. Five of the top 20 hospital companies did not exist in 1980. In 1985 fewer than 40 percent of America's hospitals were formally aligned in multiunit systems. In 10 years that percentage may double. Enormous opportunities lie ahead. Most hospitals have been satisfied with net profitability levels of 5 to 6 percent, low by the standards of most industries. Some HPOs in the hospital industry have achieved greater than 25 percent annual returns, coupled with double-digit growth rates. The first rule of the game the New Hospital will play is to throw the old rules away. The old limits and the old paradigm are gone.

The health industry is young, and the future is alive with possibilities for the high-performance organization.

REFERENCES AND SUGGESTED READINGS

Brozovich, John P., and Shortell, Stephen M. "How to Create More Humane and Productive Health Care Environments." *Health Care Management Review*, Fall 1984, pp. 43–53.

Cavanagh, Richard E., and Clifford, Donald K., Jr. "Lessons from America's Midsized Growth Companies." *McKinsey Quarterly*, Autumn 1983.

*Deal, Terrence E., and Kennedy, Allen A. *Corporate Cultures*. Reading, Mass.: Addison-Wesley, 1982.

*Deal, Terrence E., Kennedy, Allen A., and Spiegel, Arthur H., III. "How to Create an Outstanding Hospital Culture." *Hospital Forum*, January/February 1982, pp. 24–31.

*Galbraith, Jay R. "Designing the Innovating Organization." *Organizational Dynamics*, Winter 1982, pp. 5–25.

*Johnson, Kathryn E., and Berger, Judith D. "The Entrepreneurial Spirit." *Future Perspectives*. Washington, D.C.: Foundation of Association Executives, 1985, pp. 133–147.

*Kaiser, Leland R. "Organizational Cultures—Sensitive Managers Can Improve the Working Environment." *Hospital Forum*, March/April 1982, pp. 13–17.

*Kaiser, Leland R. "Innovation in the Hospital." *Hospital Forum*, March/April 1981, pp. 7–11.

*Levering, Robert, Moskowitz, Milton, and Katz, Michael. *The 100 Best Companies to Work for in America*. New York: Addison-Wesley, 1984.

*O'Toole, James. *Vanguard Management*. New York: Doubleday, 1985.

*Ouchi, William G. *Theory Z*. New York: Addison-Wesley, 1981.

*Peters, Tom, and Austin, Nancy. *A Passion for Excellence*. New York: Random House, 1985.

*Pinchot, Gifford, III. *Intrapreneuring*. New York: Harper & Row, 1985.

*Strum, Dennis W., and Coile, Russell C., Jr. "Transferring Lessons from High Performance Organizations." *Hospital Forum*, May/June, 1984, pp. 62–64.

Tibbitts, Samuel J. "Vision." 1983 Annual Report Lutheran Hospital Society of Southern California, Los Angeles.

*Timmel, Ned, and Brozovich, John. "Managing through Values." *Hospital Forum*, May/June 1984, pp. 31–39.

*Vaill, Peter. "The Purposing of High-Performance Systems." *Organizational Dynamics*, Autumn 1982, pp. 23–39.

---

*Suggested reading.

Chapter 21
Transition Management

21

If John Naisbitt, author of the best-selling *Megatrends* (1982) is right, this is "a time of parenthesis"—when the old industrial society is waning and a new socioeconomic order is being established. It is a watershed period, affecting many values and ways of thinking.

Look at the signals of change. Intermountain Health Systems, a nonprofit multihealth corporation, joint ventures a hospital project with for-profit giant Hospital Corporation of America. Catholic orders sell their hospitals to for-profit chains in Omaha and Nebraska, and for a profit. Greatwest Hospitals in California sells its hospitals to purchase a Michigan HMO and becomes Health Care USA, a national health maintenance organization.

In these changing times, Americans are rewriting the rulebooks of business and life. Yankelovich's book, *New Rules* (1981), is based on a nationwide survey of consumer beliefs and preferences. It affirms what many suspected already: rising consumer skepticism (public interest Nader groups), declining confidence in established institutions (alternative schools, wellness healers), and cutting out the middleman (factory outlets, street merchants).

The underground economy is substantial. The Internal Revenue Service estimates that more than $250 billion in business takes place off the books, some 12 percent of all money earned legally. That estimate may be too low; it could be 25 to 35 percent of the gross national product in cash and barter. Even big businesses now routinely swap products and services with vendors, independently and through international barter brokers.

NO RULES

The health industry is likewise in transition. The first rule of the new game is there are no rules about who will do business with whom. The established

247

boundaries of professional domain are breaking down. In bucolic Battle Creek, Michigan, hospitals are erecting ambulatory care centers across the street from competitors. Medical staff in the San Fernando Valley, California, are building free-standing diagnostic imaging centers in competition with their own hospital. National Medical Enterprises proposes to joint venture a new private hospital with the University of Southern California.

In the face of uncertainty, organizations must be reprogrammed and renewed, repositioning themselves for the future—but which future? Each industry, each firm has many possible futures. The goal is to define the intentional future the organization wants and align new structures, market strategies, and products in the desired direction (Figure 21–1).

TRANSITION MANAGEMENT

Transition management is a planned, rational process. It considers the future as well as the present. The tools of transition management are market analysis, decision analysis, and strategic and capital planning. The products of transition management are a defined sense of purpose and organizational goals, strategic objectives, and an action program. Transition management builds on the organization's history and experience. It is seldom a dry or academic process.

When supermanager Harold Geneen took over ITT, it was a sleepy communications company with $766 million in business, more than half of it in telephone systems in South America. Geneen set a goal of an annual growth rate of 10 percent—and for an astonishing 58 consecutive quarters, he made it—transforming ITT into a $22 billion giant. Transition management is simply good management in a changing environment.

By the standards of modern business management Harold Geneen was a caveman. Geneen would bully his senior managers for hours in the pit, a huge conference table seating 150, where every one of ITT's 250 profit centers had to report quarterly. In contrast Peter Ueberroth, head of the Los Angeles Olympic Organizing Committee (LAOOC), accomplished the miraculous—making a profit on the Olympics—through his skills as a master diplomat. Never once was there an open fight during a meeting of the LAOCC, not for seven years. Different styles,

Figure 21–1 The Intentional Organization

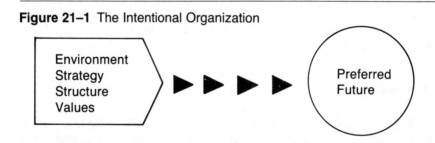

different strategies; each in their way, in their environment, and in their organization was appropriate and successful. In transition management there are four patterns (Figure 21–2).

Type 1: Venturer

The venturer manager takes advantage of any and all tactics that might generate new revenues or recover slipping margins. The venturer style is high energy and visibility. The trick is to convince everyone that the organization is dynamic, not dying. It is an opportunistic, entrepreneurial style. Not all the tactics may be thought through; problems may only be deferred. The venturer manager may sacrifice long-range growth and development for expedient problem solving.

RCA typifies the venturer style. Under its last four executives, each of whom pursued a different strategy, the company has been diversified, divested, directed toward long-term goals, and redirected toward short-term goals—all in the space of 10 years. Despite all that motion RCA's performance has remained marginal.

National Gypsum has been more successful, reaping the rewards for being bold when others went slow. During the recession of the early 1980s, Gypsum launched a $280 million expansion program while smaller competitors shut down. When housing starts rose, Gypsum was ready for the surge that pushed the wholesale price of wallboard from $2.09 in 1982 to $3.43 in 1984.

In the health industry Los Angeles-based Lutheran Hospital Society of Southern California (LHS) has been a whirlwind of entrepreneurship. In the process it has expanded from a pair of community hospitals to a multihospital system of more than 1,000 beds. LHS built or bought urgent care centers, long-term care programs, home health care, occupational and mental health programs, preferred provider organizations, and consulting services. Its health maintenance organization is California's fastest-growing HMO, with more than 100,000 members. Recently reorganized as LHS Corp, this health organization is not risk-adverse and strives to be among the first to take new directions.

Figure 21–2 Styles of Transition Management

	Short-Range	Long-Range
Proactive	Type 1 Venturer	Type 3 Developer
Reactive	Type 2 Guardsman	Type 4 Preservationist

Type 2: Guardsman

Of the four styles the guardsman is most concerned with protecting the status quo. The guardsman style is low visibility and conflict avoiding. The guardsman manager may choose a foxhole technique in the face of change, reducing staff and expenses to the minimum to stretch resources in hopes that the environment will improve. When the marketplace becomes turbulent, the guardsman style is to go slow and take few risks.

After the Del Webb Corporation went to the edge of financial disaster with an ill-conceived plan to expand its gambling casino business, this hotel chain is moving cautiously. In the process Del Webb sold two Nevada hotels, a block of Atlantic City real estate, and slashed debt from $280 to $92 million, finally putting the company back in the black in 1983. The company plans new business development but this time is staying closer to its base business.

Republic Health Corporation hopes to create a national hospital management company using the Guardsman philosophy. It buys facilities that are overweight with excess costs and debt. Turning losers into winners was a successful strategy for Hospital Affiliates International, acquired in 1981 by the Hospital Corporation of America, where key Republic executives learned the strategy. Assets of Republic ballooned from $19 million to $249 million in two years, while gross revenues grew tenfold. Republic's cost cutting has averaged 10 to 13 percent on the 18 hospitals it bought from HCA in 1983 and turned a predicted $6 million loss to a $4 million profit one year later.

Type 3: Builder

The builder style is an organization developer with a long-range perspective. The strategies are future-oriented, anticipating changes in the environment and moving boldly toward them. Builders broaden the base of business. They are willing to take risks on a multimillion dollar scale and to wait years for the payoff. The builder is not afraid to cut losses, close unprofitable divisions, shed clienteles, and root out deadwood. Investments in new systems yield future cost efficiencies for competitive advantage. Research brings new methods and products to keep it ahead of the industry.

Supermanager Roger Smith, chief executive officer of General Motors, is widely hailed for his leadership of the nation's number 1 automaker. Convinced that a technology-driven revolution is coming into auto manufacturing, Smith is injecting cutting-edge technology across GM's sprawling divisions. GM has invested $45 billion since 1980 in retooling and robotics. Seeking venture partners who could bring new technology to GM, the company is now making autos with Toyota and Isuzu. A joint venture with Japanese robot manufacturer Fanuc, Ltd., has resulted in a new company, GMFanuc, which is the leading U.S. robot vendor. Smith's $75 billion company made $3.7 billion last year, the biggest profit ever made in U.S. industry.

For years, believes Corporate President Richard Eamer, the stock of National Medical Enterprises, the nation's third-largest health chain, has been valued below competitors. NME's diversification activities made stock analysts nervous, as NME ventured away from its hospital business base into other health-related fields. NME bought Hillhaven, the second largest nursing home company, to give it a major position in long-term care. It acquired a number of companies to create new product lines in home health, durable medical equipment, ambulatory care and surgery, rehabilitation, psychiatric hospitals, and a health maintenance organization. Now that it has the pieces, founder Richard Eamer's strategy is integration. Despite a toughening economy for the health industry in 1984, NME posted 20 percent net revenues for the year. And hospitals were only responsible for 50 percent of its revenues.

Type 4: Preservationist

The preservationist approach is a careful and rational approach to conserve the long-range future of the organization. Strategy choices are more likely to reflect persistence than innovation. New directions may be ventured, but they must reflect the feel and traditions of the organization. The preservationist style is conservative. Competitors can be outlasted. The firm has the staying power and resources to withstand fluctuations in the marketplace. Preservationist managers like big deals with powerful allies. They build from within, seldom by acquisition, except at the megadeal level. Preservationist organizations are bureaucratic but powerful. The style fits best in industries where change is relatively slow or where the market is dominated by a few large firms.

When Esmark, Inc., put a price on its head by agreeing to a $2.4 billion leveraged buyout, market analysts picked Dart & Kraft as the logical company to jump in with a higher bid. But Dart & Kraft Chairman John Richman ruled out the Esmark bid in a matter of hours. He did not want the food giant to become a conglomerate. Dart & Kraft intends to increase earnings from the inside—developing new products, cutting costs, and increasing market share. The goal is 18 percent return on capital, up from today's 13.3 percent return. Kraft cut its European plants from 17 to 13 and divested its $500 million fresh milk business, whose performance had been lackluster. Although the food industry is rumbling with multibillion dollar mergers and acquisitions—such as Nestle's $3 billion takeover of Carnation—the Dart & Kraft Corporation is sticking to its knitting and its base business.

Medical Center Hospitals, a subsidiary of the Alliance Health System of Norfolk, Virginia, has a strongly traditional corporate culture. David Bernd, voted the young administrator of the year in 1984 by the American College of Hospital

Administrators, uses quality circles and task forces to increase efficiency. Bernd set a goal of zero rate increases; profits would come from managing expenses. To spur the involvement of managers, Bernd's Norfolk General Hospital created four teams to compete with business plans and bottom lines. The green team is drawn from cardiology, trauma, physical medicine, and psychiatry. Gold, red, and blue teams each represent significant clusters of hospital product lines. Norfolk General achieved a 4 percent net return last year, and Alliance Health System's $47 million bond issue was one of 10 hospital issues in the nation to get an AA rating.

HUMAN FACTORS IN TRANSITION: THE ANALOGY OF GRIEVING

Top managers often do not understand why, despite an urgent crisis and need to change, their organizations do not respond and move to meet the challenge. Berkeley-based organizational psychologist Robert Bramson uses the analogy of grieving to explain why human factors often impede transition management:

Stage 1: **Denial and isolation.** Initial feelings of it can't be true are a natural extension of the self-deception of immortality. During the denial phase individuals and organizations may continue business as usual despite the fact that it only defers needed action to begin adaptive activity.

Stage 2: **Anger.** When the first stage of denial cannot be maintained any longer, it gives way to feelings of anger, envy, and resentment. For those who devoted their life to their program or company, change is a bitter pill. Angry employees may ventilate in ways that are noisy or embarrassing to the organization.

Stage 3: **Bargaining.** The next phase, bargaining, may postpone the inevitable, however briefly. The phase usually does not last long; its only harm is that it delays acceptance and realistic action.

Stage 4: **Depression.** When the need for change can no longer be effectively denied and bargaining has not worked, anger is replaced with a sense of great loss. The result of these feelings of helplessness and loss is depression. But it counters irrational hope and brings understanding that bargaining is futile. During the depression phase, calls to action are still premature.

Stage 5: **Acceptance.** Acceptance of reality comes with time, as individuals and organizations work through the stages of grieving. The process can be facilitated with support and understanding but cannot be leapfrogged intellectually. Acceptance should not be mistaken for a happy stage, but it does provide a base on which individuals can act positively in their own behalf and the organization can initiate the needed changes to move into the future.

TRANSITION MANAGEMENT HALL OF FAME

Virtually every hero in *Fortune* magazine's hall of fame for U.S. business leadership overcame significant adversity in the climb to the top. One of the classic stories of transition management involves Ray Kroc, called the Henry Ford of the service sector. Kroc was a 52-year-old distributor of milkshake mixers when he met the McDonald brothers, operators of a small chain of hamburger stands based in San Bernardino, California. Kroc became their agent in recruiting new franchisees.

By 1961, feeling that the McDonald brothers were obstructing his efforts to expand the chain, he bought them out for $2.7 million, which he borrowed at exorbitant rates—the ultimate cost topping $14 million. Kroc's persistence paid off. At his death in 1984 he was worth more than $500 million. Which style of transition manager was Ray Kroc? He was a builder, for certain—a choice he made at age 60, proving that transition managers make their own futures.

TIME OF TRANSITION: COMPUTERIZING THE ORACLE

One of the oldest ways to foretell the future is the I Ching, a book of Chinese proverbs written 4,000 years ago. In the traditional version coins are thrown and the I Ching consulted on important decisions. Years of training were necessary to become a master of the art. A new software program, ORACLE, computerizes the I Ching for the information era. Is nothing sacred? When they start computerizing the wisdom of the ages, it is clear we live in a time of transition.

STRATEGIES FOR THE NEW HOSPITAL

Time for a change. It is widely recognized that the health industry is in a period of transition. Where the industry is heading is less certain. There are a number of scenarios, with the alternatives varying by region and political and economic factors. Health care managers have a reasonable question: Is this a time to act decisively or a time to wait to let the dust settle? Two things seem certain: those who act first have the first opportunity to be leaders in the new order and they also take the biggest risks. There is no right answer. In recently deregulated industries many companies underestimated how rapidly change would occur. There is a lesson here for hospitals: act now.

No one best way to manage transition. The private-sector experience with changing market conditions underscores there is no ideal way to manage under uncertainty. There are at least four effective management styles for transition. Each of them can be appropriate in a particular industry or situation. Think of them as a repertoire of strategies and tactics useful for a variety of conditions. The choice should be the individual manager's who knows the territory best and has differing comfort levels with various styles.

Contingency planning. The health industry may prefer to believe deregulation is coming, but it should be prudent enough to protect itself against reregulation. Legislative and governmental relations have slipped in hospitals' priorities in the past few years. The general shift toward conservative government in Washington and many state capitals only masks the central fact that government is a major purchaser of health care. Like all enterprises government is self-interested in managing its costs. The health industry needs to reinvigorate its governmental advocacy efforts and to maintain a reasonably consistent front against the regulators.

Human factors. The greatest single obstacle to change in the health industry is human nature. As the business of health care becomes more focused on business and less on health care, there is genuine resistance by the health professional rank and file. Change may be inevitable, but it will almost always be resisted. The more significant the turn in direction, the more prolonged may be the resistance. Plan for it, work through it, and take the time needed to bring all employees, medical staff, and trustees along.

REFERENCES AND SUGGESTED READINGS

*Bibeault, Donald B. *Corporate Turnaround*. New York: McGraw-Hill, 1982.

*Coile, Russell C. Jr. "Transition Management: A Guide to Agency Self-Preservation and Self-Renewal." San Francisco: Western Center for Health Planning, 1981.

*Coile, Russell C. Jr. "Human Factors in Transition Management." San Francisco: Western Center for Health Planning, 1982.

*"Dart & Kraft Turns Back to Its Basic Business—Food." *Business Week*, June 11, 1984.

*"General Motors Moves into a New Era." *Business Week*, July 16, 1984.

*Johnson, Donald E.L. "Managers with Participative Skills Will Thrive in Cost-Conscious Market." *Modern Healthcare*, March 1984.

*Kaiser, Leland R. "Living for Survival." San Francisco: Western Center for Health Planning, June 1982.

*Kimberly, John R., and Quinn, Robert E. *New Futures: The Challenge of Managing Corporate Transitions*. Homewood, Ill.: Dow Jones-Irwin, 1984.

*Kuntz, Esther Fritz. "HealthWest's Team Uses Management Specialties to Cook Up New Ventures." *Modern Healthcare*, November 1983.

*LaViolette, Suzanne. "Republic Trims Fat from Its Hospitals to Get Them in Shape for Competition." *Modern Healthcare*, December 1983.

*Levine, Charles H. "Organizational Decline and Cutback Management." *Public Administration Review*, July/August 1978.

*Louis, Arthur M. "Hall of Fame for U.S. Business Leadership." *Fortune*, April 4, 1983.

Naisbitt, John. *Megatrends*. New York: Warner Books, 1982.

*"National Gypsum: Reaping Its Reward after Stocking Up for the Recovery." *Business Week*, September 24, 1984.

*"The New Food Giants." *Business Week*, September 24, 1984.

*Punch, Linda. "DRG's First Six Months: Many Hospitals Are Doing Better Than They'd Expected." *Modern Healthcare*, June 1984.

*"RCA: Will it Ever Be a Top Performer?" *Business Week*, April 2, 1984.

*Rosenblatt, Robert A. "Underground Economy: $250 Billion; IRS Moves to Narrow Gap Generated by Tax Cheats." *Los Angeles Times*, December 13, 1984.

Yankelovich, Daniel. *New Rules*. New York: Random House, 1981.

---

*Suggested reading.

Part IV

Scenarios for the Year 2001

Chapter 22
Designing the Future

22

Future scenarios can illuminate what all this means for tomorrow. While no one scenario of the future will likely become dominant, each illustrates an extreme. The future will be a mix of trends and conditions. There will be distinct regional variations, and micromarkets may be contrary to the larger environment. The managers of tomorrow's health care organizations must be sensitive to these differences and be flexible in corporate design and management methods. The challenge of coaligning the New Hospital with the changing environment, as James Thompson (1967) put it, is shooting at a moving target from horseback—a process of continual adjustment.

When futurists talk about the future, they frequently use scenarios to bring it to life. Projections, assumptions, and expert estimates are artfully blended in a dramatic fashion to illustrate a set of future options. The scenarios read like science fiction, with an important difference. They are carefully constructed, sometimes at considerable expense, to guide present actions toward a desired future.

In the health field three studies generated alternative scenarios for the future of the health care system beyond the year 2020, as outlined in Table 22–1. The TAP and Health Futures Project (TAP 1980) scenarios are especially well-developed. Each is based on data and expert opinion to illuminate and extend already evident trends. The forecasts of the Health Futures Project are based on four social and economic scenarios, which are composites of data sets originally developed by the Stanford Research Institute and Professor James Dator. The TAP scenarios have been expanded to include a fourth possibility, the conglomerates scenario and linked it to the four economic futures developed by the Health Futures Project, into an integrated set (Table 22–2).

Each of the four scenarios for the health care system in the year 2001 will be described briefly to illustrate how present trends can lead to different alternative environments.

Table 22–1 Health Industry Scenario Developers

Scenario Developer	Scenario 1	Scenario 2	Scenario 3	Scenario 4
Trends Analysis Program (TAP)	Medical technology	Wellness	National health	
Health Futures Project	Continued growth	Transformation	Disciplined society	Decline and stagnation
Edmunds	Curative	Counsel on technology	Mysticism Good living	Private entrepreneurship

Table 22–2 Health Care 2001: Four Scenarios

Scenario	Socioeconomic Futures	Future Health Care Systems
Scenario 1	Coming boom	High-technology
Scenario 2	Completion	Conglomerates
Scenario 3	Reregulation	Cost control
Scenario 4	Voluntary simplicity	Wellness

SCENARIO 1: HIGH-TECHNOLOGY

Technological advances have eradicated many diseases, and by the year 2001 society appears to be on the verge of overcoming death itself. Genetic engineering has virtually eliminated birth defects. Improved tranquilizers have reduced mental health problems and eliminated state mental hospitals. Space explorations have stimulated another cycle of bioengineering advances. Brain-machine and body-machine interfaces through miniaturized computers extend human potential far beyond what was thought possible. Breakthrough technologies that eliminate handicaps are extended to areas such as heart replacements and elimination of senility through neurotransplants.

The price for technological solutions is steep, requiring more than 20 percent of the gross national product for health. There is an active public-private partnership between the federal government and private industry, with joint funding of third-sector organizations in new health industries like genetic engineering, sharing the profits between them. The computer has replaced the physician as the primary diagnostician and therapist, with nurse practitioners and other paraprofessionals providing much of the hands-on care. Cable television and personal computers provide the linkage for routine health care, especially of the chronically ill. The use of hospital clinics and emergency rooms have declined dramatically as consumers use cable TV and two-way in-home communications to ask health questions and are given health advice by remote care givers.

Although there are complaints by some who claim technology has eroded the citizen's abilities to take care of their own health, most are willing to pay the price for the benefits of high technology.

SCENARIO 2: CONGLOMERATES

Continuing economic stagnation and decline are the conditions that bring about real competition in the health care marketplace in the 1980s and 1990s. The number of hospital failures is smaller than expected, but many fall prey to takeover by one of the megasystems that come to dominate the health care scene. By the year 2001 four multinational corporations have emerged.

HMO International is the giant of health maintenance organizations, with 50 million life care subscribers dependent on the health care conglomerate. When the federal government withdrew its funding and special incentives for HMOs in the late 1980s, the plan picked up a number of bankrupt or undercapitalized HMOs for a few cents on the dollar. Now giant of its field, HMO International is negotiating with Great Britain to take over its health system.

The second conglomerate, International Medical Enterprises, is the result of a joint venture between several of the largest proprietary hospital chains and commercial insurance carriers that occurred in the late 1980s when the indemnity companies saw the handwriting on the wall. IME controls almost half of the nation's hospitals, but only about 35 percent of the beds, running them consistently above 80 percent occupancy.

Associated Health Network is the third major health corporation, the result of a merger of Blue Cross with several of the largest nonprofit multiinstitutional systems. It is running second in profitability to IME.

The fourth megasystem, American Health Federation, has been organized by the American Hospital Association as a national health care corporation in a joint venture with the American Medical Association. Lack of effective controls over hospital use and costs, however, is undermining its financial viability, and by the year 2001 American Health Federation is tottering on the edge of financial disaster. The federal government operates the fifth megasystem, Fedcare, having consolidated the Veterans Hospitals with the Department of Defense facilities into one national military health system.

In this scenario public hospitals have disappeared, either closed or sold off by financially beleaguered governments. Consumers get what they can pay for, and the poor now get fewer doctor visits and have longer hospital stays than the middle class. Technology such as organ transplants is available but expensive. Many large employers have differential health benefits. Executive policies cover much more than rank-and-file workers have been able to negotiate.

Business coalitions in a number of urban areas developed joint purchasing agreements with local hospital systems. They drove the price of hospital care down and reduced hospital use significantly. The problem of cost shifting has reversed, with the federal government now paying more than its share of Medicare and Medicaid in the states that have still not enacted mandatory hospital rate review to achieve equity among payers.

In this competitive marketplace customers must look out for their own self-interests. The megasystems' caveat emptor attitude has reinforced wider public recognition of the importance of life styles, and modest gains in life expectancy have resulted. Despite increasing competition health is still a growth industry, taking 15 percent of GNP. Cancer and heart disease have declined, despite the absence of breakthrough medical technologies before the year 2001.

SCENARIO 3: REREGULATION

In the third scenario government has intervened on the public's behalf to provide health care services. The mixed regulatory strategies of employing both cost controls and competition were inadequate to prevent a breakdown in the health care system and the economy in the late 1980s. Frustrated that medical costs continued to rise at more than double the consumer price index, the federal administration in 1990 instituted mandatory rate review and price control for all Medicare and Medicaid patients. Within five years governmental control had been extended to all patients, and the public takeover of the health care system accelerated.

The proprietary hospital chains were early victims of the rate freeze. As their profits declined drastically, the chains lobbied for a federal buy-out. Congress provided a one-time fund of $100 billion, and both proprietaries and hard-pressed community hospitals took advantage of the program. More than 2,500 of the nation's 6,000 hospitals were acquired in a brief period, and only a few were kept open. Persistent governmental pressures on rates forced most other nonprofit and municipal hospitals to throw in the towel and voluntarily surrender to public takeover, with the federal government buying out their debt. In less than 10 years only 15 percent of the nation's hospitals were still in private ownership.

Physicians have become salaried employees, bargaining in guilds and unions with their public employers. Clinical trials are now required by federal legislation to determine which therapies are actually effective, and impact statements are required for new technologies or policies before they can be initiated.

Even before the year 2000 the government began to intervene directly in the individual health decisions. Risk and cost-benefit analysis was required for costly therapies, with centralized rationing and control. The convergence of health data systems into one public system made possible preventive interventions with families and individuals. Those with antisocial or criminal tendencies are now monitored and controlled. Genetic engineering ensures against birth defects. Cost control has been achieved by direct governmental action. While there are persistent problems of queuing and shortages, the public is generally adapted to the national health system in the year 2001.

SCENARIO 4: WELLNESS

In the fourth scenario a cultural transformation toward voluntary simplicity has had a pervasive influence in reforming health attitudes. The wellness movement symbolizes the gains of this new social ethic.

Recognizing the physical and environmental etiology of disease, a shift was made beginning in the 1980s away from a disease oriented medical system to health enhancement. Employers, recognizing the contributions of work place stress and health hazards, have taken responsibility to eliminate them.

Hospitals have shrunk dramatically in numbers and importance except for a few regional repair centers. Most others, including the venerable Mayo Clinic, have become health education and fitness centers. Decentralization among the provider organizations results in a cottage system of health programs accessible to those who need them. Health insurance and public payment systems like Medicare now spend less than 25 percent on hospital and institutional health services. Health education, fitness, and mental health programs receive most of the nation's health investment.

The payoff is already evident by the year 2001: life expectancy gains plus major declines in chronic illnesses have resulted in dramatic improvements in productivity within the overall economy. Rising consciousness about diet, life style, and the mind and body connection has reduced mortality rates. A new respect for the environment has dramatically enhanced the quality of life. The wellness system has successfully encouraged people to take effective responsibility for their own health.

PLANNING FOR ALTERNATIVE FUTURES

Which of these futures will occur? All are possible, but in their extreme form, none are likely to dominate as clearly as the scenarios suggest. Signals of each of these possible futures are evident today.

The New Hospital can choose which of these scenarios, or others, would be preferable. Which is best aligned with the organization's vision of its own future? What strategies and structures create the paths to the preferred future? How should the organization hedge its bets and plan for contingencies? What wild card events could spoil even the best-laid plans?

There is a pervasive concern that the best days of the hospital industry are over. What is true is the golden age of cost reimbursement is finished. The door of competition is open, and there is no closing it. For the New Hospital the path to the future will not be found in the rear-view mirror. To quote one of America's most-admired social observers, humorist Will Rogers, "The future lies ahead."

REFERENCES AND SUGGESTED READINGS

*Ackoff, Russell L. *Creating the Corporate Future*. New York: John Wiley & Sons, 1981.

*Bennis, Warren G., Benne, Kenneth D., and Chin, Robert, eds. *The Planning Of Change*. New York: Holt, Rinehart & Winston, 1961.

Bezold, Clement, and Goldschmidt, Peter G. "Health Futures Project." Washington, D.C.: Institute for Alternative Futures, 1980.

*Cetron, Marvin, and O'Toole, Thomas. *Encounters with the Future: A Forecast of Life into the 21st Century*. New York: McGraw-Hill, 1983.

*Coile, Russell C. Jr. "Forecast 85." Futures Program, Center for Health Management Research, Lutheran Hospital Society of Southern California, Los Angeles, California, March 1984.

"Health Care: Three Reports from 2030 A.D." Trends Analysis Program, American Council of Life Insurance, Washington, D.C., TAP 19, Spring 1980.

*Jaeger, B. Jon. "The Concept of Corporate Planning." *Health Care Management Review*, Summer 1982, pp. 19–27.

*Johnson, Richard L. "Old Memories and New Dreams: Economies for Non-Profit Hospitals." *Health Matrix* 3, no. 1 (Spring 1985):15–21.

*Kimberly, John R., and Quinn, Robert E. *New Futures: The Challenge of Managing Corporate Transitions*. Homewood, Ill.: Dow Jones-Irwin, 1984.

*Koehn, Hank. "Medicine in the 21th Century: A Snapshot Scenario." Security Pacific National Bank, Los Angeles, California, December 1981.

*Nanus, Burt. "Quest—Quick Environmental Scanning Technique." *Long Range Planning* 15, no. 2 (April 1982):39–45.

*Ney, Jan, and Coile, Russell C. Jr. "Forecast 86." Center for Health Management Research, Lutheran Hospital Society of Southern California, Los Angeles, California, 1985.

*Pointer, Dennis. "Preparing for the New Age." *Hospital Forum*, November/December 1984, pp. 60–61.

*Scheffler, Richard M., et al. "Future Scenarios for the Economy and the Health Care System." Institute of Medicine, Washington, D.C., Background paper 20, 1982.

*Schmid, Gregory, and Poulin, Mary. "Health Care Services Environment: Hospital Utilization to 1995." Final Report to the Robert Wood Johnson Foundation, Institute for the Future, Menlo Park, California, June 1983.

*Selbert, Roger. "Less Medicine = More Health." *Future Scan*. Futures Research Division, Security Pacific National Bank, Los Angeles, no. 443, August 19, 1985.

*Steiner, George A. *Strategic Planning: What Every Manager Must Know*. New York: Free Press, 1979.

Thompson, James D. *Organizations in Action*. New York: McGraw-Hill, 1967.

*"Toward an Unlimited Future: A Report of the Global One Hundred.'' Business International Corporation, New York, August 1983.

*Wilner, Diane. ''Scenario-Building: A Tool for Shaping the Future.'' *Hospital Forum*, November/ December 1984, pp. 57–59.

*Wilson, Ian H. ''Scenarios.'' In *Handbook of Futures Research*, edited by Jib Fowles. Westport, Conn.: Greenwood Press, 1978.

---

*Suggested reading.

Chapter 23

Failures of Foresight

23

In the future the margin for strategic error will be smaller, and the price for failure will be higher. The largest default in municipal bond history occurred in 1984, when the Washington Public Power Supply System (WPPSS) announced it could not make the first payment on $2.25 billion in bonds. The syndicate put together to underwrite the WPPSS bonds contained some of the biggest names on Wall Street: Merrill Lynch, Goldman Sachs, Salomon Brothers, Smith Barney, Blyth Eastman, and Paine Webber. Virtually every brokerage house of any size participated in the huge offerings. The cost of the project was spread across 88 utilities in the Pacific Northwest. Each had signed a contract promising to pay— even if the new nuclear power facilities were never built—but only two utilities had made any payments to WPPSS, totaling a bare $9,435.

The WPPSS project was conceived to meet the electric power needs of the Northwest into the twenty-first century. It fell victim to the growing antinuclear movement, compounded by mismanagement and horrendous cost overruns in construction costs. Finally, construction was halted in 1983 on the first two nuclear plants. The WPPSS project teetered, looking in vain for a Chrysler-style federal bailout, then went down for good.

Rumors of impending trouble were rife in the industry for at least three years before default. Like the Titanic, everyone believed the WPPSS project was too big to be allowed to sink. The "WHOOPS" fiasco left egg all over the biggest faces on Wall Street.

ENERGY POLICY: A FAILURE OF FORESIGHT

The WPPSS default did not happen overnight. Today's energy situation is the result of a failure of foresight—not because current conditions could not be anticipated—but because the United States did not act on available foresight. There is no critical energy shortage today, but another repeat of the oil crisis of 1974 is predicted as early as 1990.

In this time when America should be preparing for an energy-gap future, it has instead become even more dependent on foreign oil. Gasoline consumption is returning to 1974 levels as consumers lose the sense of urgency about conservation. Nuclear power is not being increased. The antinuclear movement has brought the nuclear industry to its knees. No new plants are on the drawing boards, and older plants are not being replaced.

New initiatives in solar, wind, and geothermal energy are out of political favor. Private-sector development of synthetic fuels has been canceled as not financially feasible. Pilot synfuel projects have been written off at considerable expense by Exxon and other oil companies that tried to implement the president's energy independence strategy.

Shortages Widely Predicted

Before the massive disruption of the oil embargo in 1973–74, many forecasts indicated that U.S. dependence on foreign oil was growing at an alarming rate. There was little variation among nearly 20 public and private organizations analyzing energy consumption.

This gloomy consensus among experts was worsened by their realization that nuclear energy was coming along more slowly than expected (in fact, it would slow to a halt by 1981). The experts saw this clearly in the early 1970s, yet it was impossible to alert a sleeping America to the potential criticality of the emerging conditions. In 1973, when President Nixon declared a major energy crisis, many thought his action was a political ploy designed to distract attention from Watergate.

Forecasters' Mistakes

Once the oil crisis had galvanized the attention of American consumers and Congress, President Carter launched an energy independence initiative across a broad front. Numerous alternatives would be explored. The private sector made major capital investments in support of the new policy.

Unfortunately forecasts by both the National Academy of Engineering and Project Independence were nowhere near their targets. The former overestimated the power of technology and the latter the power of the price mechanism.

Other serendipitous factors helped postpone round 2 of the forecasted energy crunch. The natural gas shortage was not as bad as originally feared. Mexican, North Sea, and Alaska oil came along on schedule. OPEC's stranglehold on supply eroded as the Arab coalition split. The willingness of Saudi Arabia to break with OPEC made foreign oil reasonably plentiful. Consumers eased their consumption rates of power and gasoline. Oil prices actually fell, and at least a temporary glut of oil developed, which held down gas prices in the mid-1980s.

Foresight versus Farsight

If it's not raining, who needs an umbrella? That attitude is understandable but dangerously shortsighted. Americans today are skeptical of doomsday forecasts of another energy crisis ahead. The experience of the 1970s should make it quite clear that long-term energy conditions will not right themselves without major policy interventions. No forces in the world economic system will bring all energy supply and demand into balance painlessly.

Selwyn Enzer (1979) of the USC Center for Futures Research believes we have too much foresight (the predictions of experts) and not enough farsight (real understanding of how alternative futures may occur and could be influenced). As the events at Three-Mile Island demonstrate, too much certainty (foresight) can block the development of a farsighted posture. Since the experts thought the possibility of a meltdown remote, there was no plan for such a contingency (farsight).

EARLY WARNING

Disaster seldom strikes entirely without warning. Strategic planning and prudent management look for early signs of change in market conditions, consumer preferences, new technology. When a company declares itself insolvent, it usually blames a single disaster that no one could have predicted. In many instances the problems were long in coming and no surprise to anyone. Yet somehow the enterprise failed.

Early warning signs of danger abound. Financial consultant C.J. Thompson (1982) outlines a checklist for possible corporate insolvency:

Management

- board out of balance with business
- board with minimal responsibility
- overreliance on management

Operations

- overtrading
- erosion of margins

- outsized project
- high gearing (debt service)
- resistance to change and new technology
- short-term borrowing
- deterioration of service

Accounting

- inadequate, erroneous, or out-of-date
- cash flow
- unsystematic payment of creditors collection of debtors
- creative accounting and beneficial adjustments

The Zeta Factor

Detecting potential business weaknesses before a crisis develops can be profitable—for securities analysts, junk bond investors, and turnaround management specialists—and for the company in trouble. There are two basic approaches: (1) company-specific financial analysis looking for slippage and (2) industry analysis for vulnerability in products and markets. Both the micro- and macro-analyses are valuable. New Jersey–based Zeta Services weights a number of financial ratios that were unearthed in studying more than 50 companies that folded or were taken over by banks. The ratios are combined to come up with a Zeta score that assesses the likelihood of insolvency. Developer of the Z-score, Edward Altman (1983), claims it accurately signaled virtually all major business failures in a five-year period, including Penn-Dixie (1980) and McLouth Steel (1981). The Zeta model is now a proprietary service with more than 40 subscribers. The Zeta factor also singles out insolvencies that have not and may never come to pass. Between 12 to 15 percent of the more than 2,400 publicly traded firms have a negative Zeta score.

The Z-score has its competitors. Drexel has a macroanalytic viewpoint, emphasizing market perceptions. Its market adjusted debt (MAD) ratio is a barometer of how a company's stock changes in quality, alerting analysts to discrepancies between what the market thinks (stock price) and what actually appears on the company's books (debt security). Market ratings are serious business. When a company becomes too highly leveraged, or expands or acquires very rapidly, Standard & Poor may place a corporation on the dreaded credit watch list, making further borrowing more costly and difficult, even if the company's current position is still financially positive.

LESSONS FROM TROUBLED COMPANIES

Positive cash flow has become the top priority for both businessmen and bankers in today's economic environment. Many businesses are scrambling to elude financial failure, which in recent years has toppled companies in unprecedented numbers (Dolan 1983).

Year	*1932*	*1979*	*1980*	*1981*	*1982*	*1983*
Failed businesses (per 10,000)	154	28	42	61	89	100

In tandem with these business failures, bank loan losses, and nonperforming loans, those on which interest payments have not been met for a protracted time more than tripled in 1983. Most lending institutions cannot safely absorb such a default rate. The near-collapse of Continental Illinois, the nation's sixth-largest bank, illustrates the danger.

The resurging economy will not automatically pump life back into sagging corporate finances. In a prophetic article in the *Harvard Business Review*, Charles Williams (1984) identified 50 companies in serious financial trouble, including the following:

More than $1 billion in total debt

- Penn Central
- W.T. Grant
- Itel
- Dome Petroleum
- International Harvester
- Eastern Airlines

$100–999 million in total debt

- Braniff
- Continental Airlines
- Manville
- Sambo's Restaurants
- Memorex

Less than $100 million in total debt

- Allied Supermarkets
- First National Bank of Midland

- Rolls-Royce Ltd.
- Data Access Systems

A Harvest of Troubles

International Harvester (IH), one of America's oldest manufacturers of agricultural equipment, set a record for slippage into hot financial water. In 1979 IH had record sales of $8 billion and net income of $370 million. A six-month strike and the developing recession led to sharply lower sales and a net loss of $397 million only one year later. IH boosted its total debt from $1.4 billion to $2.2 billion in 1980 to avoid financial catastrophe. Despite higher sales in 1981, IH again experienced severe losses of $393 million. IH and its credit company built up borrowings of $3.8 billion. Financial restructuring in 1981 locked in the lenders to seeing IH through the crisis. 1982 was worse—much worse, with total losses of $1.6 billion. Fiscal losses from the sale of assets and industrial restructuring essentially eliminated IH's net worth in 1982.

Further financial restructuring based on sharing the pain helped somewhat. Banks made concessions, including converting $350 million of debt into warrants for future purchase of stock. Further losses in 1983 of $485 million forced another financial restructuring, rescheduling payment of most of the corporate debt.

What Harvester failed to see was that the booming success of the agriculture industry in the 1970s contained the seeds of future grief. Increasing productivity created a glut of farm products, driving prices down. Improved agricultural capacity worldwide reduced demand for U.S. food exports. Harvester finally saw the light. It sold the farm implements division and is regrouping around truck manufacturing. In 1985 Harvester finally got back in the black, making its first profits in five years. It sold the farm implements business and renamed the company Navistar to convey a new future-oriented image. Now Harvester's hopes for the future are still slim but brightening. So hope its lenders, who have mortgaged their own futures in tandem with Harvester.

The Osborne Domino

Two years after Adam Osborne's computer company began its meteoric rise to become a $100 million concern, it took an equally precipitous fall. The Osborne personal computer was a genuine innovation. Author of a popular computer industry magazine column, Osborne noted the lack of portability among the new microcomputers. He decided to fill this niche himself and went one better than his competitors by packaging the device with built-in software. At its peak, the company was selling 100,000 units a month. Customers loved it.

Despite its popularity Osborne was already in trouble. A new rival, Kaypro, jumped into Osborne's market with more features and a lower price. Other competitors followed swiftly. Soon there were nearly 40 portables. The big companies responded by price cutting, which little Osborne could not match. Osborne introduced its improved model, the Executive, but broke the news before it could deliver the product. This flattened sales of the old machines and killed interest in a stock offering for desperately needed capital. Chapter 11 bankruptcy filing followed.

The Osborne failure triggered a fire alarm in the overbuilt small computer industry. Was the Osborne the first domino? Mattel, Atari, and Texas Instruments have since taken themselves out, after suffering huge losses, and others like Commodore and Eagle are shaky. Industry experts had predicted since 1983 that a shakeout was imminent—and they were right. The personal computer industry is following a time-old pattern of innovation-growth-consolidation. But Adam Osborne never believed he would experience this roller-coaster first-hand until his growth peaked and he took the plunge down the experience curve himself.

FIVE BIGGEST MISTAKES TO AVOID

Is the business climate more risky today? Many industry observers believe there is less room for error. The marketplace is considerably less forgiving than it was in the past, in the airlines, banking, communications—and health care.

Business writer David Weber (1984) interviewed experts across a variety of businesses and distilled five of the biggest mistakes to avoid in business:

1. Don't try to do too much.
2. It's time to be bold.
3. Overhire rather than underhire.
4. Avoid betting on inflation.
5. Try not to relax.

MEGAMARKET SHIFTS

This is the era of bigness—megatrends, superpowers, and the big bun. Much of this is just hype, but beware, for some changes going on right in front of us are genuinely revolutionary.

Airlines, banking, communications, and public power utilities are experiencing revolutionary market shifts. The experiences of these deregulated industries are instructive for health care. They are experiencing levels of competition undreamed of in 1980.

The safety nets of regulatory protection these companies have traditionally enjoyed have been cut away or lowered perilously close to the ground. Strategic error by management can lead to failure. Look at Braniff, Continental Illinois Bank, and WPPSS.

The New Shape of Banking

Bankers are not supposed to be smart: they are supposed to be safe. Well, the era of the 5.25 percent passbook savings account is over. Since 1980 deregulation has unleashed entrepreneurship in the staid world of banking. Imagine making money on your checking account? In 1980 that didn't exist. Today every bank offers it. Banking has aggressively invaded consumer finance and securities brokerage and is eyeing the insurance market. Sears is a bank now (it was already the world's largest financial services corporation). Automated tellers are popping up on every corner. These robot tellers can process 2,000 transactions a day, versus 300 for a human teller.

Citicorp is a model of innovation in banking. Its retail bank, a $79 million loser as recently as 1980, was ahead $202 million in 1983, by pursuing Chairman Walter Wriston's Five I's strategy: gain a major position in institutional, individual and investment banking, then attack insurance and information.

The near failure and $7.5 billion rescue of giant Continental Illinois has jolted the banking industry. Will banks move as aggressively as Citicorp tomorrow? Most banking industry experts believe that the marketplace has dramatically shifted, and there will be no turning back.

Life in Life Insurance?

There are few more conservative industries than life insurance, but Prudential's rock doesn't look much like Gibraltar any more. The nation's largest life insurer recently unveiled a sleek, abstract version of its famous logo—a dynamic rock is what Pru's chairman calls it.

The pattern of change is equally tumultuous in health insurance. In the 1980s the health insurance industry's biggest competitors is its customers—major employers who have become self-insured. As a result, providing administrative services only (ASO) is one of the most successful lines of business for the indemnity carriers. To cope with the competitive attack of HMOs and PPOs, the insurers are rapidly counterattacking with development and acquisition of their own HMOs and PPOs, and experimenting with a wide range of joint ventures to redirect and redesign their futures.

POSTSCRIPT: THE SEER-SUCKER THEORY OF FORECASTING

Despite evidence to the contrary some companies do take planning seriously. They look for the early signs of change and plan accordingly. When the weather forecaster predicts rain, these companies carry an umbrella. Nonetheless there is some evidence to suggest that at least occasionally the experts can be wrong.

Scott Armstrong (1980) advances his own seer-sucker theory of forecasting: "No matter how much evidence exists that seers do not exist, suckers will pay for the existence of seers." Is he right? There is certainly a large body of evidence that forecasters are often wrong. In the 1984 presidential debate candidates Reagan and Mondale argued over whose experts were wrong more often and missed the mark more widely. Both were right.

Forecasters can err. It would be a greater mistake, however, to ignore the future just because it cannot always be predicted with precision. Keeping the window on the future open is essential for strategic management. If the future is anywhere near as uncertain and difficult as the present, we had better keep at least one eye on the horizon.

STRATEGIES FOR THE NEW HOSPITAL

Foresight essential. In periods of uncertainty the value of information goes up. Decisions are always made with incomplete knowledge of the outcomes. When the marketplace is reasonably well-known and conditions stable, there is less risk. The health industry is in a period of transition from a relatively stable cost-reimbursement environment into an unknown future in which both demand and payment are shifting. More than ever, health organizations need to keep their eyes open to the future.

Alternative futures. There is more than one possible future. The health industry is complex, as is the environment. The prudent organization will plan based on alternative futures, hedging its bets.

Second opinions on the future. Every health organization should test its own biases about the future by calling in outside experts. The experts will disagree— that can be predicted with almost 100 percent certainty. What is important is not which expert is right, but the process of gaining more information so that the management and board can confirm or disconfirm their opinions. Those who are well-informed will make the best strategic choices.

Fatal mistakes. As the case histories of business failure indicate, management mistakes today can be fatal. There is less margin for error today. Major capital investments and diversification decisions need careful analysis. There are also hazards in sitting still, while competitors move. This is a time for close attention to strategic management.

Vision. While others are losing their heads all around, keep yours. The future is uncertain, but that will also create new opportunities for those with vision and management discipline. The strategically managed organization has a high-level awareness of the environment and the market, then picks its own future and steers toward it.

REFERENCES AND SUGGESTED READINGS

Altman, Edward I. "Exploring the Road to Bankruptcy." *Journal of Business Strategy*, Fall 1983.

*"Are Utilities Obsolete?" *Business Week*, May 21, 1984.

Armstrong, J. Scott. "The Seer-Sucker Theory: The Value of Experts in Forecasting." *Technology Review*, June/July 1980.

Dolan, Patrick F. "A Four-Phased Rescue Plan for Today's Troubled Companies." *Journal of Business Strategy*, Summer 1983.

Enzer, Selwyn. "Energy Policy—a Failure of Foresight," Center for Futures Research, Graduate School of Business Administration, University of Southern California, June 27, 1979.

*"The Fallout from 'WHOOPS.' " *Business Week*, July 11, 1983.

*"A Fiasco That May Rock Municipal Bonds." *Business Week*, February 7, 1983.

*Harman, Willis. *An Incomplete Guide to the Future*. New York: W.W. Norton & Co., 1979.

*Hawken, Paul, Oglivy, James, and Schwartz, Peter. *Seven Tomorrows*, New York: Bantam, 1982.

*Hogan, Mike. "Banking: Only the Strong Survive." *California Business*, April 1983.

*Hogan, Mike. "Osborne Computer Crashes." *California Business*, November 1983.

*Kahn, Herman, et al. *The Next 200 Years*. New York: William Morrow & Co., 1976.

*"The New Shape of Banking." *Business Week*, June 18, 1984.

*Rohrer, Julie. "The Imperfect Art of Forecasting Bankruptcies." *Institutional Investor*, September 1982.

Thompson, C.J. "Danger Signs of Corporate Insolvency." *Financial Executive*, June 1982.

*"The Upheaval in Health Care." *Business Week*, July 25, 1983

*"The Upheaval in Life Insurance." *Business Week*, June 25, 1984.

Weber, David. "Five Biggest Business Mistakes to Avoid in 1984." *California Business*, January 1984.

Williams, Charles M. "When the Mighty Stumble." *Harvard Business Review*, July-August 1984.

---

*Suggested reading.

Index

About the Author

Russell C. Coile, Jr., MBA, is the founder and president of the Health Forecasting Group, which provides strategic information on emerging markets and advanced management practices in the health industry. As the first corporate futurist in the health field, he is a frequent author and speaker on aspects of health and the future, and consults with a broad range of U.S. health care companies.

His column, "The Leading Edge" appears regularly in *Healthcare Forum* magazine. He hosted the miniseries on "Intrapreneurship and Entrepreneurship," and has been seen on several programs on the Hospital Satellite Network.

Prior to forming his own consulting firm, Mr. Coile was the director of the Center for Health Management Research for the Lutheran Hospital Society of Southern California where he established the first futures research program in the health industry. During the past 15 years he has held a variety of senior positions as a management consultant, planner, and educator in the health field.

Receiving his BA from Johns Hopkins University, Mr. Coile holds an MBA in Health Care Administration from George Washington University. He is now completing doctoral work at the University of Southern California where he is a member of the health care administration faculty.